THE UNIVERSITY OF CHICAGO

ORIENTAL INSTITUTE PUBLICATIONS

VOLUME XCVII

THE UNIVERSITY OF CHICAGO
ORIENTAL INSTITUTE PUBLICATIONS
VOLUME XCVII

NIPPUR

II

THE NORTH TEMPLE AND SOUNDING E

Excavations of the Joint Expedition to Nippur
of
The American Schools of Oriental Research
and
The Oriental Institute of the University of Chicago

BY
DONALD E. McCOWN
RICHARD C. HAINES and ROBERT D. BIGGS
assisted by ELIZABETH F. CARTER

THE ORIENTAL INSTITUTE · CHICAGO · ILLINOIS

International Standard Book Number: 0-918986-04-4
Library of Congress Catalog Card Number: 77-74719

THE ORIENTAL INSTITUTE, CHICAGO

© 1978 by The University of Chicago. All rights reserved.
Published 1978. Printed in the United States of America.

BECAUSE of printing difficulties, the publication of this volume was delayed well beyond the initially scheduled date. Professor Haines was able to read through all of the proofs of the text, but he died on February 15, 1977, before the final version of the book went to press. This volume is dedicated to the memory of this painstaking and devoted archeologist and expedition leader, who gave so much of the last three decades of his life to the work at Nippur.

JOHN A. BRINKMAN
Director, Oriental Institute
February 20, 1977

FOREWORD

In the present volume, the presentation of the pottery, objects, and burial material was reorganized so as to agree with changes that had been made from Dr. McCown's original manuscript when the first volume of *Nippur* was published. The changes consisted in placing the descriptions of pottery and objects opposite the plates, and including in the text untyped, unillustrated objects and a complete list of burials. No factual changes were made in Dr. McCown's descriptions, observations, or conclusions.

The reorganization was very capably done by Elizabeth Carter, and her knowledge of the material and her thoroughness have greatly contributed to the value of this report. I am also thankful for the very fine hand of Ann Wharton Epstein, who drew all the smaller-scaled architectural plans of the excavations, and grateful for the listing and checking done by my wife, Irene. Professor Robert Biggs's chapter on the epigraphic material is a happy inclusion, for we can now present a complete report of the excavation of the North Temple and Sounding E. We all wish to express our appreciation of Jean Eckenfels, the Editorial Secretary of the Oriental Institute, for carefully editing the manuscript and shepherding it to publication.

RICHARD C. HAINES

CHICAGO
September 1971

PREFACE

DURING the third season of excavation at Nippur an Early Dynastic temple was discovered in the northwestern part of the Religious Quarter which became the site of the major activity of the fourth season. This volume details the findings and results uncovered at this temple by the joint expedition of the Oriental Institute of the University of Chicago and the Baghdad School of the American Schools of Oriental Research.

The digging season lasted from November 14, 1953, to March 15, 1954. Mr. Richard C. Haines was again architect and my chief assistant. Professor Thorkild Jacobsen, senior epigrapher, was assisted by Dr. Vaughn Crawford, and both of them played an active part in the supervision of the excavations. Mrs. Irene Haines was again recorder. We were happy to have with us Sayyid Izzadin Sandouq as representative of the Directorate General of Antiquities; his help in drawing pottery and other objects was invaluable.

As in the past, we owe to Dr. Naji al-Asil, Director General of Antiquities, and his staff the pleasure of their friendship as well as much valuable help. To Professor Carl Kraeling, Director of the Oriental Institute, and to Professor Albrecht Goetze, Chairman of the Baghdad School Committee of the American Schools, we owe the support that made the fourth season of excavations at Nippur possible.

The first task on the resumption of excavations in the North Temple area (the designation given the region of the Early Dynastic temple) was to expand the area of excavations to be sure that it included all the territory of the temple or complex surrounding that building. This involved rapid digging of levels dating around the middle of the first millennium B.C. A second phase ensued with the excavation of levels from the third millennium around the North Temple proper. When we were satisfied that they were composed mainly of private houses, work was concentrated on the North Temple and proceeded as far as time allowed.

From information gained in the third season it was clear that the third millennium temple and its surroundings differed in character from the later remains in the region. Therefore, though the excavation area was the same, different designations were used (1) for levels and in recording finds for the third millennium and older remains and (2) those in and after the Third Dynasty of Ur. The designation SE distinguishes the architecture and finds of the Third Dynasty of Ur and following. NT designates the architecture and finds from Akkadian and older levels. The numbering of levels begins at the top, and NT level I precedes in time the lowest SE level.

The second objective in the fourth season was to remove encumbrances superimposed on the temple of Inanna of Duranki. Since the excavation of the Inanna Temple will be the main work of the fifth season, all finds from that area will be published in a future volume when that temple has been excavated.

DONALD E. MCCOWN
Field Director

CHICAGO
1955

TABLE OF CONTENTS

	PAGE
LIST OF PLATES	xiii
LIST OF ABBREVIATIONS	xv
TECHNICAL NOTES	1
I. THE STRUCTURAL REMAINS IN NT LEVELS X–I. *Richard C. Haines*	3
The Protoliterate Period	3
The Early Dynastic Period	3
Early Dynastic I	4
NT Level X	4
NT Level IX	4
NT Level VIII	6
Early Dynastic II	8
NT Level VII	8
NT Level VI	9
NT Level V	11
Early Dynastic III	17
NT Level IV	17
NT Level III	21
The Akkadian Period	23
NT Level II	23
NT Level I	24
II. THE OBJECTS FROM NT LEVELS X–I. *Donald E. McCown*	27
Pottery and the Dating of Levels	27
Tablets and the Dating of Levels	29
Stone Vessels	29
Seals and Seal Impressions	30
Sculpture	32
Baked Clay Figurines and Models	32
Personal Ornaments	33
Other Small Objects	33
III. THE STRUCTURAL REMAINS IN SE LEVELS VI–I. *Richard C. Haines*	35
The Ur III–Old Babylonian Periods	35
SE Level VI	36
The Kassite Period	37
SE Level V	37
The Erosion of the Surface	38
SE Level IV	38

The Neo-Babylonian Period	39
SE Level III	39
The Achaemenian Period	39
SE Level II	39
The Seleucid Period	41
SE Level I	41
IV. THE OBJECTS FROM SE LEVELS VI–I. *Donald E. McCown*	43
Pottery	43
Tablets and Coins and the Dating of Levels	47
Stone, Metal, and Glass Vessels	48
Seals and Seal Impressions	49
Baked Clay Figurines, Plaques, and Model	49
Personal Ornaments	51
Other Small Objects	52
V. THE BURIALS. *Donald E. McCown*	53
Earth Burials	53
Tub Burials	53
Jar Burials	54
Bowl Burials	55
Slipper Coffins	55
List of Burials and Their Contents	55
VI. HISTORY OF THE NORTH TEMPLE. *Donald E. McCown*	69
VII. THE CUNEIFORM INSCRIPTIONS. *Robert D. Biggs*	71
INDEX OF CATALOGUE NUMBERS	97
GENERAL INDEX	104

LIST OF PLATES

1. Plan of Eastern Nippur showing excavated areas, 1954
2. *A*. Site of Sounding E and the North Temple. *B*. Sounding E trench
3. *A*. Findspot of stone statuettes in NT level III. *B*. The cella of the North Temple, at NT levels IV and III. *C*. Pottery *in situ* in the box altar, at NT level IV
4. *A*. View of the cella area at NT level IX. *B*. View of the cella area at NT levels IX and VIII
5. *A*. The cella at NT level VIII. *B*. Detail of the hexagonal platform in the cella at NT level VIII
6. *A*. The temple at NT levels IX to VII. *B*. The northeast part of the temple
7. *A*. The stepped altar at NT level VII. *B*. The pot on the lower step of the altar. *C*. The entrance to the anterooms of the cella at NT level VIII
8. *A*. Entrance corridor to the temple at NT level VI. *B*. Doorway between entrance corridor and temple courtyard at NT level V
9. *A*. Furnace for melting bitumen in locus 116, NT level V. *B*. Cutaway view of furnace. *C*. A modern bitumen furnace in the village of Afak
10. The temple at NT level V
11. The temple at NT level IV
12. The temple at NT level V. *A*. An offering table in the ablution room. *B*. Circular offering tables and ramplike construction in the courtyard
13. The circular offering tables in courtyard of the temple at NT level V. *A*. Table partially cut away to show successive plasterings. *B*. Table cut away to show core and original plastering
14. Cella of the temple at NT level V 2–1. *A*. Southeast part showing stand, entrance doorway, and altar. *B*. Northwest part showing offering table and basin
15. The cella at NT level V. *A*. The altar with step partially cut away to show successive mud plasterings. *B*. Detail of core of freestanding offering table
16. *A*. Foundation layer for bitumen oval in cella at NT level V 4. *B*. The northwest part of the cella at NT level V 4
17. Northwest part of the cella. *A*. Foundation layer for oval platform at NT level IV 1. *B*. Oval platform at NT level III 2
18. Ovens in the temple kitchen. *A*. At NT level V 2–1. *B*. At NT level IV 2
19. Ovens in the temple kitchen. *A*. At NT level IV 1. *B*. At NT level III 1. *C*. At NT level II
20. Ablution places in the temple. *A*. At NT level V 4. *B*. At NT level IV 1
21. Ablution places in the temple. *A*. At NT level III 2. *B*. At NT level III 1
22. *A*. View of NT levels III and II with NT level IV temple in middle distance. *B*. Oven in room 49 at NT level IV 1. *C*. Rooms 48 and 152 at NT level II
23. *A*. View of NT level I cut by SE level V. *B*. View of NT levels III and II with southwest wall of SE level VI platform
24. *A*. Southwest wall of SE level VI platform. *B*. Detail of through joint in southeast part of wall
25. Northwest part of SE level II. *A*. View showing saw-toothed wall and intrusive kilns. *B*. Saw-toothed wall at SE level II 1. *C*. Intrusive kilns at SE level II 4–2

26. Plans of NT levels X (*A*), IX 2 (*B*), IX 1 (*C*), and alterations to IX 1 (*D*)
27. Plans of NT level VIII 2 (*A*) and 1 (*B*)
28. Plans of NT levels VII (*A*) and VI (*B*)
29. Plans of NT level V 4–3 (*A*) and 2–1 (*B*)
30. Plans of the temple at NT level IV 3–2 (*A*) and 1 (*B*)
31. Plan of NT level IV 1
32. Plan of the temple at NT levels III (*A*) and II (*B*)
33. Plan of NT level III
34. Plan of NT level II
35. Plan of NT level I
36. Plans of SE levels VI (*A*) and V (*B*)
37. Plan of SE level III
38. Plan of SE level II 4–2
39. Plan of SE level II 1
40. Plan of SE level I 3–2
41. Plan of SE level I 1
42. NT structural details
43. NT and SE sections A–A, B–B, and C–C
44–46. Pottery from NT levels
47–48. Pottery and stone vessels from NT levels
49–55. Pottery from SE levels
56. Pottery, stone, bronze, and glass vessels from SE levels
57–58. Pottery from SE levels
59–62. Objects from NT and SE levels
63. Potsherd, cylinder seals, and seal impressions from NT levels
64–65. Seal impressions from NT levels
66. Seal impressions and stone sculptures from NT levels
67–69. Stone sculptures from NT levels
70. Stone sculptures and other objects from NT levels
71. Baked-clay figurines and other objects from NT and SE levels
72. Baked-clay figurines and plaque from NT and SE levels
73. Baked-clay figurines, plaque, and molds from SE levels
74. Baked-clay figurines and other objects from SE levels
75. Burial jars and slipper coffins from SE burials
76. Slipper coffins and incantation bowl from SE levels
77. Incantation bowl and other objects

LIST OF ABBREVIATIONS

Archaeology V   Archaeology V (summer, 1952).

Kish "A"   MACKAY, ERNEST. Report on the Excavation of the "A" Cemetery at Kish, Mesopotamia, *and* A Sumerian Palace and the "A" Cemetery at Kish, Mesopotamia (Field Museum of Natural History. Anthropology, Memoirs, I 1–2 [Chicago, 1925–29]).

OBI   HILPRECHT, H. V. Old Babylonian Inscriptions Chiefly from Nippur (The Babylonian Expedition of the University of Pennsylvania. Series A: Cuneiform Texts, I [Philadelphia, 1893–96]).

OIP   Chicago. University. Oriental Institute. Oriental Institute Publications (Chicago, 1924–).

OIP LX   FRANKFORT, HENRI. More Sculpture from the Diyala Region (Chicago, 1943).

OIP LXIII   DELOUGAZ, PINHAS. Pottery from the Diyala Region (Chicago, 1952).

UE II   WOOLLEY, C. LEONARD. The Royal Cemetery. Text and Plates (London, 1934).

Vol. I   MCCOWN, DONALD E. and HAINES, RICHARD C. Nippur I: Temple of Enlil, Scribal Quarter, and Soundings. (*OIP* LXXVIII [Chicago, 1967]).

TECHNICAL NOTES

SOUNDING E (see Vol. I, p. 150) was originally a 5 × 12 meter trench laid out in a gentle wadi on the northeast side of a low-lying ridge in the northwest section of the Religious Quarter (Pls. 1, 2 A). Excavation was begun on December 18, 1951, and by January 7 we had reached a buttressed wall founded about 6 meters below the surface of the mound (Pl. 2 B). To investigate the mound northeast of the facing, we jumped about 8 meters and continued northeastward in a narrower trench, which ended at the lower end of the wadi, where it was joined by another wadi from the south. By the middle of January we were finding walls of plano-convex bricks some 2 meters higher than the baked-brick base of the facing. We enlarged the area and soon realized that we were digging in the cella of a temple built of plano-convex bricks. On February 5 we found a cache of Early Dynastic stone statuettes just outside the southeast wall of the cella (Pl. 3 A). We extended the dig still farther to learn more about the plan of the temple (Pl. 3 B and C). The excavations were closed in the middle of March, 1952.

When digging was resumed in the fall of 1953, the excavation was enlarged again to the size shown in Plate 1. We needed to know the limits of the baked-brick facing and the extent of the earlier temple complex. By the middle of January we had not reached the level of the temple floors excavated the previous season, and it was evident that further digging had to be limited to the immediate vicinity of the temple. By March 1, five building levels of the temple, each with many floors and minor structural alterations, were cleared, and a major wall appeared beneath the sanctuary, dividing it into two parts. The southeastern part looked the more promising, and the excavation was extended in that direction. A large rectangular room was found, but it contained neither temple furniture nor an altar. Except for a few probings and a sounding to virgin soil, little could be done in the time that remained. The excavations were stopped on March 15, 1954.

The structural remains were mapped with an alidade and a plane table from bench marks established with a transit. The bench marks are part of a triangulation of eastern Nippur which includes bench marks in the Enlil Temple area and the Scribal Quarter. Some of the mapping points are shown on the plans with a cross (+) so that they may aid in the plans' orientation and superposition. Datum is the same as that used in Volume I; that is, an arbitrary elevation of 100 m. was established at the northwest corner stake of TA in the Scribal Quarter. The digging followed, as nearly as possible, the major building levels which, because of small structural changes, often had to be divided into several floors. The levels were assigned roman numerals beginning at the top of the mound.

The area was given two designations, "SE" and "NT," abbreviations of Sounding E and North Temple. Only one area is involved; Sounding E is the upper of two horizontally divided sections, and its earliest level follows in time the latest level of North Temple (see p. 35). One of these designations precedes the room, level, and floor numbers in a locus designation. For example, NT 107 IX 1 signifies the North Temple, room 107, level IX, floor 1. The letter "B" signifies a burial. The number preceding the letter indicates the season and the number following the letter is the serial number of the burial. The burials are shown on the plans of the levels in which they were found and not on the plans of the levels to which they are attributed. No burials are shown on the sections.

There are three object catalogues: the general catalogue designated by the letter "N," the discard catalogue by "D," and the pot catalogue by "P." The identifying number of an object is formed by giving first the number of the season, next the specific catalogue in which the object is recorded, and then the serial number in that catalogue. For example, 4P 294 signifies entry 294 in the pot catalogue of the fourth season. (In the discard catalogue we recorded objects which we intended to discard after they had been measured, described and, sometimes, photographed or drawn. Many have been kept, however, for study purposes.) A fourth catalogue of cuneiform tablets and other inscribed materials is designated by the letters "NT," preceded by the number of the season and followed by the number of that item in the catalogue.

I

THE STRUCTURAL REMAINS IN NT LEVELS X–I

By RICHARD C. HAINES

In the NT levels, the structural remains were of particular interest because of a small temple found in the area. The time of its founding was uncertain. The Protoliterate materials were found only in a small pit and, although there were several floors, there were no indications of the kind of structures the floors belonged to. The same was also true of the higher floors in the pit containing Early Dynastic I materials. Above the pit a sufficient area was cleared to recognize a structure that was a temple. Its founding cannot be surely dated but probably it was during the latter part of the Early Dynastic I period. The temple was rebuilt many times and was in use during the remainder of the Early Dynastic period and the Akkadian period as well.

In the upper NT levels the excavated area was large enough to include structures other than the temple. They seemed to be of a domestic character.

THE PROTOLITERATE PERIOD

Protoliterate materials were found only in test pit NT 132 (Pl. 43 A). Floors 17–15 have been assigned to this period; floor 14, at el. 81.32 m., may be either Protoliterate or Early Dynastic I (p. 29).[1] The locus was small, about 1.40 × 2.10 m., and little was learned about the buildings. Usually the floors were thin ashy layers with almost no accumulation of debris.

Floor 17, at el. 80.27 m., was the lowest floor that we found. Below it, there was approximately 65 cm. of clay soil with no potsherds or organic materials in it. Below the clay there was a fine buff-gray sand. We dug into this for almost 30 cm., to el. 79.30 m., and stopped. In all probability we had reached virgin soil.

At floor 16, the floor area had a covering of bitumen, which securely placed the findspot of a seal impression (4D 378) in the floor below. Laid unbaked bricks were also found in the northeast part of the pit. They were not plano-convex but rectangular in shape and measured 13.5 × 23 × 9 cm.

THE EARLY DYNASTIC PERIOD

The greater part of our excavations in the NT levels fall within the range of the Early Dynastic period. The earliest materials were found below NT level X (in NT 132, floor 14) and the latest in NT level III, an occupational accumulation of about 5.5 m. The structural remains can be divided into the temple and the residential buildings around the temple. The founding of the temple is unknown. The nature of the structure in NT level IX was uncertain, but it may have been a temple; the structure in NT level VIII certainly was. The

---

[1] When a level may belong to either one period or another, it is included in the range of both periods and usually mentioned in the discussion of the earlier period.

temple continued, in its various rebuildings, beyond the end of the Early Dynastic period. Residential buildings were uncovered only in NT levels IV and III.

The construction of the Early Dynastic North Temple was similar in many ways to that of other Early Dynastic temples. The walls were built of unbaked plano-convex bricks and sometimes, but not always, placed on a projecting footing. The bricks were of very poor quality with little or no binding material and sometimes with more ash than earth. The bricks which could be measured were 15–16 cm. wide, 21–23 cm. long, 5–6.5 cm. thick at the center and 3–4 cm. at the sides. In some walls the bricks were laid in flat courses, in other walls in a herringbone pattern. The method of brick-laying was too infrequently recognized to discover a pattern of use for the two, if there was one. The flat-laid bricks were in alternating courses of stretchers and headers with broken bricks filling the inner part of the wall. It would have been impossible to trace the walls with any certainty if they had not been covered with many layers of a good clay plaster. The floors were also made up of many layers of clay plaster which continued without a break up the walls in a somewhat thinner coating. Sometimes the clay floor was placed on a layer of fairly clean fill, especially when the floor was the first one laid after a repair or alteration to the building. There was very little occupational debris on the floors, and it was almost free of potsherds and other artifacts. Door pivots, either of stone or baked brick, were rare, and it is probable that many of the openings were closed with cloth or matting or not at all.

In the residential buildings the wall construction was similar to that in the temple. The plano-convex bricks were the same size and were also laid flat or in a herringbone pattern. The bricks seemed to be of a better quality, but the examples came only from the upper levels of the period, NT levels IV and III. In several instances in level III the plano-convex bricks were replaced by small oval lumps of clay 13–17 × 19–23 × 4–8 cm. The floors were mostly clay mixed with straw put down in layers 1–2 cm. thick. The plaster coatings on the walls and floors were thicker and not so numerous as they were in the temple.

EARLY DYNASTIC I

The range of Early Dynastic I extended from floor 14 in test pit NT 132 to NT level VIII (p. 29). The early and middle parts of the period were excavated only in test pit NT 132; in the levels toward the end of the period we had excavated a sizeable area.

Floor 14 in NT 132 may or may not be Early Dynastic I, but floors 13–3 certainly were. If we use absolute elevation as our main criterion, we may correlate NT 132 floors 8, 7, and 5 with NT levels X 2, X 1, and IX 2 in loci NT 163 and 164. NT 132 floors 4, 3, and 1 equate with NT levels IX 1b, IX 1a, and VIII 2 in locus NT 123. Since NT level VIII may be either Early Dynastic I or II, the same is also true of NT 132 floors 2 and 1.

NT LEVEL X

Except for NT 132, we reached NT level X only in loci 163 and 164 (Pls. 26 A, 43 A, B). The west corner of the room and part of the southwest wall were excavated but not enough to suggest any particular type of building. Two floors were recorded. Floor 2, of tamped earth with some ash, had a slightly dished, circular hearth hardened and blackened by fire, at el. 82.32 m. The hearths at el. 82.40 and 82.45 m. belonged to floor 1, which covered a somewhat larger area at el. 82.45–82.50 m.

NT LEVEL IX

NT level IX represents a time of complicated and not very well understood building activity. The changes could best be seen in the large room on the southwest, locus 121, where two floors were identified. Floor 2, at el. 82.75 m., was found in loci 163 and 164, where there were no walls within the excavated area to delimit it. An unbaked-brick fill in the northeast half of room 121 seemed to be laid against the northeast and northwest walls of NT level IX (Pl. 4 A). The fill had a good southwest face and two bonded walls extended southwestward and continued beyond the limit of the excavation (Pls. 26 B, 43 A, B). Southwest of the fill there were additional floors between floors 2 and 1 (at least four in a 20-cm. build-up). There was also a laid unbaked-brick fill in rooms 124 and 136 (and presumably also 123), but whether the fill abutted the NT level IX walls was not determined. The reason for the fill was not apparent.

At floor 1 more of the building was excavated, but the plan was not yet very clear (Pl. 26 C). In later levels the entrance was in the north part of the complex. It might have been there in NT level IX, too, and if so, room 137 was an anteroom to courtyard 131. An entrance into the building on the southwest is problematical. It may have been beyond the end of the bench on the southwest side of the courtyard, where the wall was not much higher than the floors on either side, or it may have been farther to the southeast in the unexcavated part of the complex. The circulation inside the structure may be complete except for a way into room 124. There were indications that there had been a doorway between rooms 121 and 124, but it could not be clearly defined and must remain uncertain. It was certain, however, that there was no opening between rooms 124 and 123 or 136 at this time.

Above the fill of floor 2, two clay floors, very close together, were labeled 1a and 1b. The plan was the same for both floors except that at floor 1a the northwest and southwest walls of room 121 were rebuilt slightly out of line with those at floor 1b (Pl. 26 D). Floor 1b was at el. 83.10 m. in room 121 and 83.00 m. in room 123; floor 1a sloped from el. 83.17 m. in room 121 to 83.10 m. in 123 to 82.95 m. at the far side of courtyard 131 and to 82.90 m. in the northwest part of room 137. At the time of excavation it seemed that floor 2 of the NT level VIII temple descended by steps and slopes from the cella to the lowest excavated floor in the courtyard, a floor which correlated well with the floors of NT level IX 1a. So it has been assumed that the level of the courtyard did not rise significantly during the IX 1a–VIII 2 occupation.

In room 137, only one floor was excavated. A rectangular depression at the end of a wall stub jutting out from the southwest wall contained much ash and probably was a hearth. More than usual ash and burned material was found in the room debris although there were no signs of burning on the walls. The bench in the west corner of the room was 55 cm. wide, 25 cm. high, 105 cm. long, and rounded at its east corner.

The only feature in the excavated part of the courtyard was a mud-plastered unbaked-brick bench, 85 cm. wide and 40 cm. high. Although the NT level VIII door construction had cut into the level IX bench, enough remained of the bench and the wall face behind it to indicate that a doorway such as that in the level above did not exist in NT level IX.

Along the southwest wall of room 123 there were several unbaked-brick curbs or wall stubs built on floor 1a. They extended 25–30 cm. into the room and were formed by placing single bricks on edge with one end against the wall face. The sides and front ends were covered with mud plaster, but the tops had been cut off by the construction of the NT level VIII wall.

Similar wall stubs were also found on floor 1a against the southwest wall of room 136. The room extended beyond the southeast limit of the excavation, and the south corner was found by tunneling. In the tunnel we also located the opening between rooms 136 and 121. Floor 1b (el. 83.07 m.) was laid directly upon the brick filling in floor 2 and consisted of two layers of clay totaling 5 cm. in thickness. Floor 1a (el. 83.20 m.) was also a layer of clay, about 2 cm. thick, and was laid on the ash and occupational debris above 1b. Circular, slightly dished hearths were found on both floors.

A similar hearth was also found on the rather uneven floor 1b in room 121. Here, too, we had to tunnel to find the east and south corners of the room. The room was rectangular, 3.65 m. wide and 10.40 m. long, and partly underlay the sanctuary of the temple in the levels above. We were not able to tunnel along all the southeast face for fear of a cave-in, and we found no indications of an altar or other cult installations in the room. Since we have learned that the earliest Inanna temple at Nippur was closely patterned on a house directly below it,[2] we are somewhat hesitant to call this building, with an overburden of temples but without appropriate furniture, a temple. The good clay floors and the small amount of ash, potsherds, and accumulation of floor debris suggest, however, that the building was not a private house.

It is possible that area 122 was not part of the building at NT level IX. Although the floors were clay, they were covered with a heavier layer of ash and debris than we found in other parts of the excavation. There were good floors at 1b and 1a (el. 83.07 and 83.25 m.). The unbaked-brick table(?) on the northeast side of the locus was founded on floor 1a; the top was destroyed by the level VIII rebuilding. The two semicircular bins built against the southeast wall belong to a slightly higher floor, at el. 85.35 m. (Pl. 4 B).

NT Level VIII

At NT level VIII, the plan was comprehensible and surely that of a temple (Pls. 6, 27). The entrance still may be questioned but its most logical place would be in the north immediately below the entrance in NT level VII. A newly constructed wall limited the building on the southeast, and a drain tile leading from locus 132 to the courtyard indicated that the unexcavated area on the northwest was included in the temple precinct. If the entrance was in the north, room 137 was a vestibule or anteroom for the main courtyard 131. On the southwest a doorway flanked by towers gave access, through antecellae 123 and 124, to the cella, 107. There was the usual Early Dynastic approach to the altar but not so usual was the position of the doorway in the long wall near the altar end of the room. There was insufficient evidence to determine whether any room was a kitchen. Although there was a hearth in room 133, on the southeast, it is probable that the kitchen was in the unexcavated area on the northwest.

The numerous thin layers of clay which made up the floors of the level have been divided into two floors (three in cella 107) corresponding to the major changes made during the occupation of the level. Floor 2 was at el. 82.95 m. at the northeast wall of courtyard 131 and rose to el. 83.55 m. in cella 107. In addition to a slope in the floor there were two risers, 7 cm. and 20 cm., before the doorway between the courtyard and room 123 (Pl. 7 C) and another, 15 cm., in the doorway between rooms 123 and 124. Floor 1 rose from el. 83.25 m. in courtyard 131 to el. 83.65 m. in cella 107. In addition to a sloping floor there were two risers, 7 cm. and 12 cm., in the doorway from the courtyard to room 123.

Floor 2 in room 137 was at the same general level as it had been in NT level IX. The level IX hearth may have been no longer used since there was a corner binlike construction filled with ash in the south part of the room. Floor 1, about 18 cm. above floor 2, was defined by a heavy layer of burned debris; the walls on the west were not preserved at that height.

The size of courtyard 131 was determined in NT level VIII, although it was not entirely excavated. It was never clear whether the northeast wall of the court was rebuilt when the new southeast wall was constructed. Floor 2 at level VIII was no more than an added layer

---

[2]"The Inanna Temple at Nippur," *The Illustrated London News,* September 9, 1961, p. 408.

of clay on the level IX floor. Although drains did not exist in the excavated floor of the courtyard, a drain tile passing through the northwest wall did empty from locus 132 into the west corner of the court. The tile was baked clay, 15 cm. in diameter, and extended 25 cm. into the courtyard; the top clay floor coating was brought up over the tile. Floor 1 was raised 30–35 cm. above the level of floor 2 and covered the level IX bench against the southwest wall.

In room 123 there was a limestone pivot block at the north jamb of the doorway in the northeast wall at floor 2. The stone, 8 × 8.5 × 3 cm., was set upon a potsherd as a base. During its use the stone had been turned over and was worn completely through; the depression in the top of the stone was 3 cm. in diameter.

In room 133, floor 2 was made up of three layers of clay totaling 4 cm. laid over a layer of gray ash on floor 1a at level IX. At NT level VIII 1 the wall between rooms 126 and 133 did not exist, and these loci became a large room or open space southeast of the cella. A good light gray clay floor partially laid on a bed of potsherds covered the area. At floor 1 the northeast portion of the room was closed off with unbaked-brick walls creating two small rooms. Both rooms were plastered, and there were no doorways into them. The walls were laid against the existing level VIII walls and were the normal width, except on the northwest, where the brickwork was 1.20 m. thick; it filled the doorway into room 123 and effectively closed off this area from the rooms of the temple on the northwest.

In NT level VIII the cella, or room 107, lay to the northwest of the comparable room in NT level IX, over parts of loci 121 and 122. The side walls were built upon those of level IX; the southeast wall was placed on a footing 20 cm. deep and projecting 15–20 cm. beyond the wall face on both sides (Pl. 43 B); the northwest wall was built directly on the level IX debris.

Three floors were recognized, none of which was quite level. In the northwest end of the room there was a slope of about 10 cm. downward from the northeast to the southwest. From the northwest wall to the southeast, there was a rise of 13 cm. to the center of the room and then a drop of 7 cm. to the area in front of the altar step. Floor 3, the lowest floor in the cella, was a clay layer placed upon the debris of level IX and was about 5 cm. below the lowest plastering on the doorsill.

The unbaked-brick altar against the southeast wall of the cella was founded at floor 3 and continued unchanged throughout the level. It was 1.30 m. wide and 90 cm. deep; it was preserved up to 28 cm. high (Pl. 4 B). The step in front of the altar was built of one course of unbaked bricks 12 × 21 × 3–5 cm. and was plastered. The step was given a coating of plaster each time the floor plaster was renewed so that the step riser remained approximately 6 cm. high throughout the level. At floor 3 the edge of the step was rounded and the plasterings "flowed" from the floor to the top of the step. In floors 2 and 1 the edge of the step was more sharply defined. In contrast to the step, which received many replasterings, the altar itself was given very few coats, and at floor 1 the step extended several centimeters on each side of the altar.

In the center of the room at floor 3 there was a circular hearth 75 cm. in diameter and about 5 cm. deep (Pls. 4 B, 27 A). It had been burned to a black and red-orange. At floor 2 the hearth was covered with an unbaked-brick platform raised slightly above the floor of the room. The platform, about two-thirds preserved, was undoubtedly hexagonal in shape, although there was no evidence for the sixth side (Pl. 5 A, B). The platform was 2.00–2.30 m. across and was preserved 8–12 cm. high, that is, to the clay layer of floor 1. This may have been its original height, or it may have been cut down when floor 1 was laid. We did not find a hearth at floor 2, but directly above the platform there was one, 65 cm. in diameter, on floor 1.

EARLY DYNASTIC II

It was not possible to separate Early Dynastic II from Early Dynastic I or III, and NT level VIII may be either Early Dynastic I or II and NT level V may be either Early Dynastic II or III. NT levels VII and VI were definitely assigned to Early Dynastic II (p. 29). In NT levels VII and VI, the temple plan, which had been changing somewhat through NT levels IX 1, VIII 2, and VIII 1, seemed to have developed into a layout which was acceptable in the remaining Early Dynastic levels. The cella was no longer raised above the courtyard, as it had been in level VIII, and the intervening antecellae were dispensed with. Although a kitchen and an ablution place may have existed in the unexcavated parts of NT levels IX 1 and VIII, they were recognized for the first time in the Early Dynastic II levels. A blocked opening in the northwest wall of locus 127 at NT level VII suggested that there were additional rooms at that level, but since the direction of the wall changed at that place, the through joints in the brickwork may have represented a stage in the building of the wall rather than the construction of a door opening later filled in. The other limits of the temple complex remained the same throughout Early Dynastic II.

NT Level VII

In NT level VII the temple plan was understandable although uncertain in places (Pl. 28 A). The entrance to the temple was from the northeast through a corridor which opened into a large rectangular space (9.5 × 12.5 m.) in front of the cella. At a lower floor the space was compartmented by very poorly preserved walls into several rooms. It seemed that the northeastern portion of the area was divided into two parts, locus 127, which may have been roofed, and courtyard 111. Room 125, with a drain tile through one wall, may have been an ablution place and room 135, with a fire pit in the floor, may have been a kitchen. Room 123, which was directly over the antecellae in NT level VIII, was also an anteroom to the cella. The walls were not preserved at floor 1, and there were indications that the space in front of the cella was not divided into rooms at floor 1. The cella occupied the same position that it had in NT level VIII.

Two well defined floors could be followed through the complex. At floor 2 there was a gradual rise from el. 83.55 m. in room 130 to el. 83.65 m. in courtyard 111, and el. 83.75 m. in cella 107. Floor 1 varied only a little throughout the building. It was at el. 83.85 m. in room 130, el. 83.80 m. in courtyard 111, and el. 83.85 m. in cella 107.

The northeast end of corridor 130 was not excavated and the actual entrance to the temple remained unknown. A preserved northwest jamb and a crushed baked-clay drain tile below the level of the sill indicated the doorway into room 127. The slope of the drain could not be determined from the one broken tile, and whether the drain continued beneath floor 2 of the room was not investigated.

In courtyard 111, there seemed to be a low rectangular platform against the southeast wall. Only the west corner remained, and it was preserved for a height of 10 cm. At floor 1 the wall between courtyard 111 and room 123 was partly overlain by a freestanding table. Both the table and a stand against the southeast wall were built of unbaked bricks covered with layers of clay plaster; the tops were not preserved. The stand was built of at least 3 courses of stacked, unbonded bricks, and the sides were covered with layers of clay that totaled 6 cm. in thickness.

In room 135 a small fire pit sunk below floor 2 provided a cooking place in that room. The ash-covered bottom of the pit sloped down from the floor of the room to a depth of 10–12 cm. at its semicircular end. The pit was 27 cm. wide and 40 cm. long. The partially preserved bench against the southwest wall was built from floor 1.

At floor 2 most of the southeast part of room 125 was occupied by an unbaked-brick platform bordered with bricks placed on edge and filled with other carelessly laid bricks to a height of 25 cm. The floor sloped from el. 83.65 m. at the southwest to el. 83.57 m. at the drain tile passing through the northeast wall. The drain tile was made of baked clay and was 20 cm. in diameter. No opening was found into the room, but there may have been a doorway above the drain (with a sill about 25 cm. above the floor). Floor 1 was level with the top of the platform at el. 83.85 m.

The walls of cella 107 were rebuilt at NT level VII. The entrance doorway was much narrower than it had been in NT level VIII and was balanced by a niche in the northwest part of the wall. The niche, 62 cm. wide and 17 cm. deep, was filled up and plastered over at floor 1. The new altar was placed directly above the altar at level VIII. It was built of unbaked bricks 15.5 × 23.5 × 3.5–5.5 cm. and measured about 1.60 m. wide and 1.17 m. deep. A step of unbaked bricks was built across the front of the altar and continued on the southwest to fill the space between the altar and the southwest wall. A pot, 4P 297 (Pl. 44:7), had been set into the step at the west corner of the altar (Pl. 7 A, B). At floor 2 the step was at el. 83.82 m., and at floor 1 at el. 83.90 m., flush with the top of the pot. The altar was preserved to el. 84.05 m. The offering table against the southwest wall was founded at floor 2 and was used only in the early part of the level, for it was completely covered by floor 1. The L-shaped curb northwest of the entrance doorway was founded on floor 2 at el. 83.77 m. It was made of two courses of unbaked brick and was replastered at the same time that the floor plasterings were renewed. At floor 1, el. 83.90 m., the top of the curb was at el. 84.13 m. The reason for the curb's location was never clear. At floor 2 the hearth in the center of the room was an oval with axes of 75 cm. and 100 cm. Between floors 2 and 1 there was a layer of dark gray-buff clay 10 cm. thick. Above this the hearth at floor 1 was 58 cm. in diameter, dished about 3 cm. below the floor, and was burned black, with a fire-reddened clay beneath. North and east of the hearth, there were small slightly squared, low-domed mounds made of a piece of unbaked brick covered with a thick mud-plaster coating. These seem to be the earliest recognized examples of the better-developed round offering tables in NT level VI (p. 11).

Very definitely, loci 126 and 133 were outside the temple complex at NT level VII. Neither room was completely excavated. On the northeast side of room 126 there was a wall, or more probably a bench, with only a southwest face. It was founded at el. 83.68 m. on floor 2 and was 27 cm. high. On the northeast the brick filling seemed to be bonded with the lower courses of the wall separating these two loci.

NT LEVEL VI

The temple, except for the southwest wall of the cella, was rebuilt at NT level VI (Pl. 28 B) following the outline that was established in NT level VII. There were a few differences; the entrance corridor was wider, the northeast wall was farther to the northeast, and a kitchen, locus 119, now occupied the east corner of the courtyard. In addition to the kitchen we found two installations not evident in the earlier plans: an ablution place and a curious clay-plastered ramp in front of an offering table or courtyard altar. These two items may have been represented at NT level VII by the low platform on floor 2 in room 125 and the freestanding table on floor 1 in courtyard 111, but this is not certain. The kind of installations we found in the NT level VII cella were also present in NT level VI. It is odd that there was no wall between loci 110 and 111. Only vestiges of a wall were found in NT level VII, but it represented a construction that was present in all the Early Dynastic temple plans after NT level VI.

There was a layer of earth and unbaked-brick debris between the top floor of NT level VII and the lowest floor of NT level VI. The lowest floor, floor 2, could be followed from room 130 at el. 83.95 m. to courtyards 110 at el. 84.05 m. and 111 at el. 84.08 m. to cella 107 at el. 84.02–84.13 m. Floor 1 also varied little, from room 130 at el. 84.15 m. to courtyards 110 at el. 84.15 m. and 111 at el. 84.17 m. to cella 107 at el. 84.17–84.22 m.

In corridor 130 the ledge at the southeast wall, the bench(?) against the northwest wall, and the pedestal in the west corner of the room belonged to floor 2 and did not appear above floor 1 (Pl. 8 A). At floor 1 a fireplace was formed around the pedestal below the level of the floor (Pl. 42 D). The sides and bottom of the fireplace and the exposed part of the pedestal were burned to a light red and black.

In locus 110 an ablution place 1.60 m. in diameter was built on floor 1. It had a one-course foundation of broken baked bricks, which was leveled off with potsherds and finally coated with bitumen. The bitumen, only partially preserved, was about 8 cm. higher than the surrounding clay floor. The east part of the construction had been destroyed when the drain pit of a superimposed ablution place was built in NT level V.

An early stage in the construction of a round offering table was found at floor 2 in the northeast part of courtyard 111. It was 90 cm. in diameter and 15 cm. high at the center of its slightly domed top. The circular table probably continued to floor 1, although its existence at that floor was not recorded. Near the south corner of the courtyard there was a bench against the southeast wall at floor 2. It measured 1.10 m. long and 42 cm. wide. At floor 1 the bench was replaced with a larger one 1.45 m. long and 55 cm. wide. The offering table or courtyard altar against the southeast wall was built at floor 2 and remained unchanged during the occupation of both floors. In front of the table a ramp started at floor level 3.10 m. from the southeast wall and sloped up at a rate of 1 in 3.5–4.0 toward the table. It stopped 52 cm. short of the table, and the normal floor was found between the two constructions. Both the table and the vertical sides of the ramp were coated with mud plaster. The sloping top of the ramp had the same coatings of clay plaster as the floor. The ramp was in existence during the entire level, and the upper part of it was destroyed by the construction of an NT level V ramp. A similar ramp was found at Khafajah in Nintu Temple V.[3] No satisfactory explanation of the ramps' use has yet been offered.

Locus 119, southeast of the courtyard, was the first in a series of kitchens. At level VI its only feature was a hearth in the eastern part of the room. A doorway into the room was not found. The southwest wall, at the place where there was a doorway in NT level V, was not in good condition nor preserved very high. If a doorway existed there, an unbaked-brick sill may have been raised one course above floor 2. At floor 1 the wall had been destroyed when the foundation courses of a new wall were built at NT level V.

Apparently the same southwest wall of cella 107 was used in NT levels VII and VI, for a rebuilding line was impossible to find. The other three walls were rebuilt at NT level VI. The northeast wall was thinner than the corresponding one in the level below and was chamfered at the exterior corner of the southeast jamb of the doorway. The exterior corner of the other jamb was destroyed and has been indicated by broken lines on Pl. 28 B. There was a niche 62 cm. wide and 13 cm. deep in the northeast wall in about the same position as the niche in level VII 2. As usual, there was a succession of floor plasterings. The lowest, called floor 2, was a yellowish sandy layer covered with a layer of dark red clay about 4 cm. thick. Another yellowish sandy layer 5–15 cm. higher was called floor 1, although there were a few patches of floors above that. The highest floor, recognizable only at a burned area, was 7 cm. above floor 1. The altar, not exactly aligned with the one in NT level VII, was 1.55 m. wide and 1.25 m. deep. At floor 2 the step was built with bricks laid flat at the edge and filled in with others set on the narrow side. The step was 30 cm. wide, and its tread was 15 cm. above the floor. At floor 1 the clay plasterings had increased the length and width of the step by 5 cm., and it projected beyond the side of the altar in the upper

---

[3] Pinhas Delougaz and Seton Lloyd, *Pre-Sargonid Temples in the Diyala Region* (*OIP* LVIII [Chicago, 1952]) p. 96 and Fig. 89.

floors. Northwest of the entrance doorway another L-shaped curb was built over the one at level VII. It was made with an unbaked-brick core one course high covered with repeated plasterings which reached a height of 11 cm. above the floor level. The hearths in the center of the room were not very well defined but were roughly 50–60 cm. in diameter. Just northeast of the one on floor 2 there were two offering tables 45–50 cm. in diameter at the bottom and 5–7 cm. smaller at the top. They were made with a core of unbaked bricks only one course high and covered with layers of plaster. Above each one there was a small shapeless fragment of brick which was all that remained of the tables at floor 1.

NT LEVEL V

The temple walls were completely rebuilt at NT level V, most of them on projecting foundation courses (Pls. 10, 29 A, 43 A and B). The plan was a further development of the one already seen in NT level VI. The location of the entrance corridor, the ablution place, the courtyard, the kitchen, and the cella remained the same. But a new wall divided the courtyard area, and there may have been a roof over that part containing the ablution place, which was rectangular instead of circular, as it had been in NT level VI. The courtyard contained the same features that were found there at the lower level: a bench, a rectangular offering table with a ramp in front of it, and two round offering tables instead of one. The kitchen hearth was replaced by a fireplace construction. At the west corner of the courtyard an anteroom was added for a second entrance to the cella. Whether this doorway, which was in the more customary location for a cella, was the main entrance was not certain. Although neither doorway was recessed in NT level V, the door nearer the altar was recessed in NT levels IV and III, and this decorative treatment was transferred to the opening of the anteroom at the farther doorway in NT level II. It should also be noticed that the position of the cella "furniture" suggested a pattern of moving from the northwest end of the room to the altar in the southeast. This new second entrance probably became the one in normal use in the rebuilt temple of NT level V. In the cella the altar and hearth remained as in the level below, but the two circular offering tables were replaced by a rectangular one. Two new curbs and a large bitumen-paved oval were added.

The numerous clay plasterings were grouped into floors 1 to 4 mainly to record the introduction of new elements and the various changes made during the occupation of the level V temple, but the succession of floor plasterings in the courtyard and cella showed no signs of interruption in their build-up during the entire level V occupation. The floor plaster turned up at the walls and continued as wall plaster. The floor plasterings were clay with no straw; the wall plaster was mud mixed with straw. Since the walls were replastered whenever a new floor coating was laid, the wall plaster became very thick, 6–7 cm. in places. The walls were made of unbaked bricks 14–15 cm. wide, 20–21 cm. long, and 5 cm. thick in the center and 2–3 cm. at the sides. Since the triangular room on the north (locus 128) was incorporated into the temple complex only at floors 4 and 3 and the kitchen was rebuilt for floors 2 and 1, the two lower floors are shown on one plan (Pl. 29 A) and the two upper floors on another (Pl. 29 B). Only in the cella and the kitchen, 107 and 119, could floors 4 and 3 be separated; in the other loci they were treated as one. Floors 4 and 3 were at el. 84.33 m. in corridor 130, at el. 84.35–84.50 m. in room 110 and courtyard 111. Floor 4 was at el. 84.50–84.52 m. in cella 107 and floor 3 at el. 84.60–84.67 m. Floor 2 was recorded at el. 84.52 m. in corridor 130, at el. 84.42–84.50 m. in room 110, at el. 84.50–84.67 m. in courtyard 111, and at el. 84.75–84.77 m. in cella 107. Floor 1 was at el. 84.85 m. in corridor 130, at el. 84.80 m. in room 110, at el. 84.62–84.75 m. in courtyard 111, and at el. 84.80–84.87 m. in cella 107.

Corridor 130 was much narrower at this level than in the level below. Very little of the northwest wall and the doorway into room 110 was preserved. The southwest jamb of the doorway was missing, and the face of the northwest wall of room 110 continued through the opening without an opposing northwest jamb. There was a drain through the opening at floor 4. The bottom of the drain, slightly below the floor, was at el. 84.27 m. in room 110 and at el. 84.24 m. in room 130, a difference hardly great enough to determine the direction of flow. The drain was about 15 cm. wide and had sides formed of potsherds which were preserved at one place to a height of 10 cm. (Pl. 8 *B*). At floor 2 there was a baked-brick pivot block on the northwest side of the opening at el. 84.43 m.

A small triangular room, locus 128, northwest of room 110 was formed by a thin screen wall (35 cm.) built between two converging structural walls. The room was included in the temple at floor 4 by means of a doorway which connected it with room 110. There was a baked-brick pivot block inside room 128 at floor 4. There was no doorway, and the room no longer existed at floor 2.

Locus 110 was a long narrow room (3.70 × 11.15 m.) between the entrance corridor and the anteroom in front of the cella. A doorway existed between the room and the courtyard next to it at all floors, and there may have been another opening at the south corner of the room where a well, dug sometime later, destroyed part of the dividing wall. The reconstruction on the plan offers a suggestion of what may have been there. In the room there was an unbaked-brick bench against the northeast wall at floor 4, an ablution place at floors 4 to 2, an unbaked-brick stand against the northwest wall at floor 2, and a large offering table or altar against the southeast wall at floors 2 and 1.

The ablution place (Pl. 20 *A*, 42 *B*) was built on floor 4; first the area was outlined with a foundation stretcher course of baked bricks placed just below the floor level. A similar course surrounded the drain pit. Then the area was edged with a header course of baked bricks placed upon the lower one. The baked bricks were 17 cm. wide, 22 cm. long, 6.0–7.5 cm. thick at the center and 4 cm. thick at the edge. Inside the edging bricks was clay plaster, put down in two layers totaling 5 cm. in thickness, which provided a base for the final coating of bitumen. The sides and bottom of the depression for the drain pit were formed with potsherds. The bottom of the pit was raised about 7 cm. with broken bricks. This may have been an attempt to construct a French drain, although no hole was found in the bottom of the pit. The broken baked bricks were probably put in just to make the finished drain pit shallower. The depression was also lined with two layers of clay as a base for the finish coating of bitumen. Although the bitumen coat was only partially preserved, it originally covered the entire ablution place and turned down with a battered face to the floor of the room. The floor of the room was at el. 84.30–84.33 m., the top of the ablution place at el. 84.38–84.42 m., and the bottom of the drain pit at el. 84.03 m. A few baked bricks at el. 84.45 m. were all that remained of the ablution place as it was rebuilt at floor 2. These bricks were a little larger than the ones used in the lower construction; they measured 17 × 26 × 4–6 cm. and had a thumb or knuckle impression on top.

The offering table (or perhaps altar, since it was not repeatedly plastered) was a large rectangle (1.80 × 1.20 m.) and had one rounded exterior corner (Pl. 12 *A*). The table was founded at floor 2 (el. 84.47 m.) and was preserved to its full height (el. 85.23 m.). This was about 45 cm. above floor 1. The table was made of unbaked bricks laid to a good face but poorly laid inside. There was a thin coating of reddish mud plaster on the sides and on the top where the surface was preserved on the southwest as well as a small patch on the southeast behind the table.

Courtyard 111, in front of the cella, was approximately 5.50 m. wide and 8.75 m. long. Alcove 118 did not appear to have a special function; no means of access was found but it must have been from locus 103. Upon floor 1 a thin partition wall (30 cm.) was built across the northeast end of the courtyard, apparently to screen the kitchen area from the area in front of the cella, creating locus 103. This made the route from the kitchen to the cella a circuitous one, and all the traffic from the entrance to the cella had to enter courtyard 111 at the place where the wall had been destroyed by the later well. Locus 109 was separated from the ablution room and the courtyard by a wall, T-shaped in plan and plastered on all its faces, projecting from the northwest wall. Locus 109 was more like an alcove off the courtyard than an anteroom of the cella. The separation of the alcove from the courtyard was strengthened, however, at floors 2 and 1 by two mud-plastered pedestals southeast of the opening into locus 109. The freestanding pedestal was 27 × 35 cm. and 23 cm. high; the engaged one was 27 × 20 cm. and 31 cm. high. Their use was not clear unless they were placed there to suggest a barrier at the opening to the courtyard. It is not unreasonable to assume a third pedestal at the end of the wall between locus 110 and the courtyard. Unfortunately, this area had been destroyed. (See the development of the plan at this place in NT levels IV and III, Pls. 30 and 32.) In room 109 there was a hearth at floor 1 which was not present at the lower floors.

The features in courtyard 111 were founded at floor 4 and continued into floor 1 without being rebuilt. The bench and offering table against the southeast wall were not preserved much higher than floor 1, but the highest floors stopped against them and their shapes were certain. The ramp in front of the offering table was similar to the one in NT level VI except that the slope of the ramp was a little steeper, about 1 in 3. Plate 12 B shows the ramp at floor 1 and the courtyard floor at floor 2. The beginning of the ramp can be seen on the left; the right half has been destroyed. The many plasterings of the sides of the ramp, offering table, and the bench measured about 10 cm. in thickness. The two circular offering tables (Pl. 12 B) were fashioned on a small core of unbaked bricks, and their increase in size was due to the many coatings of mud plaster they received (Pl. 13 A, B). At floor 4 the southwestern table had a roughly circular core of two courses of unbaked brick 35 cm. in diameter and 12 cm. high. The original plaster coating was a thick one, slightly domed at the top. It was 52 cm. in diameter at the bottom, 38 cm. in diameter at the top, and 15 cm. high. At floor 1 the table was 103 cm. in diameter at the bottom, 78 cm. in diameter at the top, and 45 cm. high.

We never completely understood the building sequence of the kitchen and the southeast wall of the courtyard at NT level V. At floor 4 the northeast and southeast walls of the courtyard and kitchen 119 were built over the corresponding walls in NT level VI. The other two kitchen walls did not align with the ones below, and the kitchen was some 75 cm. narrower. At floor 2 the kitchen walls were rebuilt on a projecting footing founded at the floor 3 level. The southeast kitchen wall was inside a newly built continuation of the courtyard's southeast wall, which had been in use since floor 4 and then was rebuilt at floor 1. Floor 4 of the kitchen rose from el. 84.35 m. at the doorway to 84.42 m. at the northeast end of the room; at floor 3 it rose from el. 84.47 m. to el. 84.55 m. After the walls of the kitchen were rebuilt the upper two floors were well above the corresponding floors in the courtyard. Floor 2 sloped upward from el. 84.72 m. at the kitchen doorsill to el. 84.85 m. at the northeast wall. At floor 1 a step had to be introduced to take care of the increasing difference in the floor levels. In the courtyard, locus 103, floor 1 was at el. 84.64 m. At the step in front of the kitchen door it was at el. 84.80 m., rose to el. 84.90 m. at the doorsill, and 85.00 m. at the northeast wall of the kitchen.

The lower kitchen, locus 119, had one fireplace and part of a second preserved against the northeast wall. The partition walls were preserved no more than 10 cm. above floor 3. The one preserved fireplace was about 1.00 m. square and had an opening 55 cm. wide. The upper kitchen had a small fireplace, 45 × 82 cm., in the west corner of the room. It was built at floor 2 and was preserved to just above floor 1. The circular hearth beside the fireplace occurred only at floor 2. The walls of the oval oven-like construction in the north corner of the room (Pl. 18 A) were founded at floor 2 and preserved about 10 cm. above floor 1—not enough to show whether the oven was domed or not. There were two burned floors in the oven, one at el. 84.97 m. and the other at el. 85.09 m. In the east corner of the room there was an unbaked-brick platform, one course high, at floor 1.

The cella, locus 107, was 3.90 m. wide and 9.45 m. long (Pl. 10 A). Before the first floor was put down, the debris of the NT level VI cella was covered with a 7–8 cm. layer of clean earth fill. The floors were made of many clay plasterings, one on the other with no ash or debris between. Floor 4, the lowest floor in the cella, can be equated with the lowest floor in the courtyard. Floor 3, however, was also associated with the lower plasterings in the courtyard. At floor 3 the necessary slope in the doorsill was aided by building up the southwest side of the sill with two courses of unbaked bricks. At floor 2 (el. 84.70 m.) a broken baked brick at the southeast jamb of the doorway to the courtyard was used as a pivot block. It was only slightly worn on a very small point. Small brick fragments may have been placed around the pivot block so that it could be used as the layers of clay rose higher (Pl. 14 A). At floor 2 the northeast wall was rebuilt with a course of unbaked bricks projecting slightly on the courtyard side (see Pl. 13 B near the top). At floor 1 the southwest wall, or at least part of it, was rebuilt.

The features in the cella were laid out on floor 4, and all of them continued in use throughout level V, although some changed slightly. The repeated plasterings on the floor around the bitumen-paved oval on floor 4 created a basin in the upper floors; the L-shaped curb northwest of the doorway to the courtyard was filled in at floor 1 to form a table against the northwest wall; and the curb separating an alcove, locus 108, from the rest of the cella disappeared in the floor plasterings by floor 1. The only feature added in the cella at floor 1 was a bench against the southwest wall, which was probably installed when the wall was rebuilt. At floor 3 all the features in the cella were given a wash of white paint, probably gypsum. Even the floor was painted white at that time. Patches of white paint were found on other plasterings, but none were as widely preserved as at floor 3.

A thin curb projecting at a right angle from the northeast wall just southeast of the doorway to room 109 was founded at floor 4. The curb was 15 cm. thick, projected almost 80 cm. from the wall face, and was made of two courses of unbaked bricks. Above this the curb was made entirely of many coatings of mud plaster, and in the repeated coatings a semicircular pedestal was formed on the southwest side of the curb. At floor 1 the pedestal was 50 cm. in diameter, 25 cm. high on the northwest side and sloped down to a height of 5 cm. on the southwest.

At floor 4 the bitumen-coated oval in the northwestern part of the cella had an irregular edge and large patches of the bitumen were missing (Pl. 16 B). Its axes measured about 1.65 m. and 1.90 m. The drain pit in the center, also coated with bitumen, was 42 cm. in diameter at the top, 35 cm. in diameter at the bottom, and 18 cm. deep. The bitumen coating was applied to the lowest clay plastering of the room (el. 84.50 m.), which just covered a prepared foundation around and under the drain pit. The foundation was made of baked bricks, most of them broken, but two measurable ones were 17 × 29 × 3.5–7.5 cm. and 20 × 30 × 3.5–7.5 cm. Under the drain pit there was a pad of broken bricks 35 cm. in diameter, and the sides were formed by two courses of brick. The lower surround was about 60 cm. in diameter and the upper one, just below the clay plastering, was 118 cm. in diameter (Pl. 16 A). The foundation course was not as large as the bitumen oval above it (it is shown on Pl. 29 A in broken lines). The construction of the oval is in many ways similar to that of the ablution place in locus 110 at NT levels VI and V. As the floors of the cella rose with repeated plasterings, an attempt was made to maintain the level of the bitumen oval, and a basin developed. The clay floor plasterings turned down to form the plastered sides of the basin, and at the bottom there was a build-up on the bitumen of very thin layers, 1 to 2 mm. thick, of a fine-grained clay. They did, however, follow the contour of the bitumen into the central drainage pit. At the upper floors the basin was encircled by two courses of unbaked brick, first a course of stretchers and then a course of headers (Pl. 14 B). The plaster on the sides of the basin continued over the unbaked bricks and was flush with the floor. There was no evidence that the sides of the basin were ever above the floor level. At floor 1, the bottom of the basin was at el. 84.63 m. and the floor of the room at el. 84.87 m.

The freestanding offering table was built just southeast of the bitumen-paved oval. At floor 4 (el. 84.52 m.) the core of the table was 38 cm. wide, 98 cm. long, and 15 cm. high. Two-thirds of the core was built of two courses of unbaked bricks 14 × 21 × 3–5 cm. The width was made up of one row of stretchers and one row of headers with their position interchanged in the second course. The remaining third of the core, on the northwest, consisted of sherds of large pots placed flat and on edge (Pl. 15 B). Those sherds placed on edge formed a box 9–11 cm. wide, 16 cm. long, and 20 cm. deep, which was covered with a few other sherds laid flat. Nothing but earthy debris was found inside. At floor 1 (el. 84.83 m.) after at least 15 and probably more plasterings, the table was 75–82 cm. wide, 117 cm. long, and 24 cm. high. At least five separate hearths were recognized in the series of clay floor plasterings, all of them southwest of the freestanding table. The lowest was slightly northwest of the middle three, which were placed one over the other; the highest was farther to the southeast.

The L-shaped curb projecting from the northeast wall at floor 4 to floor 2 was similar in shape and construction to the one built at the same place in NT level VI. The curb was 23–28 cm. thick at its base, 14–15 cm. thick at its slightly rounded top, and 19–20 cm. high. At floor 1, it was filled in to form an offering table projecting 85–90 cm. from the wall and measuring 72 cm. wide and 12 cm. high. The curb separating alcove 108 from the rest of the cella was built at floor 4 on a core of unbaked bricks covered with many clay plasterings. The core was one brick wide and two courses high. Sixteen plasterings were counted from floor 4 to floor 2 (Pl. 42 C; the number of plasterings shown above floor 2 is approximate). The curb began to decrease in height after floor 3 and by floor 1 was lost entirely and the difference in floor level between the two loci was taken care of by a simple slope. In the series of plasterings, numbered from the earliest, the fourth, fifth, sixth, and tenth were covered with a white wash.

The altar was built of unbaked bricks not bonded with the southeast and southwest walls of the cella. A through joint in the brickwork of the altar and irregularity in the brick-laying southwest of the joint suggested that the altar stood away from the southwest wall (Pl. 14 A). This was probably so even though it could not be definitely ascertained. If so, the space between the altar and the southwest wall may have been higher than the step in front of the altar but lower than the altar itself. This would have been a somewhat more elaborate arrangement than we found in NT levels VI and VII. The side and front of the altar were given several coatings of plaster; neither the original height of the altar nor the space southwest of it was preserved. The step construction, placed against the plaster face of the altar, consisted of three courses of unbaked bricks, 15 × 20 × 3–5 cm. The step was about 50 cm. wide and 17 cm. high. At its southwest end there were four courses of bricks which created a riser about 12 cm. high and an intermediate level between the step and the space between the altar and the southwest wall. The step was given many clay plasterings from 0.5 to 1.0 cm. thick. The projection of the step beyond the northeast side of the altar was due to the build-up of clay plasterings on the step which the altar did not have. At floor 4 (el. 84.50 m.) the top of the step was at about el. 84.68 m. and the intermediate level was at el. 84.80 m. Floor 3 was given a white wash and that one particular plastering could be followed with certainty. At that time the floor was at el. 84.60–84.65 m., the top of the step in front of the altar was at el. 84.78 m., and the intermediate level was at el. 84.91 m. At floor 1 (el. 84.85 m.) the top of the step was at el. 84.96 m., not much below the preserved height of the altar itself.

The bench against the southwest wall was built at floor 1. It was made of unbaked bricks, bluish in color and without straw. The mud plaster on the face of the bench was 13–14 cm. thick, not from many plasterings but from a thick layer (9–10 cm.) of plaster which was applied over the earlier plasterings and brought the face of the bench flush with its 15 cm. high projecting base.

At NT level V the excavation extended beyond the limits of the temple complex on all sides, except perhaps on the northeast at the mound's edge. On the southeast there was little of interest; on the southwest an open place contained the fragmentary remains of an oven and a bitumen furnace; on the northwest a continuation of the open place was bitumen-paved and, northeast of that, there were two rooms, only partially excavated, of a complex extending to the northwest.

In the open place on the southwest, locus 116, two floors were recorded; the lower one was at el. 84.57 m. and the upper one at el. 84.87 m. Both were earthen floors covered with black ash. At the lower floor we found the remains of an oven 2.05 m. in diameter. Its bottom was one course of laid unbaked brick, and its walls were one brick thick; both were reddened by fire. At the upper floor a roughly circular hearth 95 cm. in diameter was at el. 84.87 m., and a bitumen furnace (Pls. 9 *A*, 42 *A*) was built from a floor at el. 85.00 m. The firebox, below the level of the floor, was built of unbaked bricks and roofed with a brick arch (Pl. 9 *B*). There should have been a draft hole at the rear of the firebox, but we could not find it. The rectangular mud-plastered pan where the bitumen was melted was formed over the firebox by standing unbaked bricks on end. The bottom of the pan sloped gently down to the front of the furnace and was covered with many thin layers of bitumen. The furnace was surprisingly like a modern one built beside the canal in the village of Afak to heat bitumen to recoat the bottom of a boat (Pl. 9 *C*).

Northwest of the temple, locus 115 was a continuation of the open area. There, we recorded earth floors, usually recognizable by the accumulation of ash on them, at el. 84.33 and 84.78 m. A still higher floor sloped upward from el. 84.85 m. at the northwest edge of the excavation to el. 85.05 m. at the temple wall. It was covered with a large irregular patch of bitumen over a vertical drain made from the upper part of a large storage jar. There was no opening within the limits of the excavation between the open area and the rooms on the northeast. There were two floors in rooms 114 and 113, the lower one at el. 84.50–84.62 m. and the upper one at el. 84.80–84.82 m. In room 114 traces of a white wash were found on the plaster on floor 2 and the southwest wall. The unbaked-brick table or platform against the southeast wall was 32 cm. high and was covered by floor 1. There were no features in room 113 at floor 2. The room was partitioned at floor 1 and southwest 113 was filled with a platform with a raised central section. The central section was 20 cm. high and built with two courses of unbaked brick; the end sections were 10 cm. high and built with a single course. Both were covered with several coatings of mud plaster. The partially exposed shelf built against the northeast wall was 5 cm. high and was made of several coats of mud plaster. The northwest complex was not excavated enough to indicate its character, but rooms 114 and 113 did not seem to be part of the usual private house.

EARLY DYNASTIC III

Although NT level V may have been Early Dynastic II or III, NT levels IV and III definitely belonged to the latter period (p. 29). At the upper floor of NT level IV the excavated area extended beyond the immediate vicinity of the temple and indicated the domestic character of the surrounding buildings. In the expanded area it was evident that the boundaries of the temple remained very much as they had been at NT level V.

For the first time the doorway from the courtyard of the temple to the cella was set in a double recess, and the second entrance was definitely provided with anterooms. Also at NT level IV we found a "box" altar, with unbaked-brick walls and a hollow space inside, like that found in Shrine I of the Abu Temple at Tell Asmar in Early Dynastic II.[4]

NT LEVEL IV

In NT level IV there were two and, in some places, three major floors. Floor 3 was found in the northeast part of the temple and in the areas northeast and southwest of the temple complex where it corresponded to the bottom of the footings of the temple walls. If there were similar floors northwest and southeast of the cella, they were not recognized. At floor 2 (Pl. 30 A) the area excavated around the temple was slightly larger than it had been at NT level V and was still larger at floor 1 (Pl. 30 B). A few rooms at the extreme northwest limit of the excavation were also dug at NT level IV floor 1 (Pl. 31).

THE TEMPLE

The walls of the NT level V temple were completely torn down, and a new temple was built at NT level IV (Pl. 11 A and B). The new walls were not necessarily built upon those of the older temple; many were shifted and often the orientation was slightly changed. With few exceptions the main walls were built on projecting footings 25–45 cm. deep. The width of projection varied, especially since the footings and walls were not always aligned.

The plan of the temple was not materially changed. The entrance corridor was replaced by a larger room, the southwest part of the ablution room was partitioned off and, during the later occupation of the level, there was a doorway into one of the rooms northwest of the temple. The entrances to the cella were somewhat altered, as we have mentioned, and the main features in the cella were built anew. Even though there was a thick layer of debris and fill between the NT level V and level IV floors, the bitumen-paved oval, the freestanding offering table, and the altar were in their customary places. We did not, however, find a hearth in the cella at this level. The many clay layers that made up the floors and the thick accumulation of straw-tempered mud plaster on the unbaked-brick walls were usual conditions already common in the early temple construction.

Whereas the accumulation of clay layers in the cella could be divided into only two floors there were three floors traceable throughout the rest of the temple. Floor 3 was at el. 85.25 m. in room 68, at el. 85.20–85.40 m. in room 86, at el. 85.25–85.35 m. in courtyard 64 and merged with floor 2 at the entrance to cella 60. Floor 2 was at el. 85.50 m. in room 68, at el. 85.42–85.55 m. in room 86, at el. 85.25–85.60 m. in courtyard 64, and at el. 85.63 m. in cella 60. Floor 1 was at el. 85.73 m. in room 68, at el. 85.67–85.73 m. in room 67, at el. 85.38–85.80 m. in courtyard 64, and at el. 85.78 m. in cella 60.

The corridor entrance to the temple no longer existed at NT level IV. Although the northeast wall of room 68 was not preserved at floors 3 and 2, the wall fragment at floor 1

---

[4] Delougaz and Lloyd, *Pre-Sargonid Temples in the Diyala Region*, p. 183.

suggested that the long axis of the room was at right angles to the circulation. At floor 3 there was an open drain edged with baked bricks in line with the doorway in the southwest wall. Its direction of flow was not certain. Just under floor 1 part of another drain was found in the doorway. It consisted of an incomplete drain tile 45 cm. long and 16 cm. in diameter at the intact end and 22 cm. in diameter at the broken end. The drain was extended northeastward by baked bricks placed on edge. At the northeast jamb of the doorway, there was a pivot stone (el. 85.71 m.) in room 67.

Unfortunately, the room southwest of room 68 was given two loci numbers: 67 at floor 1 and 86 at floors 2 and 3. The only feature in room 86/67 itself was an ablution place in the same location as those at NT levels VI and V. The NT level IV ablution place was built at floor 3 on a pad of broken potsherds. It was outlined on the northeast and northwest by a baked-brick curb preserved two courses high. On the southwest there was a raised sill formed with a single course of baked bricks. We did not find a drain pit belonging to the floor 3 basin. If there was one, it was probably in the same position as the one at floor 1. The basin had been covered with bitumen, most of which was destroyed. Small potsherds had been placed upright against the inside of the curb and the southeast wall to provide a sort of cant, and the bitumen on the bottom of the basin continued over it and up the sides of the curb and wall for a few centimeters. The bitumen also continued over the sill and ended with an irregular edge on the floor of the room. The bottom of the ablution basin was at el. 85.22–85.31 m., the top of the curbs at el. 85.45–85.47 m., and the sill at el. 85.28 m. The floor of room 86 was at el. 85.20 m. southwest of the basin, at el. 85.30 m. northwest of the basin, and rose to el. 85.40 m. at the east corner of the room. The line of the northwest baked-brick curb was continued in unbaked brick to form the edge of a platform, locus 85, northeast of the ablution basin. The floor of the platform was at el. 85.55 m. and a few paving bricks were preserved at that level. At floor 2 the basin remained at the same elevation, and the higher clay floors turned down over the curbs to it. In locus 85 only a small patch of floor plaster was preserved, and it was covered with a white wash. At floor 1 another ablution place was built of rather irregularly laid baked bricks with one small patch of bitumen coating preserved at el. 85.73 m. The baked bricks measured 23.5 × 35 × 3–5 cm. A large jar fragment 60 cm. in diameter and 52 cm. high placed just below the baked-brick paving served as a drain pit. Northeast of the ablution place the floor turned up over a line of unbaked bricks to form a very low platform similar to the one at floor 2. Later, an additional course of baked bricks was laid in the ablution place (Pl. 20 B), and a low unbaked-brick wall was built on the northwest side of the platform, separating it from the rest of the room. The benchlike construction along the northeast wall was also rebuilt at this time. New floors, 8 cm. above floor 1 on the platform and 5 cm. above in the east corner of the room, showed traces of a white wash or plaster.

At floors 3 and 2, a doorway was not preserved between room 86 and courtyard 64, but, since a doorway did exist at NT levels V and IV 1, one has been reconstructed. In courtyard 64 the large hearth at floor 2 was the only one recorded in the courtyard. The bench and offering table with a ramp construction in front of it were similar to those in NT level V, but there were no circular offering tables such as we found in the lower level. The entrance from the courtyard to the cella was doubly recessed. The recesses were formed in the brickwork and were so heavily plastered that a sharp definition of planes was lost. The rather awkwardly defined areas at the west corner of the courtyard in NT level V were formalized into two rooms, 63 and 61, which served as anterooms for the second entrance to the cella.

The kitchen walls were rebuilt at floor 3 and again at floor 1. In locus 66 there was not a recognizable floor 3, but beneath floor 2 there was an unbaked-brick filling from 20 to 30 cm. thick which rose from el. 85.40 m. to el. 85.65 m. in its southwest-northeast run. When the kitchen walls were rebuilt at floor 1, the exterior west corner was rounded, and the wall face bulged beyond the normal wall line. Although there was only the one face in the length of the preserved wall (35 cm.), it was treated as a curbing on the plan, and a continuation of the normal face was reconstructed.

On floor 2 in the kitchen there was an oval oven with unbaked-brick walls 18 cm. in thickness and preserved about 28 cm. high (Pl. 18 B). In that height the wall overhung its base by 12 cm. in what seemed to be a dome construction; the bricks were partly laid radially and partly corbelled. The inside plaster was burned to a red color, and the clay floor layers were blackened by fire. At floor 1 there was part of a larger oval or circular oven that must have almost filled the room (Pl. 19 A). The lowest course of the surrounding wall, the only course preserved, was laid on edge, and the original floor was placed on a layer of broken baked bricks and potsherds. In the west corner of the room there was a small fireplace, 32 cm. long, 22 cm. wide, and 20 cm. deep, burned red inside.

The walls of the cella, locus 60, were rebuilt on projecting footings at NT level IV. The unbaked bricks, measured in the southeast wall, were 16 × 21 × 5.0–6.5 cm. In the lowest four courses the bricks were laid flat, and above that they were laid on edge in a herringbone pattern as high as the wall was preserved. For no apparent reason the top of the projecting footings were at higher elevations at the ends of the room than the top of those under the side walls. This made it necessary to raise the floors and created a sharp slope in the sill of the doorway between the courtyard and the cella. Floor 2 in the courtyard at the cella doorway was at el. 85.25 m. and rose to el. 85.63 m. in the cella. Floor 1 in the courtyard was at el. 85.38 m. and rose to el. 85.75 m. in the cella. Above the debris of NT level V the lowest floor (NT level IV 2) was a 6-cm. layer of reddish clay that had been covered with several thin clay plasterings before a higher floor, floor 1, was established. Floor 1 was a 5-cm. layer of reddish clay on top of a 5.5-cm. layer of yellowish sand and had also been replastered several times with thin coatings of clay.

At floor 2 the features in the cella consisted of a long offering table against the northeast wall, a freestanding offering table in the center of the room, a box altar with a step in front near the south corner, and an enclosed space in the east corner. The same features continued at floor 1 except that the offering table against the northeast wall was shortened, small pedestals set off the northwest end of the room, and a raised bitumen-paved oval was built above the one in NT level V. We should have found a similar construction at floor 2, but the space below the floor 1 oval was much disturbed and, if there was evidence of a floor 2 oval, we missed it. The offering tables and pedestals were given several coats of mud plaster, often totaling 5 cm. in thickness. Small bits of white plaster were found on the walls, floor, and offering tables at floor 1.

The altar, which was built at floor 2 and continued in use throughout the level, was 2.05 m. wide and extended 1.60 m. into the room. It was a hollow box sitting on a solid foundation of unbaked bricks (locus 96). The box was formed of unbaked bricks laid flat in the northeast wall and in an irregular herringbone pattern in the northwest one. The southwest wall was destroyed, and part of the box was disturbed by a previously dug hole. The exterior walls were plastered, but only the northeast one was given repeated coatings; the inner faces were not plastered. The box contained nine baked-clay jars: 3P 528–30, 536, 538, 557–59, and 565 (Pl. 3 C). The solid coursing of unbaked bricks over the box was above the NT level III floor and may have been the lower part of an altar built at that level. The unbaked-brick step in front of the altar continued southwestward and filled the space between the altar and the southwest wall. Floor 2 in front of the altar was at el. 85.63 m. and the top of the step was at el. 85.70 m. Floor 1 was at el. 85.75 m. and the step at el. 85.80 m. At floor 1 a stand was built on the step, free of the altar face. The sides were plastered but the top was destroyed 12 cm. above its base. Also at floor 1 the space along the southwest wall was raised above the regular step and became lost in the plasterings of the NT level III step. The top of the box altar was destroyed at el. 86.12 m.

At floor 1 the offering table against the northeast wall was shortened, perhaps to provide additional space at the northwest end of the room. A freestanding pedestal near the northeast wall and another midway across the room seem to provide a sort of separation between the northwest end of the room and the rest of the cella. This separation is accentuated if a third pedestal is reconstructed at the southwest wall where the wall and floor plasterings were destroyed. In fact, there was a third pedestal at the southwest wall in a similar set of pedestals at level III 1 (Pl. 32 A). The pedestals were made of unbaked bricks and covered with plaster. That on the northeast was 35 cm. square at the base, and its sides sloped in slightly. It was destroyed 30 cm. above its base. The center one (Pl. 17 A) was 22 × 25 cm. at the base, its sides also sloped in slightly, and it was destroyed 25 cm. above its base.

Just southeast of the central pedestal was the raised oval built on floor 1 (Pls. 17 A, 42 F). It was made of unbaked bricks 15 × 22.5 × 4–6.5 cm. The sides were covered with bitumen, which turned outward at the floor level and inward at the top, and so its actual height could be measured. Most of the bitumen top coating was gone, and a layer of large potsherds, which served as a foundation for the bitumen, was exposed. In the center of the oval there was a circular drain pit with its bitumen coating well preserved. At some time the pit was partially filled with debris and its rim was lined with large potsherds placed at an angle as if to wedge a jar tightly into the depression. A second ring of potsherds had been put in at a later date, apparently for wedging in another jar, and similar sherds were found on top of the oval as well. There were enough sherds found to restore in drawing the shape of the jar that was probably the first one wedged into the depression (Pl. 46:3).

OTHER STRUCTURES

In the excavated area around the temple, there was little of interest. At NT level IV 2 in locus 147 the circular paving of baked bricks was around the neck of a large jar used as a drain. In locus 99 there was an unbaked-brick bench with rounded ends which was 23 cm. high. In locus 80 the trench (2.30 m. wide) extending southwest was all that remained of the exploratory trench dug in 1952. Beyond the trench to the southwest, a narrow tunnel was dug to find the inside of the SE level VI baked-brick facing. In the tunnel we found the south corner of NT locus 80 and about two meters beyond that a wall 1.10 m. thick, also built of plano-convex bricks (Pl. 43 A). At floor 1 in locus 142, a large oven filled the northeast end of the room. The sides of the oven were 40 cm. high and burned red.

In the northwest part of the dig several rooms were excavated down to NT level IV 1. Most of the rooms belonged to a single dwelling unit. If there was a courtyard in the excavation probably it was locus 56, since the large oven had to be serviced from that room. The doorway between loci 50 and 49 was blocked, apparently when the oven was built. The oven was placed on a one-course oval foundation of unbaked bricks laid on edge (Pl. 42 E), and the vertical walls were built of unbaked bricks 15.5 × 23 × 3–5 cm. laid in alternating horizontal and herringbone courses. In the low dome above, the bricks were all laid as headers on an increasingly steeper bed, until, by the seventh course, the highest one preserved, the bricks were at an angle of 30° (Pl. 22 B). The inside of the oven was covered with mud plaster 1.0–2.5 cm. thick. The floor was also mud plaster put down in four coatings, each one burned black. The oven opening was closed with an irregular mass of unbaked brick. A stair, of which the lower three risers were preserved, was built in locus 56 after the oven was in use and after there was an accumulation of ash on the floor.

NT LEVEL III

The structural remains of NT level III were exposed in most of the area. The destruction caused by the north-south wadi was apparent (Pl. 32 A). Other than the temple, the half-preserved building southwest of the temple was the largest structure in the excavation; the northwest complex seemed to be made up of several small units (Pl. 33). Two floors could be traced throughout the level, but they were not preserved in all the rooms or, in some instances, may not have been recognized.

THE TEMPLE

It appeared that some of the NT level IV walls were used during all of NT level III, that some were torn down and replaced at floor 2, and others were used until level III 1 and rebuilt at that time. There was no change in the general plan. There was a new ablution place at floor 2 which was rebuilt and changed at floor 1. The doorway from the courtyard to the cella was much narrower than before, and the proportions of the double recesses were changed. The raised oval at the northwest end of the cella was rebuilt at floor 2 but was not found at floor 1. The small pedestals built at level IV 1 were used at level III 2 and replaced with larger ones at level III 1. Also, it appeared that the level IV altar was not rebuilt until level III 1. There was not a clear separation between the level IV and level III temple constructions such as we had found between VI and V or between V and IV.

Floor 2 was at el. 86.10 m. in room 68, at el. 85.98–86.10 m. in room 67, at el. 85.82–86.02 m. in courtyard 64, and at el. 85.85 m. in cella 60. Floor 1 was found at el. 86.37 m. in room 68, at el. 86.40 m. in room 67, and at el. 86.12 m. in cella 60; it did not exist in courtyard 64.

At NT level III 1 the southwest wall of locus 69 was built of two rows of vertical reeds about 8 cm. apart with an exterior facing of unbaked bricks. The space between the reeds was filled with earth. It was the only instance of this kind of wall construction found in the excavation. At level III 1 the lower part of a bread oven also was found in the south corner of locus 68.

The ablution place in room 67 at NT level III 2 was built of baked bricks coated with a layer of bitumen (Pl. 21 A). The floor of the ablution place was raised 10 cm. above the floor of the room. The bitumen turned out on the floor and rounded in at the top, and the sides were sloped in 3 cm. About 45 cm. in from the southeast and southwest edges the floor was broken, and the central part of the platform was somewhat lower. A definite upcurve at the edge of the bitumen coating in the central part showed that the change in level was intentional. Presumably this wide edging, so plainly visible at the south corner, continued around the platform, but this was not certain. Near the southeast edge there was an oval of bitumen, with axes of 34 and 37 cm., raised 2 cm. above the edging, which widened at that place. (In Pl. 21 A, a small dish is sitting on the oval. It was placed there to indicate where a water jar may have stood.) In the central part of the platform the top of the drain was at el. 86.02 m., and the floor at the south corner was at el. 86.03 m. The edging was at el. 86.15 m. at the south corner, at el. 86.06 m. on the northwest and at el. 86.12 m. on the northeast. The top of the bitumen oval was at el. 86.16 m. The drain was built of four courses of baked brick. The drain hole in the topmost course was 15 cm. square and in each succeeding course was stepped back enough so that the lowest course was supported by a baked-clay vertical drain tile, 65 cm. in diameter at the top, 70 cm. in diameter at the bottom, and 45 cm. high. The drain tile was sitting on a course of baked bricks placed on edge and a lower course laid flat.

At floor 1 another ablution place was built on top of the one at floor 2 (Pl. 21 B). Less than half of it was preserved, but it seems to have been a space about 85 cm. wide, 1.20 m. long, open on the northeast, and closed in a semicircle on the southwest. In one place the baked-brick side was preserved for four courses. Less than half of the brick floor remained in place, and the level III 2 drain could have been used. The baked bricks in this construction measured 15.5 × 23.5 × 3.5–5 cm. The original height of the side was not certain, and no traces of bitumen or other coating were found on the baked bricks. The floor of the ablution place was at el. 86.09 m., and the top of the side construction was at el. 86.41 m.

There were no features in courtyard 64 at NT level III. In kitchen 65 a patch of the oven floor (el. 86.10 m.) and a fragment of the oven wall were found at floor 2. The remains of a circular bread oven, 70 cm. in diameter and 32 cm. preserved height, were also found at floor 2. The highest of the series of oven floors (el. 86.30 m.) was found at floor 1.

The features in NT 60 at level III 2 were, in most instances, the same that existed at level IV 1. In the cella level III 2 seemed to belong in the series of level IV floors rather than in that of level III, but the designations given at the time of excavation have been kept. The pedestals and offering tables of level IV 1 continued into level III 2. A new oval was built over the one in level IV (Pls. 17 *B* and 42 *F*). It was the same size as the earlier one but was built of unbaked bricks without a drain pit and was plastered with a layer of mud plaster about 7 cm. thick. The upper part was destroyed 11 cm. above level III 2. The top of the step in front of the altar was at el. 86.05 m., and its face was a series of three projecting planes; the one with the greatest projection was at the southwest wall. Only a 12-cm. space separated it from an offering table built against the southwest wall. Level III 1 covered all the features in the cella (except the altar) that had existed at level III 2. Two large unbaked pedestals, 40 × 45 cm., preserved 16–20 cm. high, replaced the ones of NT level IV. A third pedestal was attached to a long bench built against the southwest wall. Between the bench and the altar, a new offering table was built over the one at level III 2. Floor 1 continued over the step in front of the altar to the altar face. The altar was a solid block that filled the south corner of the room. It was preserved to el. 86.24 m. Since this was no more than 12 cm. above floor 1, we may have found the step and foundation courses of a box altar similar to the one built in NT level IV.

In locus 99, just southeast of the cella wall, we found a cache of stone statuettes (catalog numbers 3N 402–6) at el. 86.15 m. (Pl. 3 *A*). The statuettes may have been discarded outside the temple at level III 1, or they may have been buried from level II when the temple was rebuilt. If they were buried from level II, and if the limits of the cella were as we have reconstructed them, the statuettes were buried beneath the floor in the southeastern end of the cella.

OTHER STRUCTURES

In the northwest part of the excavated area the walls were better preserved than those of the temple were, but, even so, the building complex could not be resolved into its separate dwelling units with any certainty (Pls. 22 *A* and 23 *B*). We may not have found some of the doorways, and others may have been destroyed by the foundation courses of later rebuildings. The units seemed to consist of four or more rooms; the incomplete building southwest of the temple must have had at least six. The walls were of unbaked bricks 17–18 cm. wide, 23 cm. long, 6–8 cm. thick at the center and 4 cm. thick at the edge. Some of the walls were built of hand-fashioned bricks that averaged 13 × 19 × 8 cm. The bricks were laid flat or in a herringbone pattern but not in any recognized order.

The floors, mostly made of clay usually mixed with some straw, were put down in layers 1 or 2 cm. thick. It was impossible to trace a particular floor throughout the entire area, but it seemed that there were two major ones. The floors sloped up slightly from the temple. Level III 2 rose from about el. 86.00 m. at the temple to el. 86.30 m. in the northwest part of the excavation, and level III 1 from about el. 86.25 m. at the temple to el. 86.50 m. in the northwest.

Unfortunately, the structure southwest of the temple was partly destroyed when an SE level V retaining wall was founded lower than the NT level III floor. It was the most impressive non-temple structure in the excavation. The plan was recognizable as a dwelling with a single range of rooms around a central courtyard. The one floor that could be assigned to level III was at el. 85.97–86.15 m. Against the northeast wall of the courtyard, an unbaked-brick bench, 30 cm. high, partly blocked the doorway to room 47. In the central part of the courtyard a fireplace, 30 × 45 cm., was sunk 14 cm. below the floor. Near the southwest wall of room 3 there was a 40-cm. square of clay, 10 cm. thick, sitting on the floor.

In the northwestern part of the excavation, locus NT 21 was an empty baked-brick tomb, which had been sunk from one of the SE levels, certainly after SE level I and probably after SE level III. The tomb, 1.50 m. wide and 2.70 m. long, was built of flat baked bricks about 30 cm. square which, through an oversight, were not measured. The walls of the tomb were founded at el. 85.70 m. and were 1.27 m. high. They were one brick thick and were laid with a good inside face. Above the walls the side bricks were laid radially in an arch in which the lower courses were also slightly corbelled. At el. 87.46 m. the bricks were laid at an angle and overhung the vertical part of the wall by 27 cm. The one end wall preserved above el. 86.97 m. sloped inward 10 cm. in a height of 53 cm.

THE AKKADIAN PERIOD

NT levels II and I were assigned to the Akkadian period (p. 29). A few wall fragments of the temple were found at NT level II, but nothing at all remained at NT level I. In the northwest there was less change in the plan of the complex between NT levels III and II than between NT II and I. In both the southwest and northwest there was sufficient continuity in the structures to suggest that there had not been an occupational break between the Early Dynastic and the Akkadian periods.

NT Level II

Although the walls in the temple area were very fragmentary at NT level II (Pl. 32 B), a corner of the kitchen and the anteroom of the cella did verify the existence of the temple at this level. The walls were rebuilt, not always following the walls of NT level III, but it appeared that the plan had not been materially changed. The other structures have much in common with those of NT level III (Pls. 22 A, 23 B, and 34). We found two floors in the southwest building and the northwest complex. A still higher floor was found only in the west corner of the excavation.

THE TEMPLE

Only the north corner of the kitchen was preserved. The walls had been rebuilt but not directly on those of NT level III. This corner of the kitchen contained the remains of two ovens, one built over the other (Pl. 19 C). The lower one was oval in plan, with axes of 1.70 m. and 2.10 m. (restored). The oven floor was at el. 86.60 m., and presumably it was floor 2. The upper oven partly overlay the northeast wall of the kitchen and may have belonged to floor 1. It was circular in plan, with a diameter of 1.35 m. The floor was entirely gone but the oven wall was founded at el. 87.00 m.

Only one jamb of the doorway to the cella was preserved, and it was not recessed. The doorway from courtyard 64 to anteroom 61, however, was set in a double recess; this was the first time that the doorway was decorated in this way. The cella walls were so fragmentary that the dimensions of the room could not be determined. As we have reconstructed it, by broken lines on the plan, the room was a little larger than it had been in the lower levels. A small patch of clay floor was preserved against the southwest wall; it was at el. 86.52 m. and has been labeled floor 2.

OTHER STRUCTURES

Although the walls of the temple were poorly preserved, many of the walls of the other structures were sufficiently well preserved to be cleaned and articulated. In the several places where this was done, the unbaked bricks were plano-convex in shape and were laid either flat or in a herringbone pattern. The bricks measured 17 × 23 × 4–7 cm. and 15 × 25 × 4–7 cm. No rectangular bricks were found.

Most floors were clay usually mixed with straw, although some tamped earth floors were found. Floor 2 varied from el. 86.65 m. to el. 86.90 m. and floor 1 from el. 86.80 m. to el. 87.05 m. The usual small fireplace was found near the center of a room and was made of baked bricks standing on edge; the top of the fireplace was usually about 10 cm. above the floor. As the floors rose and new clay layers were put in, fireplaces often were placed one over the other.

On the southwest the building around courtyard 11 had one floor (NT II 2) at el. 86.22–86.45 m. and another (NT II 1) at el. 86.72 m. The thin partition wall in room 151 was not preserved as high as floor 1, and the circular bread oven in the north corner of courtyard 11 was at floor 1. No opening was found between the main building and the addition built on the southeast side at this level, but one may have existed in the part that was destroyed. In locus 152 at floor 2, a fireplace 60 cm. square was built of unbaked bricks placed on edge against the northeast wall. There was also a circular bread oven in the east corner and a smaller fireplace, 30 × 45 cm., built of baked bricks placed on edge in the center of the room (Pl. 22 C). At floor 1 the baked-brick fireplace was replaced by a baked-clay one about the same size, and it was replaced by a third, also of baked clay. In room 48 the circular bread oven in the southeast end of the room was found at floor 1.

The isolated two-room structure (loci 24 and 39) in the west corner of the excavation was built upon a projecting footing about 20 cm. deep. The floor in the building corresponded to the top of the footing, at el. 86.87 m. One or more courses of plano-convex bricks, not aligned with the foundation, were laid horizontally above the floor level. It was evident that the footing of the building cut below the floor and destroyed some of the walls of NT level II 1. On the southeast the footing cut into a level II mass of unbaked brick which was not related to any of the other level II structures. Since the walls of the building were covered by floor 3 at NT level I, it was given a floor designation of NT post-level II 1.

NT LEVEL I

At NT level I there were fragments of walls that did not materially add to an understanding of the structural remains of the period (Pl. 35). The walls were founded at various elevations and have been divided into three periods of building activity, or floors 3, 2, and 1. Presumably there was a temple at this level, but nothing of it remained. The walls that were preserved were domestic in character but gave little idea of the structures they were a part of. The walls that were cleaned and articulated were built of unbaked plano-convex bricks covered with mud plaster. At floor 3 the bricks in the northwest wall of NT 5 measured 16 × 20 × 4–8 cm.; the bricks in the southwest wall of NT 17 measured 17 × 22 × 3–7 cm. At floor 2 the bricks in the northwest wall of NT 18 measured 16–17 cm. wide, 22–23 cm. long, and 4–7 cm. thick; the bricks were bonded by placing headers and stretchers in alternate courses. In room 6, also at floor 2, the bricks in the northeast wall measured 16 × 27–28 × 4.5–7 cm. The wall was 87 cm. wide, and in its lowest course five rows of bricks were laid parallel to the wall face. In the next course three rows of bricks were laid at right angles to the face. These two alternating courses were repeated for the preserved height of the wall. At floor 1 the southeast corner of room 6 was rebuilt with bricks which measured 16.5 cm. wide, 23.5 cm. long, 7 cm. thick at the center and 4.5 cm. at the edges.

A few of the floors in NT level I were clay, but many more were tamped earth; both types were covered with ashy debris. Floor 3 varied from el. 87.05 m. in the south to el. 87.35 m. in the northwest. On the southwest it continued southwestward until it was cut by the SE level V retaining wall. The walls of the house around courtyard 11 were preserved as high as el. 87.53 m., and a patch of floor at el. 87.25 m. may have belonged to the latest occupation of this building.

NT level I 2 and 1 were cut by the structural remains of Sounding E (Pls. 23 *A*, 35, and 36 *B*). Floor 2 varied from el. 87.37 m. in the south to el. 87.65 m. in the northwest. In the few places where we found floor 1 it varied from el. 87.50 m. in the south to el. 87.85 m. in the northwest.

II

THE OBJECTS FROM NT LEVELS X–I

By Donald E. McCown

THE levels excavated in the northwest section of the Religious Quarter dated from the Protoliterate to the Akkadian period. Since the levels varied greatly in their excavated area (see Pls. 26–35), the size of the sample available from each also varied. Test pit NT 132, which went down to virgin soil, was a shaft in which little was found but a small sample of sherds. Level X was penetrated in only a few places, and levels IX–VI were essentially inside the temple limits. In levels V and IV the main area excavated was also within the temple, but the digging included some rooms around the temple. Levels III–I were of considerable size.

POTTERY AND THE DATING OF LEVELS

The pottery sample's main value is in dating the levels excavated.[1] The earliest levels (NT 132 floors 17–14) belong to the Protoliterate period, as indicated by the occurrence of bevelled-rim bowls (*OIP* LXIII, C.002.210), the only pottery type represented in any amount.[2] In the test pit 21 sherds of bevelled-rim bowls were from floor 17, 9 from floor 16, 11 from floor 15, and 3 from floor 14. Other sherds were rare and not very distinctive, except for one painted Jamdat Nasr sherd from floor 16 and two from floor 15. The pottery gives no indication of how early in the period floor 17 might have been, but a sealing (Pl. 63:4) from floor 17 suggests an early Protoliterate date.

Illustrated examples of the pottery of the Early Dynastic I period (NT 132 floors 14–1 and NT levels X–VIII) are on Plate 44:1–6. The period is determined by the appearance of chalices (*OIP* LXIII, B.007.700, 076.700, 077.700), which are the most frequent pottery type during that period. One was found in NT 132 on floor 14, which may be either Protoliterate or Early Dynastic I. Six were found on floor 11, 3 on floor 10, 1 on floor 9, 10 on floor 7, 9 on floor 6, 6 on floor 5, 1 on floor 4, and 7 on floor 3. Forty-seven chalice bases came from level X, 111 from level IX, 7 from a mixture of material belonging to both levels IX and VIII, and 16 from level VIII. With this vessel type as the criterion there is no doubt that finds from floor 13 in NT 132 through NT level IX are Early Dynastic I, but it is not clear whether level VIII dates to Early Dynastic I or II.

Besides the characteristic chalice, another vessel represented in some amount, though not limited to Early Dynastic I, is a deep truncated conic bowl (Pl. 44:1, 10). Sixteen of these were found between floors 13 and 3 in NT 132, 12 from level X, 104 from level IX, 20 from

---

[1] When a level may belong to either one period or another, it is included in the range of both periods and usually mentioned in the discussion of the earlier period.

[2] The shape designation scheme used here is that detailed in *Pottery from the Diyala Region* (*OIP* LXIII [Chicago, 1952]) by P. P. Delougaz. These designations refer to the shapes illustrated there that our samples most closely resemble and not to the application of that scheme to our samples.

levels IX and VIII, and 21 from level VIII. They are less frequent in levels VII and VI and only sporadic in levels V through I, when much shallower bowls of the same conical shape become characteristic. Other pottery finds which confirm the Early Dynastic I dating are a strap handle on a pot neck (*OIP* LXIII, D.545.626) from NT 132 floor 12, a lug handle with an incision above on a flat jar shoulder (*OIP* LXIII, D.504.353) from floor 7, a triangular excision (*OIP* LXIII, C.014.310) from floor 5, a jar shoulder with reserved slip and oblique verticals cut by two horizontals from level X, and several scarlet-ware fragments from level VIII.

The Early Dynastic II period (NT levels VIII–V) cannot be distinguished on the basis of the pottery found in the excavation, and so the levels belonging to Early Dynastic II must be determined by a process of elimination. As will be seen, since level V may be either Early Dynastic II or III, only levels VII and VI are unquestionably Early Dynastic II. Illustrated examples of pottery found in these levels are on Plate 44:7, 8, 10.

The Early Dynastic III levels (NT levels V–III) must be determined by a relatively small number of sherds with distinctive shapes. Illustrated examples are on Plates 44:9, 11, 12, 45:1–6, 46:1–5 and 7–9, and 47:5.

In NT level V there were a considerable number of broad rope ridges (as in Pl. 45:1 and 3). These rope ridges, common also in level IV, are probably of Early Dynastic III date.

In NT level IV the so-called goddess-handled vessels are represented by narrow, fairly high, undecorated handles rising from the pot shoulder, which may have incised decoration above a broad ridge with notching. Also found in level IV were a sherd from the top of a plate stand (*OIP* LXIII, C.367.810) and a rim sherd (*OIP* LXIII, C.366.810) with a tapered rim incised with a wavy line and notching on the ridge at the bottom of the rim, from floor 2, and a sherd, probably from a plate stand, with an incised design in two zones, from floor 1.

From NT level III 2 came a vessel similar to that in Plate 46:8 except that it has a disk base, a cylinder (*OIP* LXIII, C.803.200), the plate portion of a plate stand (*OIP* LXIII, C.365.810*d*), the rim of a plate stand with notches on the rim and ridge with an incised wavy line between, and the fragment of a pilgrim flask of tan ware with buff slip (*OIP* LXIII, B.816.521*a*). From floor 1 came two rims from plate stands (see *Kish "A,"* Pl. XII:15), and the neck and handle of a pilgrim flask (*OIP* LXIII, B.816.521*a*). From an uncertain floor came the plate of a plate stand (*OIP* LXIII, C.365.810*b*) with three ridges below the rim and the neck and shoulder of a jar (see *Kish "A,"* Pl. IX:15).

The "goddess"-handled pots in level IV are the best evidence for its attribution to Early Dynastic III. In level III the pottery is much more characteristically Early Dynastic III and probably late, especially the plate stands, spouted pots, pilgrim flasks, and ridged cylinders.

The Akkadian period is represented by NT levels II and I; their date has been ascertained from tablets and seal impressions. The pottery is illustrated by examples on Plate 46:6 and Plate 47:1, 3, 4, 7. The pottery of level II was not distinctive except for the appearance of several bowls of type 1 (see Vol. I, pp. 77–78) with rims 12–17 cm. in diameter and 3–6.5 cm. high. Also in this level there was a jar with rugose slip (Pl. 63:1). Jars with a similar slip have been found in TB Akkadian levels as well as in levels dating to the Third Dynasty of Ur (Vol. I, Pl. 148:5). In level I more distinctive Akkadian shapes were found such as ridged jar shoulders (see, e.g., Vol. I, Pl. 81:9) and the upper part of a pot (*OIP* LXIII, C.467.350).

For two reasons no attempt can be made to determine the pottery sequence of the Protoliterate through the Akkadian period. In the first place the sample is too small to distinguish pottery types with any certainty. Second, the jar and pot rims and the rims of the big bowls are too nearly uniform throughout to have a useful chronological range.

A fair-sized sample of vats or big bowls which vary little in shape (Pl. 48:4–12) was found from Early Dynastic I through the Akkadian period.

The conical bowl is another vessel with a long time range. The earliest were found on floor 14 of NT 132. Throughout, their diameter varies no more than one or two centimeters from 15 cm. In NT level VI and below the ratio of diameter to height is 1:1.5. In level IV the ratio is 1.5:2, in level III it is 2:2.5, and in levels II and I the ratio of diameter to height is 2.5:3 or more, and the rim diameters are frequently less than 15 cm.

TABLETS AND THE DATING OF LEVELS

The following tablets were found in the excavation and have aided in the dating of the NT levels:

CAT. NO.	LOCUS	REMARKS
4NT 259	NT 259 VI 2	probably Fara
4NT 66	NT 61 IV 2	Fara
4NT 62–63	NT 54 IV 1	probably Fara
4NT 64	NT 76 III 1	probably Fara
4NT 55	NT 45 III 1	Fara
4NT 61	NT 29 II 2	Fara
4NT 56	NT 48 II 2	Akkadian
4NT 53	NT 3 II 1	Akkadian
4NT 59, 60	NT 48 II 1	Akkadian
4NT 31	NT 8 I 2	Akkadian
4NT 26	NT 5 I 1	Akkadian

According to the dating of these tablets, NT level III is Early Dynastic and levels II and I are Akkadian. If 4NT 56 was found *in situ* there is some question about whether the period of Sargon and his two successors is represented in this area. There was, however, no sign of architectural discontinuity between levels III 1 and II 2, and one tablet by no means securely dates a level. According to Professor Gelb, the distinctive differences between Akkadian tablets of the time of Sargon and those of the time of Naram-Sin are not found at Nippur.[3] Consequently, dating criteria useful elsewhere fail us at Nippur, and NT levels II and I may date from the time of Sargon through at least the reign of Naram-Sin.

From the pottery and the tablets we may relate the NT levels to these specific periods:

Locus NT 132	
floors 17–15	Protoliterate
floor 14	Protoliterate or Early Dynastic I
NT levels X, IX	Early Dynastic I
NT level VIII	Early Dynastic I or II
NT levels VII, VI	Early Dynastic II
NT level V	Early Dynastic II or III
NT levels IV, III	Early Dynastic III
NT levels II, I	Akkadian

STONE VESSELS

LOW TRUNCATED BOWLS

CAT. NO.	LOCUS	REMARKS
4P 295	NT 131 VIII	Pl. 47:6
4P 298	NT 120 VIII	Light greenish gray stone; d. 15.5, h. 5.2 cm.
4P 271	NT 116 V 1	Buff stone; d. 8.2, h. 2.4 cm.
4P 260	NT 77 IV 1	Gray stone with granular surface; d. 22.0, h. 8.5 cm.
4P 288	NT II 1	Buff stone with pinkish tone; d. 11.0, h. 6.4 cm.
4P 170	NT 9 I 2	White calcite; d. 19.0, h. 5.2 cm.

[3] Personal communication.

HIGH TRUNCATED CONIC BOWLS

CAT. NO.	LOCUS	REMARKS
3N 512	NT 144 IV 1	Pl. 47:9
3P 620	NT 144 IV 1	Light gray-brown, probably limestone; d. 22.0, h. 8.1 cm.
4P 276	NT III 2	Diorite; d. 23.5, preserved h. 18.2 cm.
3P 410	Debris above NT temple	Pl. 47:8
3P 428	Debris above NT temple	Light buff stone; d. 24.0, h. 8.6 cm.
3P 401	Debris above NT temple	Pl. 47:10

BOWLS WITH CONVEX, OBLIQUE SIDES

CAT. NO.	LOCUS	REMARKS
4NT 69	NT 33 II 2	Pl. 48:1
3N 509	Debris above NT temple	Gypsum, inscribed; d. 20.0, preserved h. 7.3 cm.
3P 626	Debris above NT temple	Buff stone; d. 13.0, preserved h. 5.0 cm. Similar to Pl. 48:1

MISCELLANEOUS BOWLS

CAT. NO.	LOCUS	REMARKS
4P 261	NT 77 IV 1	Pl. 48:2
4NT 67	NT I	Pl. 47:11

SEALS AND SEAL IMPRESSIONS

There is no doubt of the Akkadian character of the style of the seal impressions from NT levels II and I, excluding the few which must be the product of Early Dynastic seals. According to Frankfort's analysis of the stylistic development of Akkadian seal design, most of these seal impressions belong to a transitional style which was given up shortly after the reign of Sargon in favor of the mature Akkadian style.[4] Characteristic of the transitional style and these impressions are the bull-man in profile rather than full face, the nude hero in profile, the lion's head seen from above, heroes or bull-men struggling with more than one animal which may include antelopes, ibex, and mountain sheep, and a seal inscription not clearly set off from the rest of the design. Among these impressions only one shows the mature style unmistakably (Pl. 63:11), though doubtless some other examples are not recognizable because of the incompleteness of the designs. Among the designs worth noting are those showing rows of bull-men (Pls. 65:15, 66:3–4) and other erect figures (Pl. 66:5–6).

CAT. NO.	LOCUS	REMARKS
4D 378	NT 132 fl. 17	Seal impression; Pl. 63:4
4N 174	NT 106 V 2	Cylinder seal; Pl. 63:6
4D 315	NT 57 IV 1	Seal impression; Pl. 63:5
4N 153	NT 80 III 2	Cylinder seal; Pl. 63:8
4N 129	NT 52 III 1	Cylinder seal; black stone; design so worn it is unintelligible; h. 2.0, d. 1.0 cm.
4N 138	NT 53 III 1	Cylinder seal; Pl. 63:2
4N 122	NT 32 II 2 below burial 4B 117	Seal impression; Pl. 71:5
4N 123	NT 32 II 2 below burial 4B 117	Stamp seal; Pl. 71:6

[4] *Cylinder Seals* (London, 1965) pp. 81–86.

CAT. NO.	LOCUS	REMARKS
4N 131	NT 48 II 2	Stamp seal; Pl. 71:11
4D 195	NT 41 II 2	Seal impression; Pl. 65:7
4D 240	NT 41 II 2	Seal impression; Pl. 66:2
4D 297	NT 43 II 2	Seal impression; Pl. 66:14
4D 298	NT 43 II 2	Seal impression; Pl. 63:3
4D 300	NT 43 II 2	Seal impression; Pl. 64:9
4D 309	NT 5 II 2	Seal impression; Pl. 64:2
4D 323	NT 48 II 2	Seal impression; Pl. 66:8
	NT II 2	One indistinct impression of animal contest
4D 157	NT 43 II 1	Seal impression; Pl. 64:5
4D 199	NT 21 II 1	Seal impression; Pl. 63:7
4D 204	NT 43 II 1	Seal impression; Pl. 64:13
4D 205	NT 43 II 1	Seal impression; Pl. 65:1
4D 208	NT 43 II 1	Seal impression; Pl. 66:7
4D 214	NT 43 II 1	Seal impression; Pl. 66:13
4D 218	NT 43 II 1	Seal impression; Pl. 64:12
4D 239	NT 20 II 1	Seal impression; Pl. 66:9
4D 245	NT 43 II 1	Seal impression; Pl. 63:9
4D 250	NT 42 II 1	Seal impression; Pl. 65:2
4D 251	NT 42 II 1	Seal impression; Pl. 65:15
4D 252	NT 42 II 1	Seal impression; Pl. 66:12
4D 254	NT 42 II 1	Seal impression; Pl. 63:14
4D 255	NT 42 II 1	Seal impression; Pl. 65:3
4D 257	NT 42 II 1	Seal impression; Pl. 63:13
4D 258	NT 42 II 1	Seal impression; Pl. 66:1
4D 260	NT 43 II 1	Seal impression; Pl. 63:15
4D 264	NT 43 II 1	Seal impression; Pl. 66:4
4D 266	NT 43 II 1	Seal impression; Pl. 66:5
4D 267	NT 43 II 1	Seal impression; Pl. 66:3
4D 273	NT 43 II 1	Seal impression; Pl. 65:12
4D 274	NT 43 II 1	Seal impression; Pl. 64:6
4D 275	NT 43 II 1	Seal impression; Pl. 64:10
4D 278	NT 43 II 1	Seal impression; Pl. 64:7
4D 286	NT 43 II 1	Seal impression; Pl. 64:11
4D 287	NT 43 II 1	Seal impression; Pl. 66:10
4D 303	NT 43 II 1	Seal impression; Pl. 64:8
4D 304	NT 43 II 1	Seal impression; Pl. 65:14
4NT 269	NT 43 II 1	Seal impression; Pl. 64:3
4NT 270	NT 43 II 1	Seal impression; Pl. 64:1
	NT II 1	Twelve fragmentary impressions and ten indistinct impressions of animal contest
4N 157a	NT 16 I 3	Stamp seal; Pl. 71:13
4D 181	NT 9 I 3	Seal impression; Pl. 65:13
4D 146	NT 1 I 2	Seal impression; Pl. 65:5
4D 147	NT 1 I 2	Seal impression; Pl. 66:6
4D 148	NT 1 I 2	Seal impression; Pl. 65:8
4D 151	NT 1 I 2	Seal impression; Pl. 65:4
4D 154	NT 6 I 2	Seal impression; Pl. 65:10
4NT 268	NT 1 I 2	Seal impression; Pl. 64:4
4D 101	Debris above NT I	Seal impression; Pl. 66:11
4D 119	Debris above NT I	Seal impression; Pl. 65:6
4D 129	Debris above NT I	Seal impression; Pl. 63:11

CAT. NO.	LOCUS	REMARKS
4D 131	Debris above NT I	Seal impression; Pl. 65:9
4D 136	Debris above NT I	Seal impression; Pl. 65:11
	Debris above NT I	Four fragmentary or poor impressions of animal contest
4N 105	NT dump	Cylinder seal; Pl. 63:12

SCULPTURE

CAT. NO.	LOCUS	REMARKS
4N 186	NT 79 IV 1	Stone plaque; Pl. 59:1, 67:2
4N 155	NT 87 IV 1	Stone plaque; Pl. 66:16
4D 348	NT 61 III 2	Corner of undecorated plaque of bituminous limestone; preserved l. 12.0, preserved w. 10.0, th. 2.5 cm.
4N 110	NT 74 III 1	Stone plaque; Pl. 67:1
4N 111	NT 60 III 1	Base of stone statuette; Pl. 66:15
3N 401	NT 99 III 1	Stone statuette; Pl. 68:3

A cache of stone statuettes (3N 402–6) was found in locus 99 just southeast of NT 60 at NT level III 1. The cache was doubtless buried when the temple was rebuilt at NT level II. At that time the cella was extended southeastward, and the cache, buried within the limits of the NT level II cella, was actually placed outside of the cella boundary in NT level III (see Pl. 32).

CAT. NO.	LOCUS	REMARKS
3N 402	NT 99 III 1	Pls. 67:3, 68:1–2
3N 403	Same as 3N 402	Pl. 70:2–3
3N 404	Same as 3N 402	Pl. 69:1–2
3N 405	Same as 3N 402	Pl. 67:5
3N 406*a*	Same as 3N 402	Pl. 70:1
3N 406*b*	Same as 3N 402	Pl. 68:4

Statuettes 3N 402 and 405 are in the Early Dynastic abstract style; statuettes 3N 403 and 404 are in the more realistic Early Dynastic style.

Several other pieces were found in the debris above the temple and may also be considered as belonging to the temple inventory:

CAT. NO.	LOCUS	REMARKS
3N 274	Debris above NT temple	Limestone or shell eye inset; Pl. 59:2
3N 275	Same as 3N 274	Feet of stone statuette; Pl. 70:8
3N 328	Same as 3N 274	Stone statuette; Pl. 67:4
4N 86	Same as 3N 274	Stone statuette; Pl. 70:5
3N 476	Same as 3N 274	Stone figurine; Pl. 70:4
3N 511	Same as 3N 274	Two stone vases supported by an animal base: Pl. 69:3–5

BAKED CLAY FIGURINES AND MODELS

CAT. NO.	LOCUS	REMARKS
3N 392	NT 100 IV	Model chariot(?) wheel; Pl. 60:6
4D 249	NT 42 II 1	Figurine head; Pl. 70:9
4D 248	NT 42 II 1	Model boat prow
4D 187	NT 43 II 1	Animal figurine with legs, tail, and ears missing; l. 6.8, preserved h. 4.2 cm.
4D 159	NT 1 I 2	Female figurine with comb at back of neck, right arm

CAT. NO.	LOCUS	REMARKS
		straight down at side, left arm broken; h. (feet to middle of head) 7.5, w. 3.8 cm.
4D 26	NT I 2	Female figurine, tan ware, vertical line down back; feet (in ledge) broken; left side of waist chipped; th. 1.8 cm.

PERSONAL ORNAMENTS

CAT. NO.	LOCUS	REMARKS
4N 213	NT 133 VIII 1	Stone pendant; Pl. 59:4
4N 210	NT 111 VI 2	Shell pendant; Pl. 59:3
4N 185	NT 118 V	Separator bead; Pl. 59:10
4N 184	NT 111 V	Shell bead; Pl. 59:8
3N 506	NT 144 IV	Nine clay barrel beads, light brown ware, dark brown surface; l. 1.9, d. 1.3 cm.
3N 510	NT IV 1	Stone bead; Pl. 70:6
3D 585	NT 100 IV 1	Stone bead; Pl. 59:11
4N 118	NT 50 IV 1	Bronze pin; Pl. 59:6
4N 126	NT 75 IV 1	Bronze pin; preserved l. 6.7, d. 0.1 cm.
4N 101	NT 33 II 2	Bead; Pl. 63:10
4N 128	NT 25 II 2	Stone pendant; Pl. 59:12
4N 165	NT 27 II 2	Bronze pin; Pl. 59:5
4N 107	NT 44 II 1	Crystal pendant; Pl. 59:9
4N 157b	NT 16 I 3	Bead; d. 1.0 cm.
4N 94	Intrusive into NT 9 I 2	Bronze pendant; Pl. 74:5

OTHER SMALL OBJECTS

CAT. NO.	LOCUS	REMARKS
4D 374	NT 133 VII	Bronze chisel; Pl. 59:7
4N 189	NT V	Bronze needle, eye bent over and hammered; l. 8.8, d. 0.2 cm.
3N 409–10	NT 96 IV	Two bluish-green glazed frit disks, somewhat lentoid section; d. 2.5, 4.0, th. 0.7, 0.6 cm.; from one of the jars in a cache buried in NT IV altar (see Pl. 45:4)
4D 226	NT 61 IV 1	Bronze arrow butt; l. 5.1, w. 1.0, th. 0.6 cm.
4N 146	NT 81 IV 1	Bone spatula; Pl. 60:1
4N 119	NT 35 II 2	Bronze pin; l. 14.0, d. 0.25 cm.
4N 124	NT 32 II 2 under burial 4B 117	Bronze balance pan; concave, 4 suspension holes; d. 6.8, 0.8 cm.
4N 163	NT 27 II 2	Bronze spear head; Pl. 60:2
4N 164	NT 27 II 2	Bronze hook; Pl. 60:7
4N 125	NT 10 II	Bronze needle; l. 11.0, d. 0.3 cm.
4N 127	NT 20 II 1	Triangular sectioned flint blade, saw edge with silica polish, set in bitumen; preserved l. 4.0, h. 3.2, th. 0.7 cm.
4N 95	NT 46 II 1	Bronze chisel; Pl. 60:5
4N 82	NT 1 II 1	Stone weight(?); l. 1.3, w. 0.45 cm.
4N 92	NT 9 I 2	Fragment of gold leaf; l. 2.9, w. 1.1 cm.
3N 323	Debris above NT temple	Pierced stone disk; d. 4.2, th. 2.0 cm.
3N 481	Debris above NT temple	Bronze pin head; Pl. 70:7

CAT. NO.	LOCUS	REMARKS
4N 207	NT dump	Corner of stone palette, preserved l. 5.0, preserved w. 3.8, th. 0.9 cm.
4N 208	NT dump	Bronze tweezers; l. 4.9, w. 0.5 cm.

III

THE STRUCTURAL REMAINS IN SE LEVELS VI–I

By RICHARD C. HAINES

IN the SE levels, the problems presented by the excavation sometimes were more interesting than the structural remains uncovered. The Akkadian temple in NT level II was covered by sub-surface overburden so that there was no evidence of a temple in the SE levels. However, there were some signs that there had been a structure on the site of the earlier temple. We found a vertical drain, a well, and part of a retaining wall. The retaining wall with its buttressed facing suggested a temple platform, which was all that remained of what may have been a continuation of the temple found in the NT levels below. The platform was created by cutting away some of the stratified debris of the earlier levels in order to give a more regular shape to the area around the temple. The area was then enclosed with a retaining wall. This method of making a platform left undisturbed the NT levels II and I floors inside the retaining wall, floors that were 2.20–2.50 m. higher than those of the Third Dynasty of Ur outside the retaining wall.

The surface of the mound at this place had a decided downward slope from the southwest to the northeast with *wadis* coming in from the west, southwest, and south. They created three isolated areas in the excavation where structures were found along the southwest boundary of the excavation and an overburden of wash in a sort of basin in the central part of the excavation. Because of these conditions, we found Seleucid structures under the surface in the southwest part of the excavation and Akkadian or Early Dynastic walls below the surface no more than 15 meters to the northeast.

In the lower part of the overburden in the central part of the excavation, there was a thick layer of potsherds above the Kassite and below the Neo-Babylonian occupations. It probably represented the surface during a time when this part of the mound was unoccupied.

THE UR III–OLD BABYLONIAN PERIODS

Structural remains identified with the Third Dynasty of Ur, Isin-Larsa, and Old Babylonian periods were sparse and somewhat scattered in the excavation. Within the temple platform the only evidences of an occupation were a vertical drain and a well. A retaining wall was found near the southwest boundary of the excavation, but a deeper exploratory pit beside it yielded no structures at all.

This exploratory pit, 1 × 3 m., was dug from SE level VI, locus 4 (Pls. 36 *A*, 43 *A*) to a depth of about a meter below the base of the retaining wall. In spite of the lack of structural remains, thin ash layers indicated floors at el. 83.42 m., 83.75 m., and 84.20 m. These have been designated as SE levels IX, VIII, and VII. A mixture of potsherds was found in the pit, and the levels were not assigned to any cultural period.

SE Level VI

The vertical drain, locus 86, and the well, locus 85, can be assigned to level VI (Pl. 36 A). The vertical drain was about 1.75 m. in diameter and was filled with three baked-clay rings, each 70 cm. in diameter. The well (p. 43) was built of baked bricks and had an inside diameter of 1.45 m. The bricks were trapezoidal in shape and measured 16.5 and 22.5 cm. wide, 27.5 cm. long, and 8.5 cm. thick. The lining was preserved as high as el. 85.06 m. It was missing, however, between el. 84.73 m. and cl. 83.20 m.; presumably this part had collapsed and the bricks had fallen to the bottom of the well. Below el. 83.20 m. the lining continued downward beyond the depth of our excavation. We reached water at el. 77.60 m. and stopped digging at el. 77.20 m. The present level of the plain northeast of the excavation is about el. 84.50 m.

Southwest of the platform two earth floors were found in locus 4; the lower one was at el. 84.60 m. and the upper one at el. 85.45 m. No attempt was made to trace the floors accurately into loci 82 and 83. The lower one, floor 2, was attributed to the Third Dynasty of Ur (p. 48), but no date can be suggested for the upper one, floor 1.

The retaining wall formed one side of a platform whose extent was not learned (Pl. 24 A). A south corner was found, but little more than a meter of the southeast run was preserved (Pl. 36 A). On the northwest the wall continued beyond the boundary of our excavation, and no other indications of the wall were found in the excavation.

The retaining wall was 1.30 m. thick and was built of unbaked bricks, 16 × 24 × 8 cm., laid in alternate flat and on-edge courses. In the one place where we investigated the inner side of the wall to its base (p. 20, Pl. 43 A), it was not laid to a face and was placed upon four courses of baked bricks which continued upward on the exterior as a facing one brick thick. There were three through joints which divided the excavated part of the wall into four sections, called here the southeast, south central, north central, and northwest. In all four sections the wall faces were battered, irregularly buttressed, and stepped in one or two times from bottom to top. The buttresses projected 20 cm. from the normal face of the wall, and the steps varied from 5 to 7 cm. in width (Pl. 36 A).

The southeast section was repaired some time after it was built. The lower courses were left intact, but the upper part of the wall face was rebuilt; in some places the wall line was changed and the buttresses not aligned. The lower part of the wall was built of baked bricks measuring 16 × 26 × 7 cm. laid in courses of alternating headers and stretchers. This bond gave a good key into the unbaked-brick backing. The lower part of the wall was founded at el. 84.35–84.48 m., and there was one setback. The base was six courses high and stepped in to a face five courses high. Each part was laid with a batter of about 1 cm. In the northwesternmost run in this section there were two setbacks. The bottom face was four courses high, the middle face was five courses high, and there were two courses of a third band above that (Pl. 24 B). The baked bricks in the facing of the upper rebuilding were 17.5 × 26 × 7 cm. and were not regularly laid. In some places the bonding was similar to that in the wall face below, and in other places a course of headers alternated with a course of stretchers. Many broken bricks were used in the stretcher courses, and they gave the effect of an all-header bond with occasional stretchers in it. Most of the rebuilding was nine courses high and was laid with a batter of 3 cm., up to el. 85.82 m.

In the south central section there was a vertical joint in the baked-brick facing 5.80 m. from its northwestern end, where a rebuilding of the northwest part abutted the original brickwork. The southeast part of the facing was built with baked bricks 17 × 26 × 7 cm. laid in courses of alternating headers and stretchers. The bottom part of the facing was founded at el. 84.48–84.52 m. and was fourteen courses high laid with a batter of 5 cm. Above that there was a setback and two additional courses, up to el. 85.85 m. The repair of the northwest part was done with square bricks 30 × 30 × 7 cm. and 31 × 31 × 7 cm. and occasional rectangular bricks 16 × 25 × 7 cm. and 19 × 29 × 7 cm. The bricks appeared to be laid in a running bond with irregularities that resulted from the use of some broken bricks. A bond with the unbaked-brick wall was provided by the use of square and rectangular bricks. This part of the wall was founded at el. 84.40 m., and there were two setbacks. The base was five courses high, and the upper face was six courses high and topped off at el. 85.60 m.

The north central section of the wall was similar to the southeast section, that is, with baked bricks 16 × 26 × 7 cm. laid in courses of alternating headers and stretchers. This section was founded at el. 84.45 m. and there were two setbacks. The base was four courses high, the middle face was four courses high laid with a batter of 1 cm., and the upper face was six courses high laid with a batter of 3 cm., up to el. 86.60 m. At the southeast end of this section the base was founded at el. 84.63 m. and was only two courses high.

The northwest section was also built with baked bricks 16 × 26 × 7 cm. laid in courses of alternating headers and stretchers. This section was founded at el. 84.43 m. and there were three setbacks. The base course was four courses high, and above that there was a setback to a single course of bricks. The third band was six courses high and the fourth or top one was three courses high, and topped off at el. 85.52 m.

Although the facing, and presumably the unbaked-brick wall behind it, was built in four sections, there was little variation in elevation at the bottom of the wall. It was founded at el. 84.35 m. at the southeastern corner but lost the two lower courses between the third and fourth buttresses, and there the wall was founded at el. 84.47 m. In the northwest part of the excavation it was founded at el. 84.43 m. There was also some regularity in the top of the baked-brick facing, although it did drop three brick courses, or about 28 cm., in its run. We removed about 50 baked bricks hoping to find one with a stamp impression and identify the builder of the temple platform and the god to whom the temple was dedicated. None of the bricks was stamped, and the name of the god remained unknown. Nevertheless, the through joints in the retaining wall of the platform and the repairs in the baked-brick facing suggested that a considerable span of time was represented in the construction. It may have been built during the Third Dynasty of Ur and continued in use until Kassite times.

Either the SE level VI wall and its facing were leveled off when the SE level V wall was built or the level VI interior unbaked brickwork was left as a core and was added to and refaced to form the level V wall. The latter method of rebuilding was used in the enclosure wall of the Ekur in the Kassite period. At least it would account for an apparent continuity of construction in the SE level VI and V retaining walls, although the faces of the two walls did not correspond.

THE KASSITE PERIOD

The Kassite period was represented in the excavation by SE level V (p. 48, Pl. 36 *B*). Within the temple platform only meaningless wall fragments could be attributed to the Kassite period. The retaining wall was rebuilt, and southwest of that, at a lower elevation, we found rooms of a substantial building in the original exploratory trench.

SE Level V

Within the temple platform the wall fragments were founded at el. 86.97–87.08 m. A layer of matting had been placed in the wall at the elevation of the tamped earth floor, or 87.27 m.

The southwest retaining wall was rebuilt at SE level V, and there is a possibility that the core of the level VI wall was incorporated in the new construction. The level V wall was much thicker than the one in the lower level, 2.15 m. in the northwest and 2.70 m. in the central part. The unbaked bricks were generally somewhat larger, 17 × 25–26 × 8 cm., but they had been laid in the same way, with alternating courses of flat and on-edge bricks. The central part of the wall was founded at el. 85.90 m. and preserved to el. 86.05 m. at the southwest face and el. 86.85 m. at the northeast face. The northwest part of the wall was founded at el. 85.55 m. and preserved to el. 86.55 m. and 86.80 m. In no place was the wall face preserved any higher than the floor on the temple platform or those on the southwest.

In locus 83 we found three floors of tamped earth belonging to SE level V. The lowest, floor 3, was at el. 86.20 m., floor 2 was at el. 86.65 m., and floor 1 at el. 87.05 m. If there was a floor lower than the one recorded as floor 3, it was not recognized. In locus 4 there were four floors. The two lower ones, designated as floors 3*b* and 3*a*, were at el. 86.00 m. and 86.50 m., respectively. Floor 2 was at el. 86.75 m. and floor 1 at el. 87.05 m. Floor 2 was a coating of mud plaster; the other three were tamped earth.

Southwest of the temple platform, part of a well-constructed building was found in the original exploratory trench. Only one room and parts of two others were within the trench, and they could suggest nothing more than that they belonged to a substantial building. The southeast wall abutted an exposed exterior corner of a building that lay south of the excavation.

The corner of the south building was made of unbaked bricks 30 × 30 × 10–11 cm., and half-bricks, 15 cm. wide, were used to stagger the vertical joints. A foundation band, which projected 5 cm., was founded at el. 85.50 m., and the normal wall began at el. 86.00 m. Both the foundation and the wall were coated with mud plaster 3 cm. thick.

The walls of the northwest building were built of unbaked bricks 30 cm. square and 10 cm. thick, and the vertical joints were staggered with broken whole bricks instead of molded half-bricks. The walls were founded slightly below the floor level; in locus 3 the northeast wall was at el. 86.00 m., and the northwest wall, at el. 85.75 m., rose slightly toward the southwest. The walls were plastered with two coats of mud plaster, a base coat 2 cm. thick, and a finish coat 1 cm. thick. Two floors were recorded, and they roughly corresponded to floors 3 and 2 in loci 83 and 4. Floor 3 was found in all three rooms, at el. 86.17–86.20 m., and floor 2 in room 1 only, at el. 86.70 m. There were no floors above that. In room 2 the pivot block at the doorway to room (or courtyard) 1 was a broken baked brick. The turning area of the vertical door post was 3.5 cm. in diameter and 2 cm. deep. In room 3 the northeast wall and half of the adjoining northwest wall had a seven-course band of baked bricks which served as a damp course at the bottom of the wall. Some of the baked-brick paving was preserved in the northeast part of the room. The baked bricks were 37 × 37 × 6 cm. After the paving had been laid, the base of the southeast wall was repaired with baked bricks placed on edge on the paving and against the wall face.

THE EROSION OF THE SURFACE

In the *wadis* and the basin they formed in the central part of the excavation, the wash had carried away the occupational levels of the Kassites and the Third Dynasty of Ur and left a thick layer of potsherds from the missing cultural periods. This layer of potsherds represented the erosion of the mound's surface which occurred from the late Kassite period to the end of the Assyrian period and later. It was not a structural level but has been recorded as SE level IV.

SE Level IV

The SE level IV sherd layer was not a clearly defined area. The layer was thicker in the center of the basin, thinned out as it extended outward into the lower part of the *wadis,* and was not present at all along the southwest boundary of the excavation. In the northwest, however, it distinctly underlay the floors of SE level III.

The sherd layer is not shown on any plan but is indicated in the sections on Plate 43. The solid lines labeled SE IV show the extent of the sherd layer and the broken lines show a probable extension of the surface during the level IV interval where the sherd layer was not recognizable.

THE NEO-BABYLONIAN PERIOD

Very little evidence of the Neo-Babylonian period remained to be uncovered in the excavated area; it consisted of only three earth floors with unrelated wall fragments. All were recorded as SE level III (Pl. 37).

SE Level III

The structural remains of SE level III were found at the extreme northwest and south parts of the excavation. Only an earth floor was found in the original exploratory trench. In the rest of the excavation all signs of an SE level III occupation had been destroyed by erosion. The few wall fragments that were preserved had been built of unbaked bricks 31 × 31 × 12–13 cm. The floors were tamped earth, usually covered with a thin layer of ash. Floor 3 was recognized in SE locus 59 at el. 87.50 m. and, although there was no correlation possible, the lower wall in SE locus 69 at el. 86.05 m. was also labelled floor 3. Floor 2 in the northwest sloped from el. 88.00 m. near the northwest boundary to el. 87.73 m. in SE locus 59. The earth floor in the exploratory trench at el. 87.63 m. and the wall fragment in the south at el. 86.80 m. may also have belonged to this floor. Most of the floor 2 walls were rebuilt, and a few new walls were added at floor 1, which was found only in the northwest, at el. 88.13–88.18 m.

THE ACHAEMENIAN PERIOD

There was considerable building activity in the excavated area during the Achaemenian period. Unfortunately, the structural remains were found only in the northwest part and south corner of the excavation. The buildings were residential in character, and their plans followed the layout typical of a Mesopotamian house, that is, a range of rooms around a central courtyard. The walls were well-constructed and more substantial than those we usually found in the crowded residential quarters of earlier periods.

All the structures attributed to the Achaemenian period were recorded as SE level II (Pl. 25 A), which included two distinct building levels. The earlier one was made up of floors 4, 3, and 2 (Pl. 38), and the later one was floor 1 (Pl. 39).

SE Level II

The east corner of a building was uncovered at the northwest boundary of the excavation at floor 4. The walls were 2 m. thick and were founded at el. 87.80–88.22 m. They were built of unbaked bricks 31 × 31 × 12 cm. The only other building that was in use in the northwest area at this time was a house constructed around a courtyard (locus 65). Its walls were founded at el. 88.05–88.35 m. These two buildings have also been shown as foundations on the plan of SE level III (Pl. 37). The walls of the house were built of unbaked bricks 31 × 31 × 12 cm. and covered with mud plaster. The inside face of the southwest wall was laid on a single course of baked bricks at el. 88.23–88.29 m. The floor of the house rose from el. 88.15 m. on the northeast to el. 88.50 m. on the southwest. Southwest of the building, floor 4 sloped down to el. 88.32–88.40 m. at the southwest boundary of the excavation. The circular unbaked-brick construction in locus 67, which may have been the lower part of a pedestal or table, was founded on floor 4 at el. 88.15 m. and was preserved 60 cm. high. The square of baked bricks on the floor in locus 52 covered a vertical drain.

At floors 3 and 2, the southwest wall of the house around courtyard 65 was rebuilt at el. 88.50–88.58 m., and the house was in use at this time although the actual floors 3 and 2 were not found. The building southwest of street 51 was founded at el. 88.62 m. in the northeast and el. 88.37 m. in the southwest. The walls were built of unbaked bricks 31 × 31 × 12 cm. and were covered with mud plaster. Floor 3 ranged from el. 88.90 m. in the northeast to el. 88.65 m. in the southwest; and floor 2 from el. 89.00 to el. 88.80 m. The floors were tamped earth except in room 43, where there was a laid floor of broken unbaked bricks and clay about 10 cm. thick. A paving of baked bricks 30 × 30 × 6 cm. covered a vertical drain in room 48. The paving was four bricks square bordered with half-bricks. An open drain 17 cm. wide with sides of baked bricks on edge sloped down from the baked-brick paving to another vertical drain in SE 45. The bench against the northeast wall of room 48 was made of unbaked bricks and rose 28 cm. above the floor.

There were five kilns in SE loci 40 and 78. Of the four in locus 40, kiln 39 was the last one built; it cut through two earlier ones, one of which cut the fourth and smallest one (Pl. 25 C). All the kilns must have been below the floor level since their sides were made by lining a hole with baked-brick fragments placed on edge and plastering the inside with mud plaster about 2 cm. thick. The kilns were divided into two parts by central partitions of unbaked bricks 30 × 30 × 12 cm.; each partition had a central opening 72 cm. to 1.15 m. wide. In kiln 39 the opening was 72 cm. wide and 1.42 m. high with a roughly semicircular head (el. 88.80 m.). It was the only one in which the opening was completely preserved. The floors of the kilns ranged from el. 87.08 m. to el. 87.38 m. so that the kilns could have been constructed at SE level II 2 or 1. Evidence of a method of firing the kilns was not preserved, nor were there traces of upper ovens. All of the kiln constructions were heavily burned.

Three fragmentary buildings were found in the northwest part of the excavation at floor 1 (Pl. 39): locus 53, a rebuilding of the lower house; locus 50, built upon the eastern corner of the building below; and locus 34, built above, although not upon, a lower house. The first building, locus 53, was a rebuilding of the lower house containing courtyard 65, but the walls were not always aligned nor oriented the same. The rebuilding was done at el. 89.60–89.72 m., and the floor, which was not preserved, was probably at the same elevation. The second building, locus 50, was founded deep on a floor 4 building. The exterior wall faces were stepped in a saw-tooth manner not uncommon in the Neo-Babylonian period (Pl. 25 B).[1] An unbaked-brick bench 72 cm. wide had been added to the northeast exterior face. The unbaked bricks in the northeast wall measured 30 × 30 × 12–13 cm., and in the bench they measured 32 × 32 × 11 cm. The wall was laid with horizontal joints about 5 cm. thick and vertical joints 0.5–1.5 cm. thick. In the lower courses the bricks were laid with dry vertical joints. The walls and bench were coated with mud plaster 2.0–2.5 cm. thick. The wall was founded at el. 88.90 m. and was preserved as high as el. 91.35 m. The bottom of the bench was at el. 89.12–89.25 m. and its top was at el. 90.12 m. The earth floor in locus 33 was at el. 89.77 m. Inside the building there were parts of two rooms, 50 and 54. Both were paved with baked bricks 34 × 34 × 8 cm. The paving in room 50 was at el. 89.73 m. and in room 54 at el. 89.70 m. The third building, with rooms 34 and 35, was constructed later than

---

[1] C. L. Woolley, *Ur Excavations* IX: *The Neo-Babylonian and Persian Periods* (London, 1962) p. 44, Pl. 71.

the second building; the exterior bench was partly destroyed so that the north corner of the new building could be set. The walls were founded at el. 89.82–89.92 m. and were preserved as high as el. 91.30 m. The baked-brick threshold of the entrance doorway in the northeast wall and the tamped earth floor of room 34 were at el. 90.18 m., and the baked-brick paving over the vertical drain in courtyard 12 was at el. 90.00 m.

THE SELEUCID PERIOD

Only above the Achaemenian period remains did we find evidence of Sounding E structures spread over the excavation area (Pl. 40). The buildings were large scale, fragmentary, and contributed little to our meager knowledge of the Seleucid period at Nippur. Especially in the southwest and south where the *wadis* had developed, the walls were placed on foundations as much as 2 m. deep. In the northwest the foundations were shallower or were not used at all. There were three building levels assigned to the Seleucid period, and they all have been recorded as SE level I (p. 48). Floors 3, 2, and 1 represent the three separable periods of building activity.

SE LEVEL I

Beneath floor 3 in the southwest there was a floor that we cannot identify with any cultural period. It was only a few centimeters above the SE level IV sherd layer and, since level I was the next Sounding E stratified material in that area, a record of the floor has been included here. Along the southwest boundary the floor rose slightly toward the southeast and had a general slope downward toward the east. Under SE 22 the floor was at el. 87.07 m. and under SE 25 at el. 87.22 m. Under SE 23 and 26 the floor was at el. 86.93 m. The floor was hard-packed earth or clay, and, under SE 24, it was interrupted by a long narrow cut 20 cm. wide (Pl. 40). The cut ran in a north-south direction, continued under SE 23 and there turned eastward as far as the floor was preserved. Down the center of the cut we found a row of vertical reed stubs or the impressions of decomposed reeds that probably was part of some sort of enclosure. The reed construction could not be associated with any other construction in the excavation.

At floor 3 in loci 20 and 24–27 we found several meaningless wall fragments within the foundations of a floor 2 building. They were founded at elevations ranging from el. 87.70 to 88.27 m. None was preserved higher than el. 88.90 m. There were two floor layers, or possibly layers of fill, one about 30 cm. above the other. The lower one was at el. 87.40–87.85 m. under loci 20 and 24. The walls on the northeast side of the excavation, loci 80 and 81, did not belong with any of the other buildings but were included in floor 3. They seemed to be foundations, based at el. 87.20–87.37 m., and were preserved as high as el. 88.47 m. There were no indications of a floor.

At floor 2 building remains were found in most of the excavation. In the northwest, loci 5–11, the walls were built of unbaked bricks measuring 33 × 33 × 12 cm. and were founded at el. 90.45–90.75 m. No floors were preserved. In the southwest, loci 22–27, the building remains were part of a well-built structure which continued southwest beyond the limits of the excavation. The walls were constructed of unbaked bricks 31 × 31 × 12 cm. and were covered with mud plaster. They were 1.10–1.30 m. thick and were set upon a foundation flush with the walls on the outside and projecting 15–25 cm. on the inside. The ash-covered, tamped, earth floors were found at el. 89.62–89.75 m. in rooms 22–24. The top of the foundation was at el. 89.07–89.22 m. and the bottom at el. 86.85–87.00 m. The foundation of a rather large building was found in the southeast part of the excavation. It was built of unbaked bricks 31 × 31 × 12 cm. but was not plastered; it measured at least 16 m. in one direction and 30 m. in the other. The bottom of the foundation was at el. 86.10–86.15 m. on its exterior face and stepped up toward the inner face, where its base was at el. 87.95 m. A floor was not found, but one has been restored on the section at el. 88.20 m.

Fragments of three large buildings were found at floor 1 (Pl. 41). All had unbaked-brick walls founded well below the floor and much thicker than those usually found in domestic construction. They were a continuation of the same scale of building found at floor 2. In the northwest, loci 5–10, the walls, which appeared to be foundations, were about 1.40 m. thick. They were built of bricks 33 × 33 × 11 cm. and were not plastered. No floor was found, but it probably was at el. 91.70 m. or above. In the southwest, loci 78 and 79, the walls were about 1.50 m. thick, and the bricks measured 33 × 33 × 14 cm. and 34 × 34 × 15 cm. The bottom of the wall on the southeast (in a *wadi*) was at el. 87.50 m., the bottom of the wall between loci 78 and 79 was at el. 88.50 m., and the northwest wall of locus 79 was founded at el. 89.30 m. There were two tamped-earth floors covered with thin layers of ash. One was at el. 89.62–89.82 m. and the other at el. 89.02–89.15 m. In the southeast there was one room, locus 29, of still another building. Its walls were founded at el. 88.10 m. The baked-brick paving above the inverted jar used as a vertical drain in the east end of the room and the baked bricks outlining the rectangular fireplace against the south wall fixed the floor at el. 89.40–89.47 m. (The circular drain which cuts into the south wall near the southwest corner must have been dug from a later occupation.) Against the north wall were the lower four baked-brick treads of a stairway to a second floor or the roof. The treads averaged 20 cm. wide and the risers 11 cm. high. The stair probably was carried on an arch reaching to the east wall. If so, there would have been a total of 25 risers and approximately 2.75 meters between floors. The fireplace, the baked-clay oval vessel beside the stair, and the large jar under the stair indicated that this was a well-established kitchen.

IV

THE OBJECTS FROM SE LEVELS VI–I

By Donald E. McCown

SOMETIME after the Akkadian period (NT level 1) the mound formed by the temple and the buildings around it was converted into a platform built above the area to the west. No floors between the Akkadian and the Kassite periods were preserved within the platform, but there is some evidence of occupation in the Third Dynasty of Ur and Old Babylonian period (SE level VI) and in the Kassite (SE level V) period. The platform may have been created to raise the temple above the surrounding structures, for floors belonging to these same periods were found at a lower elevation southwest of the temple platform. The site was probably not occupied from the late Kassite to the end of the Assyrian period, and the material found in the easily recognizable "surface layer" was labelled SE level IV. The Neo-Babylonian, Achaemenian, and Seleucid periods are represented in SE levels III, II, and I.

POTTERY

Within the temple platform, a very large vertical drain (locus SE 86 on Pl. 36 A) contained many Ur III bowls of type 8A and B (see Vol. I, Pl. 82:18–23). This is the only evidence we have of an Ur III occupation on the temple platform.

Also within the temple platform there was a baked-brick well shaft (locus 85 on Pl. 36 A). An inscription of Adadshumuṣur (4NT 273) on a baked brick found in the well not far above the water level indicates that the well was in use as late as the Kassite period.

In the baked-brick shaft there were also 3 offering stands of a newly established pottery type 73 (Pl. 49:1–3), 4 crude saucers (see Vol. I, Pl. 28:4–5), and a sherd each of types 20, 31, and 39B (Vol. I, Pls. 88:1, 93:7–8, and 95:17). The fill in the well above the baked-brick lining included more pottery of the same types as well as types 40A and 47 (Vol. I, Pls. 96:5 and 98:14–16). A probable explanation of this mixture of Old Babylonian and Kassite pottery is that the well was constructed during the earlier period and used, with possible repairs on its upper part, through the Kassite period. The Old Babylonian sherds in the well shaft probably intruded with the collapse of the upper portion of the brickwork.

The SE level V wall fragments of locus 72 (see Pl. 36 B) were dated to the Kassite period by sherds mainly of type 47 (see Vol. I, Pl. 98:14–16). Probably to this time dates the baked-brick grave found in NT locus 21 (see Pl. 33) with a mixture of Early Dynastic and Kassite sherds.

Outside the temple platform on the southwest the base of the baked-brick face of the platform wall corresponds to SE level VI, and from it came sherds of type 8B (see Vol. I, Pl. 82:19). In addition, two pots (Pl. 49:4–5) and sherds of types 43A (see Vol. I, Pl. 97:6–8) and 46A (see Vol. I, Pl. 98:11–12) were also found. It is likely that SE level VI maintained much the same elevation from about the Third Dynasty of Ur down to the Kassite period.

From SE V 3 came a variant of type 46 (see Pl. 49:6) and sherds of types 46B (see Vol. I, Pl. 98:13), 43B (see Vol. I, Pl. 97:9–10) and 47 (see Vol. I, Pl. 98:14–16).

From SE V 2 came variants of type 46 (see Pl. 49:7, 9) and type 43B (see Pl. 49:10); sherds and vessels of types 46, 43B, and 47 were also found. In addition, other vessels were found which supplement the shapes of this period from Nippur (see Pls. 49:11–12, 50:1–6, 9).

At SE level IV the surface of the mound eroded during the interval from the late Kassite period to the end of the Assyrian period in the northwest and to the time of the Seleucids in the south except for a small area in the corner of the excavation. The Ur III material recognized was mainly pottery of type 8 (see Vol. I, Pl. 82:18–23) and the Kassite material was mainly pottery of type 47 (see Vol. I, Pl. 98:14–16).

Much of the pottery found in SE levels III–I belongs to types already established; a few new types have been established, and some rare and single specimens are also included.

Type 48, bowl.—For a general description, see Vol. I, Pl. 100:1–2. Two examples were found, one gray plain and one over-fired greenish buff. One was found in SE level III and the other in SE level I.

Type 49, bowl.—For a general description, see Vol. I, Pl. 100:3–6. Five examples were found; 4 had buff surfaces, and 1 had a grayish glaze with dark green on the rim. They measured 6.6–7.1 cm. high and 15.4–20.8 cm. in diameter. One was found in SE level III, and 1 each in SE II burials 4B 85, 132, and SE I burials 3B 40, 53.

Type 52, bowl.—For a general description, see Vol. I, Pl. 100:13. Six examples were found; one of these had a groove outside just below the rim, and another had a rim beveled inside. They measured 4–7.1 cm. high and 10.5–15.4 cm. in diameter. Two were found in SE level III, 1 each in SE III or II burial 4B 146 and SE II burials 4B 48, 58, 76.

Type 55, cup.—For a general description, see Vol. I, Pl. 100:20. Four examples were found, 1 in SE level III, 2 in SE level II, 1 in SE level I.

Type 56, cup.—For a general description, see Vol. I, Pl. 100:21–23. See also Pl. 51:8, below. Seven examples were found, 1 in SE level III, 3 in SE level II, 3 in kiln 39 in SE II 2. The range of examples here appeared to be later than those in the Scribal Quarter.

Type 57, pot.—For a general description, see Vol. I, Pl. 101:1–3. There were three examples with glazed designs in brown, light green, and brown and yellow, all on a white glaze base. One was found in SE III burial 4B 119, 1 in SE III or II burial 4B 110, and 1 in SE II burial 4B 91.

Type 58, narrow-necked pot.—For a general description, see Vol. I, Pl. 101:4–12. Twenty examples were found, all glazed; 4 were yellowish or gray on the body with blue-green at the neck, 3 greenish blue, 5 yellowish green, 5 silver white, 2 gray, 1 white with a design in brown. They measured 9–12 cm. high and 7.2–9.7 cm. in diameter. Four examples were found in SE level II, 2 examples in SE II burial 4B 63, and 2 on the surface, as well as 1 example each in SE III or II burials 4B 95, 111, 136, 137, 146, in SE II burials 4B 54, 72, 85, 132, and SE I burials 3B 40, 47, 93. The time range of these examples is later than that of the examples in the Scribal Quarter.

Type 59, pot with narrow neck and pointed base.—For a general description, see Vol. I, Pl. 101:15–20. See also Pls. 51:12–13, 15 and 52:2, below. The four illustrated examples measured 9.6–12.4 cm. high and 6.0–8.3 cm. in diameter. These pots are smaller than those described in Vol. I. An unillustrated example, from SE III burial 4B 119, with green and brown design on a white base glaze measured 19.9 cm. high and 9.9 cm. in diameter.

Type 60, pot.—For a general description, see Vol. I, Pl. 102:1–9. See also Pl. 52:1, below. Thirty-six examples were found; 2 had handles (similar to those in Vol. I, Pl. 102:4), 1 was glazed, and 5 were without neck ridge. One was found in SE level II, 2 in SE level I, and the remainder in graves: 1 each in SE III burials 4B 72, 73, 106, 118, 123, 124, 129, 131, 138, SE III or II burials 4B 95, 109, 111, 115, 117, 137, SE II burials 4B 54, 56, 59, 65*A*, 69, 83, 85, 86, 87, 94, 102, SE I burials 3B 54, 93, and 4B 30, 47, 60, 64, and an unnumbered burial.

Type 63, lamp.—For a general description, see Vol. I, Pl. 102:18—19. See also Pl. 52:4—5, below. Nine examples were found, 6 with buff surfaces and 3 glazed: 1 in light blue, 1 in white with yellow on neck, 1 in white. Two were found in SE III, 1 in SE II, 5 in SE I, and 1 on the surface.

Type 64, bowl.—For a general description, see Vol. I, Pl. 103:1—4. Eight examples were found, 1 with modeled rim and 7 with everted rims (5 like that in Vol. I, Pl. 103:1, 2 like that in Vol. I, Pl. 103:3). Two had buff surfaces, and the rest had gray or greenish yellow glaze. They measured 4.6—6.5 cm. high and 18—21.5 cm. in diameter. One was found in SE level III, and 1 each in SE III or II burials 4B 109, 111, 117, 137 and SE II burials 4B 54, 69, 76.

Type 65, flat saucer.—For a general description, see Vol. I, Pl. 103:8. One of these 2 examples had a buff surface and was found in SE I burial 3B 91; the other had a light green glaze and was found on the surface.

Type 66, thin ware hemispherical bowl.—For a general description, see Vol. I, Pl. 103:13—14. There were 11 examples, 5 without incised grooves. One especially thin example had a thickness of 0.4 cm. One flat saucer type was 17.7 cm. in diameter. One was found in SE level III, and 1 each in SE III burials 4B 72, 102, 123, 124, 130, SE II burials 4B 59, 78, 86, and SE I burials 3B 54, 93.

Type 67, bowl.—For a general description, see Vol. I, Pl. 103:15—17. The shape has been redefined here to include a sinuous form (see Pl. 50:8, 11) and a hemispherical shape with no constriction below the rim (see Pl. 50:10). Thirteen examples were found (5 like those in Vol. I, Pl. 103:15—17, 6 like those in Pl. 50:8, 11, and 2 like that in Pl. 50:10); 9 had incised grooves or lines. They were all found in graves: 1 each in SE III burials 4B 73, 118, 138, SE III or II burials 4B 109, 115, SE II burials 4B 65*A*, 85, 88, and SE I burials 3B 47, 48, 53, an unnumbered burial, and 4B 64.

Type 68, cup.—For a general description, see Vol. I. Pl. 103:22—24. Three examples of tan ware with plain surface or buff slip were found. They measured 6.8—9.1 cm. high and 4.9—6.6 cm. in diameter. Two were found in SE level II and 1 in SE level I.

Type 70, pot.—For a general description, see Vol. I, Pl. 104:11—18. See also Pl. 51:7, 9—11, below. All examples found are illustrated.

Type 72, pot.—For a general description, see Vol. I, Pl. 105:7. See also Pl. 51:14, 16, below. There were 15 examples uncovered. Only one of them had lug handles. All were glazed, 3 in turquoise, 2 in green, 5 in blue, 3 in gray, and 2 in silver white. Two were found in SE level II, 2 in SE III burial 4B 138, and 1 each in SE III burial 4B 130, SE III or II burials 4B 84, 104, 111, 137, SE II burials 4B 63, 132; 4 examples were found in SE II burial 4B 88. The date of these pots is a little earlier than that of similar pots from the Scribal Quarter.

Type 74, saucer.—For a general description, see Pl. 50:12, below.

Type 75, deep bowl with neck.—For a general description, see Pl. 51:1—4, below.

Type 76, truncated conic cup.—For a general description, see Pl. 51:5—6, below.

RARE AND SINGLE SPECIMENS

SAUCERS

CAT. NO.	LOCUS	REMARKS
4P 7	SE II 1	Pl. 52:8
4P 44	SE II 1	Pl. 52:11
4P 45	SE II 1	Pl. 52:10

CAT. NO.	LOCUS	REMARKS
4P 84	SE 20 I 3	Pl. 52:7
4P 12	SE I 2	Pl. 52:3
4P 1	SE I 1	Buff ware, white glaze; as in Vol. I, Pl. 103:12, but with a low ring base; h. 4.4, d. 12.5, th. 0.45 cm.
4P 15	SE I 1	Pl. 52:6
4P 16	SE surface	Pl. 52:9

BOWLS

CAT. NO.	LOCUS	REMARKS
4P 20	SE III 2	Pl. 52:16
4P 199	SE III	Pl. 52:12
4P 230	SE III burial 4B 124	Pl. 53:1
4P 256	SE III or II burial 4B 137	Pl. 52:13
4P 41	SE II 1	Greenish gray, plain; as in Vol. I, Pl. 100:13, but with rim beveled as in Vol. I, Pl. 100:11; h. 3.8, d. 10.8 cm.
4P 49	SE 33 II 1	Pl. 53:2
4P 107	SE II burial 4B 65B	Pl. 53:3
4P 169	SE II burial 4B 94	Buff ware, plain; as in Vol. I, Pl. 103:7; h. 8.7, d. 20.2 cm.

DEEP BOWLS

CAT. NO.	LOCUS	REMARKS
4P 30	SE II 2	Pl. 53:4
4P 172	SE 71 II	Pl. 53:8
4P 70	unnumbered burial intrusive into SE 50 II 2	Pl. 53:5
4P 71	Same as 4P 70	Pl. 53:6
4P 72	Same as 4P 70	Pl. 53:7

DEEP CUPS

CAT. NO.	LOCUS	REMARKS
4P 129	SE 63 II 4	As in Vol. I, Pl. 103:23, but rim with inner groove
3P 229	SE I 2	Pl. 53:9

POTS

CAT. NO.	LOCUS	REMARKS
4P 28	SE III	Pl. 53:11
4P 186	SE III burial 4B 113	Pl. 54:8
4P 222	SE III burial 4B 125	Pl. 54:3
4P 65	SE 42 II 4	Pl. 54:4
4P 31	SE II 2	Pl. 53:10
4P 32	SE II 2	Pl. 53:14
4P 50	SE 41 II 2	Pl. 53:13
4P 134	SE II burial 4B 74	Buff surface; as in Pl. 54:6, but with disk base and without lug handles; h. 10.1, d. 8.3 cm.
4P 150	SE II burial 4B 83	Pl. 54:6
4P 197	SE II burial 4B 105	Pl. 54:7
4P 234	SE II burial 4B 132	Buff ware, plain; as in Vol. I, Pl. 105:9; preserved h. 21.1, d. 14.4 cm.

TABLETS, COINS, AND THE DATING OF LEVELS

CAT. NO.	LOCUS	REMARKS
4P 173	Intrusive into SE 71 II	Pl. 54:9
4P 5	SE I 2	Pl. 54:2
4P 54	SE 19 I 2	Pl. 54:1
3P 228	SE I burial 3B 54	Pl. 53:12
3P 286	SE I burial 3B 55	Buff slip; as in Vol. I, Type 61; h. 20.5, d. 17.0 cm.
4P 8	SE surface	Pl. 54:5

JARS

CAT. NO.	LOCUS	REMARKS
3P 255	SE III	Pl. 55:4
4P 76	SE 40 II 2	Greenish buff, warped; ridge at base of neck, two incised grooves high on shoulders; as in Pl. 54:10
4P 106	SE II burial 4B 65B	Pl. 55:2
4P 163	SE II burial 4B 77	Pl. 54:10
3P 603	SE I burial 3B 93	Pl. 55:1

POTS WITH HANDLES

CAT. NO.	LOCUS	REMARKS
4P 166	SE III	Pl. 55:9
4P 59	SE III 1	Pl. 55:10
4P 167	SE II 4	Pl. 56:1
3P 613	SE II	Pl. 55:3
4P 143	SE II burial 4B 78	Pl. 55:6
4P 10	Intrusive into SE I 2	Pl. 56:2
4P 17	SE surface	Pl. 55:7
4P 220	SE dump	Pl. 55:8

MISCELLANEOUS POTTERY

CAT. NO.	LOCUS	REMARKS
4N 68	SE 58 III 2	Lid; Pl. 60:17
4N 51	Kiln in SE 40 II 2	Lid; Pl. 60:16
	Locus unknown	Vat; Pl. 71:17

TABLETS, COINS, AND THE DATING OF LEVELS

Although no floors belonging to the Ur III period were found within the temple platform, two Ur III tablets intrusive into NT levels are signs of Ur III activity within the area:

CAT. NO.	LOCUS	REMARKS
4NT 51	Intrusive into NT 22	Amar-Sin, year 4
4NT 175	NT intrusive at approx. level IV	undated

The following dated tablets were found in SE level V:

CAT. NO.	LOCUS	REMARKS
3NT 140	SE 3 V 2	Kudur-Enlil, accession year
3NT 141	Same as 3NT 140	Kadashman-Enlil (II), year 7
3NT 142	Same as 3NT 140	Kadashman-Enlil (II), year 6
3NT 143	Same as 3NT 140	Kudur-Enlil, year 5

CAT. NO.	LOCUS	REMARKS
3NT 144	Same as 3NT 140	Kudur-Enlil, year 5
3NT 145	Same as 3NT 140	Kudur-Enlil (year broken away)
3NT 146	Same as 3NT 140	Kudur-Enlil, year 2
3NT 147	Same as 3NT 140	Kudur-Enlil, accession year
3NT 148	Same as 3NT 140	Shagarakti-Shuriash, year 1
3NT 149	Same as 3NT 140	Kadashman-Enlil (II), year 6

The following datable inscriptions were found in SE levels III–I:

CAT. NO.	LOCUS	REMARKS
3NT 891	SE ca. II 4	Nebuchadnezzar II, year 15
4NT 19	SE 44 II 4	Assurbanipal, year 22
4NT 23	SE III 2	Nebuchadnezzar II, year 1
4NT 13	SE dump	Nabonidus, year not preserved
4NT 3	SE 20 I	Copy of an earlier text in Seleucid script
	SE 60 in base of SE III wall	Half-brick with Assurbanipal stamp, *OBI*, No. 28

The brick found in the base of an SE level III wall, with an Assurbanipal inscription, was probably in secondary use and suggests that SE level III was Neo-Babylonian. Level II is not dated but probably falls within the Achaemenian period. The coin 4D 28, dating to Seleucus II, and the tablet 4NT 3 probably date level I to the Seleucid period.

The following coins were found in SE level I and above:

CAT. NO.	LOCUS	REMARKS
4D 23	SE I 3	Phraataces; as in Warwick Wroth, *Catalogue of the Coins of Parthia* (London, 1903) Pl. XXIII, No. 11
4D 46	SE 22 I 3	Not identified
4D 28	SE I 2	Seleucus II; as in Edward T. Newell, *The Coinage of the Eastern Seleucid Mints* (New York, 1939) Pl. XVII, No. 2
4D 26	Above SE level I	Probably Osroes, trace of male head, reverse defaced; as in Wroth, *Catalogue of the Coins of Parthia*, Pl. XXXI, Nos. 11, 12
4D 27	Above SE level I	Not identified
3N 474	SE surface	Silver coin; d. 2.7, th. 0.5; not identified

From the pottery, tablets, and coins, we may relate the SE levels to these specific periods:

SE level VI	Ur III–Old Babylonian
SE level V	Kassite
SE level IV	Erosion of surface from Late Kassite to Neo-Babylonian
SE level III	Neo-Babylonian
SE level II	Achaemenian
SE level I	Seleucid

STONE, METAL, AND GLASS VESSELS

STONE VESSELS

CAT. NO.	LOCUS	REMARKS
3N 489	SE I burial 3B 91	Pl. 55:5
3N 490, 491	Same as 3N 489	Similar to 3N 492
3N 492	Same as 3N 489	Pl. 56:3

CAT. NO.	LOCUS	REMARKS
4NT 1	SE I 2	Pl. 48:3
4N 20	SE dump	Vase; rim d. 1.5, body d. 2.75, h. 7.0 cm.

BRONZE BOWLS

CAT. NO.	LOCUS	REMARKS
4N 113	SE III burial 4B 125	As in Vol. I, Pl. 108:17
4N 114	SE III burial 4B 129	As in Vol. I, Pl. 108:17
4N 115	SE III burial 4B 119	Pl. 56:5
4N 116	SE III burial 4B 103	As in Vol. I, Pl. 108:17
3N 365	SE (stratification uncertain)	Pl. 56:4

GLASS BOTTLES

CAT. NO.	LOCUS	REMARKS
4N 133	SE II burial 4B 77	Pl. 56:8
3N 493	SE burial 3B 98 intrusive into SE 75 *ca.* I 3	Pl. 71:19
3P 610	Same as 3N 493	As in Pl. 71:19
3P 611	Same as 3N 493	As in Pl. 71:19
3P 608	SE surface	Pl. 71:22
3P 609	SE surface	Pl. 71:21

SEALS AND SEAL IMPRESSIONS

CAT. NO.	LOCUS	REMARKS
3N 215	SE V 2	Cylinder seal; Pl. 71:14
4N 60	SE 58 III 1	Cylinder seal; Pl. 71:4
4N 98	SE III or II burial 4B 104	Cylinder seal; p. 64
4N 139*a*	SE III or II burial 4B 117	Scaraboid stamp seal; Pl. 71:7
4N 139*b*	Same as 4N 139*a*	Scaraboid stamp seal; Pl. 71:8
4N 139*c*	Same as 4N 139*a*	Scaraboid stamp seal; Pl. 71:9
4N 139*d*	Same as 4N 139*a*	Scaraboid stamp seal; Pl. 71:10
4N 46	SE 51 II 4	Alabaster cylinder seal; worn, traces of vertical figures only; l. 1.7, d. 0.75 cm.
4N 26	SE II 1	Cylinder seal; Pl. 71:1
4N 54*a*	SE II burial 4B 62	Cylinder seal; Pl. 71:2
4N 74	SE II burial 4B 76	Scaraboid stamp seal; Pl. 71:3
4N 130	SE II burial 4B 91	Cylinder seal; Pl. 71:12
4N 75	SE I	Stone stamp seal, black-gray with white veins; plano-convex; on face two concentric circles of dots, 6 inside and 12 outside; h. 1.3, d. 2.5 cm.
4N 135	SE surface	Stone cylinder seal; preserved l. 2.5, d. 1.2 cm.
4N 71	SE dump	Stone cylinder seal; l. 2.0, d. 1.5 cm.

BAKED CLAY FIGURINES, PLAQUES, AND MODEL
KASSITE FIGURINES

CAT. NO.	LOCUS	REMARKS
3N 238	SE V 3	Male; Pl. 71:15

CAT. NO.	LOCUS	REMARKS
3N 237	SE V 3	Pl. 71:16
3D 304	SE V 2	Sitting bear(?), as in Vol. I, Pl. 141:13

HELLENISTIC FIGURINES

CAT. NO.	LOCUS	REMARKS
4N 63	SE IV or III	Female; Pl. 72:6
4N 62	SE IV or III	Male; Pl. 72:8
4N 81	SE 62 III	Female; Pl. 72:1
4D 19	SE II 1	Head; Pl. 72:9
3D 698	SE II	Tambourine player; Pl. 72:2
4D 50	SE 25 I 3	Flute player; Pl. 72:3
4D 60	SE 24 I 3	Female; Pl. 72:5
4D 11	SE I 2	Male; Pl. 77:6
3N 473	SE I	Flute player; Pl. 72:4
3N 480	SE I	Female; Pl. 71:23
3D 690	SE surface	Head; Pl. 72:7
3D 692	SE surface	Head; Pl. 77:5
4D 17	SE dump	Female; Pl. 71:20; four examples; greatest h. 8.8 cm.; 1 found in SE II 2 and 2 in SE I; 1 in SE dump

ACHAEMENIAN FIGURINES

CAT. NO.	LOCUS	REMARKS
		Mold-made horse and rider; as in Vol. I, Pl. 131:2; 26 examples; 7 found in SE IV, 2 in SE III, 4 in SE II, 13 in SE I
4D 18	SE II 1	Handmade horse and rider; Pl. 72:12; 6 examples; 3 found in SE III, 1 in SE II 1, 1 in SE II, 1 in SE I
3D 697	SE II	Figure on a horse; Pl. 72:14
3N 177	SE II	Male head; Pl. 73:1–2, 4
		Tambourine player; as in Vol. I, Pl. 125:12; 9 examples from SE II and I
3N 185	SE II	Base of rhyton; Pl. 73:5
3N 163	SE II	Demon head; h. 6.7, w. 3.3, th. 4.0 cm.; similar to 3N 190
3N 184	SE dump	Demon head; h. 7.0, w. 3.0, th. 6.0 cm.; similar to 3N 190
3N 190	SE dump	Demon head; Pl. 72:10

ASSYRIAN TYPE FIGURINES

CAT. NO.	LOCUS	REMARKS
	Intrusive into NT I	Two females; as in Vol. I, Pl. 125:13
4D 192	SE IV or III	Male head; Pl. 72:11
	SE IV or III	Male; as in Vol. I, Pl. 130:14
	SE III 1	Two nursing females; as in Vol. I, Pl. 125:5
4N 65*a*	SE III	Mold for making female head; Pl. 73:9

ANIMAL FIGURINES

CAT. NO.	LOCUS	REMARKS
4D 143	SE III 1	Pl. 74:2
4N 43	SE 55 III	Monkey; Pl. 73:3; similar one found in SE II 1
4N 30	SE 49 II 4	Horse; Pl. 74:3
3N 482	SE II	Monkey; mold-made and plaquelike; in position of that in Vol. I, Pl. 143:4

CAT. NO.	LOCUS	REMARKS
4D 201	SE 68 II 4	Head; Pl. 74:4
4D 3	SE I 2	Pl. 74:1
4N 64	SE dump	Monkey; Pl. 73:7

PLAQUES

CAT. NO.	LOCUS	REMARKS
4N 67	Intrusive into NT I	Pl. 73:8; Assyrian type
4N 69	SE 61 III 2	Mold for making plaque; Pl. 73:6; Assyrian type
4N 31	SE 40 II 4	Lion; Pl. 74:6
4D 128	SE 66 II 3	Pl. 72:13; Hellenistic

MODEL

CAT. NO.	LOCUS	REMARKS
3N 508	SE surface	Model chariot, fragmentary; l. 5.8, axle w. 3.1, preserved h. 3.3 cm.

PERSONAL ORNAMENTS[1]

CAT. NO.	LOCUS	REMARKS
4N 59	SE 58 III 2	Two silver earrings; the larger d. 5.7, th. 0.3, the smaller d. 2.8, th. 0.2 cm.; similar to Pl. 74:10
4N 65*b*	SE III 1	Agate barrel bead; l. 1.5, d. 0.5 cm.
4N 45	SE 55 III 1	Obsidian ear plug; l. 3.2, head d. 0.9, shaft d. 0.7 cm.
4N 70	SE 62 III	Obsidian ear plug, rectangular head and shaft; l. 2.3, head 0.7 × 1.0, shaft 0.55 × 0.7 cm.
3N 183	SE III	Baked clay pendant, buff surface; h. 3.5, maximum th. 1.5 cm.
4N 44	SE 52 II 3	Gold-mounted bead; Pl. 61:1
4N 58	SE II 1	Baked clay disk bead; flat face with white glazed edge and black inner circle; d. 5.0, th. 0.7 cm.; similar to Pl. 61:2
3N 485	SE II	Hollow gold barrel bead; l. 1.1, d. 0.8 cm.
4N 7	SE I 3	Frit disk bead; Pl. 61:2
4N 22	SE I 3	Frit pendant; Pl. 74:7
3N 420	SE I 3	Bronze pin; l. 15.3, d. 0.5 cm.
4N 8	SE I 2	Bronze finger ring, oval bezel; d. 2.0 cm.
3N 158	SE I 2	Bronze pin; l. 5.7, w. 0.4, th. 0.15 cm.
3N 486	SE I	Bronze finger ring, oval bezel; d. 1.9 cm.
3N 426	SE surface	Frit bead; Pl. 62:2
4N 13*a*	SE surface	Frit bead; Pl. 62:5
4N 13*b*	SE surface	Frit bead; Pl. 62:7
4N 13*c*	SE surface	Shell bead; Pl. 62:6
3N 425	SE surface	Frit scaraboid pendant, light blue glaze; l. 1.0, w. 1.0, h. 0.8 cm.
3N 296	SE surface	Bone bracelet; d. 4.95, cross section w. 0.8, th. 0.4 cm.
3N 471	SE surface	Silver ring, rectangular bezel; d. 1.9 cm.
3N 484	SE dump	Stone bead, lozenge shape, incised geometric design; l. 4.6, w. 1.7, th. 0.8 cm.

[1] Except those found in burials, which are listed with the burials in the following chapter.

OTHER SMALL OBJECTS[2]

CAT. NO.	LOCUS	REMARKS
4N 158	SE 72 V	Bronze needle; l. 21.0, square cross section 0.7 × 0.7 cm.
4N 21	SE III 2	Hematite weight; l. 2.2, d. 0.35 cm.
4N 145	SE III 1	Bronze needle; Pl. 60:4
4N 61	SE 67 II 4	Bone knob; Pl. 61:10
4N 29	SE 42 II 3	Bronze balance pan, concave, suspension holes not sure; d. 9.1, th. 0.25 cm.; similar to 4N 124, listed in Chap. II
4N 23	SE 45 II 3	Bronze rod, thickened at one end; l. 12.5, d. 0.35 cm.
4N 25	SE 44 II 2	Iron chisel; Pl. 62:1
4N 19	SE 44 II 2	Bone spatula; l. 9.3, w. 2.2, th. 0.2 cm.
3N 196	SE 78 II 2	Pot firing separator; Pl. 61:8
3N 225	SE 78 II 2	Pot firing separator; d. 6.3, h. 2.2 cm.
4N 18	SE 41 II 2	Bronze rod; Pl. 60:15
4N 3	SE II 1	Bronze kohl stick, l. 13.7, d. 0.3 cm.; one end slightly thickened, d. 0.4 cm.; other end with oval flat spoon, l. 1.2, w. 0.8, th. 0.25 cm.
4N 14	SE 33 II 1	Black stone weight; l. 3.4, d. 1.1 cm.
4N 16	SE 33 II 1	Black stone weight; l. 3.7, d. 1.0 cm.
3N 182	SE II	Limestone box divided into 4 compartments, top broken; l. 4.5, w. 4.4, preserved h. 2.3 cm.
4D 202	SE 71 II	Fragments of metal implements; Pl. 60:11–14
4N 33	SE I 3	Hematite weight encircled by a thin bronze strip 1.3 cm. wide; l. 2.4, d. 0.6 cm.
3N 500	SE I 3	Limestone duck weight; neck pierced horizontally, feet indicated on bottom; l. 9.8, w. 6.3, h. 5.9 cm.
4N 28	SE 24 I 3*b*	Bone arm and hand; Pl. 61:9
4D 51	SE 25 I 2	Carved plaster; Pl. 74:13
3D 563	SE I 2	Stone spindle whorl; Pl. 60:3
4N 12	SE I 1	Stone ax; l. 4.0, h. 1.6, th. 1.5 cm.
4D 1	SE I 1	Brick stamp; Pl. 74:12
3N 349	SE surface	Bronze blade; preserved l. 9.0, w. 1.1, th. 0.2 cm.; shaft has square cross section 0.3 × 0.3 cm.
3N 505	SE surface	Bronze spatula; Pl. 74:11
3N 483	SE surface	Bone spoon handle; Pl. 62:8
4D 42	SE surface	Carved plaster; Pl. 74:14
4D 43	SE dump	Carved plaster; Pl. 74:15

[2] Except those found in burials, which are listed with the burials in the following chapter.

V

THE BURIALS

By Donald E. McCown

All of the burials found in the excavated area ranged from the Neo-Babylonian period (SE level III) to the Parthian period. Of the pre-Parthian burials, about half were Achaemenian (SE level II) and the smallest number were Seleucid (SE level I). About two-fifths of the pre-Parthian burials were in earth graves (some with brickwork), another two-fifths were in pottery tubs (and about half of those were "bathtubs"), and the rest were in jars or bowls.

After the Seleucid period the area, especially the northeastern part, was used as a cemetery by the Parthians. The burials were mainly intrusive into SE level I, but a few were deeper, in SE level II. A total of 88 burials in the cemetery were excavated. They include all the slipper-coffin burials (about one-third of those found in the cemetery), all the pointed-jar burials, 4 burials in convex jars (4B 1, 5, 10, 12), and 2 earth burials (4B 14, 42).

EARTH BURIALS

Earth graves occurred in all levels containing burials. A total of 43 were found, 7 from SE III, 4 from SE III or II, 26 from SE II, 4 from SE I, and 2 from the Parthian cemetery. Almost three-quarters were buried in plain earth graves just large enough to receive a body; for instance, a slightly flexed adult was buried in a grave 152 cm. long and 40 cm. wide. In one case (4B 70) the lower half of the body had been placed on top of an oval tub for no apparent reason. In addition to these, 6 burials (4B 54, 67, 82, 86, 101, 106) were covered with potsherds or, in one instance (4B 106), with half of a broken jar. Also, in 6 other earth burials there was some type of brickwork present.

Two graves (4B 42, 87) contained earth burials protected on one side by baked bricks standing on edge and leaning inward. The bricks measured 31 × 31 × 7 cm. Apparently a shallow alcove was dug in one side of the grave shaft to receive the body and the baked bricks, leaning at an angle over the body, provided a cover for the opening. Two other graves contained "boxes" made of unbaked bricks standing on edge and covered with a course of bricks laid flat. One "box" (4B 48) measured 180 cm. long, 42 cm. wide, and *ca.* 55 cm. deep. The other (4B 123) measured 135 cm. long and 65 cm. wide. Another burial (4B 126) was placed in an oval grave lined with one course of unbaked bricks standing on edge. The grave was 107 cm. long and 77 cm. wide.

TUB BURIALS

Tub burials are recorded as coming from SE levels III, II, and I; a total of 40 were found. They may be divided into four types: round tubs, oval tubs, long tubs with rounded ends, and tubs with one straight and one rounded end, which, for convenience, we called "bathtubs."

One round tub burial (4B 79) was found in SE II (d. *ca.* 44, h. 19 cm.); see Pl. 56:6 for a similar profile. Oval tubs occurred 9 times, 1 (4B 68) from SE III, 3 (4B 95, 115, 133) from SE III or II, and 5 (4B 74, 80, 81, 88, 105) from SE II; see Pl. 56:6 for a similar profile. The dimensions of tubs for infants were 60–70 cm. long, 36–46 cm. wide, and 10–21 cm. high, and, for adults, 86–105 cm. long, 50–60 cm. wide, and 25–60 cm. high. Three tubs (4B 68, 74, 115) had handles (see Pl. 56:6); two (4B 80, 88) were inverted over skeletons. One burial (4B 68) had two tubs, one inverted over the other, and another (4B 133) had the broken end of the tub closed with potsherds and a baked brick. Seven examples of long tubs with rounded ends (see Pl. 75:3) were found in SE I (l. 170–85, w. 40–45, h. 16–25 cm.). Each tub had a lid in two pieces. Each piece had a hole about one-third of the distance from its end; maximum height of the lid was 20 cm. Four tub burials had brickwork of unbaked bricks *ca.* 30 × 30 × 10 cm.; one (4B 28) was enclosed by bricks laid flat around the tub and forming a gable over it (see Pl. 75:4); two (4B 29, 30) were enclosed by bricks laid on edge and forming a gable over the top, and one (4B 39) was covered only by irregularly laid bricks. No brickwork was found around the other three tubs (3B 91, 105, and 4B 47).

There were 23 examples of "bathtub" burials (like those illustrated in Vol. I, Pl. 157:12–14), 7 from SE III, 11 from SE III or II, and 5 from SE I (l. 102–30, w. 44–77, h. 32–59 cm.; one small tub [4B 145] l. 84, w. 46, h. 30 cm.). One tub (4B 104) contained fragments of a wood cover; another (4B 111) had an inverted tub used as a cover; and two tubs (4B 124, 129) were inverted over the skeletons.

JAR BURIALS

Jar burials are assigned to SE levels III, II, and the Parthian cemetery; a total of 41 were found. Since most of the jars were horizontal, their position is not specifically mentioned in the burial list; occasionally, however, when jars were upright, their position is mentioned. Except for one double-jar burial, all the burials were in single jars. The jars were probably not made especially for burials since several different shapes of jars were used. They may be divided into five types: pointed jars, oval jars, and jars with convex bases, ring bases, and funnel bottoms.

Twenty-one pointed jars (see Pl. 57:1), all containing infant burials, came from the Parthian cemetery (d. 30–40, h. 60–80 cm.). Nine of these jars (4B 2–10) had a potsherd over the open end, another (4B 15) had the upper part of a jar (like that in Pl. 57:6) closing off the open end, and two (4B 27, 52) had a baked brick. There was only one double-jar burial (4B 18). Half of the jars were smeared with bitumen inside.

There were four examples of oval jars (see Vol. I, Pl. 162:3), one from SE III, one from SE II or III, and two from SE II (at rim, l. 80–92.5, w. 50–65, h. 56–64.5 cm.). All were upright burials; two jars (4B 65, 76) had convex and two (4B 109, 113) had ring bases.

The Parthian cemetery yielded 5 convex-base jars (see Pls. 57:2, 6 and 75:6; d. 25–35, h. 25–40 cm.). One jar (4B 1) had three strap handles, and two (4B 10, 12) had two strap handles. An unnumbered infant burial in SE 38 II was in a jar with one strap handle (Pl. 57:6), and another (4B 5) was in a jar with no handles at all. One of these jars (4B 10) was covered with a bowl (Pl. 57:4). Three of them (4B 5, 10, 12) were horizontal, one (4B 1) was upright, and the position of the unnumbered burial is unknown. Two additional burials (4B 89, 118), from SE III and II, were in upright jars which had their tops broken off.

There were five examples of ring-base jars (see Pl. 75:1 and Vol. I, Pl. 157:2–5), one from SE III and four from SE II (d. 50–100, base d. 30–40, h. 60–90 cm.). Two jars (4B 63, 93) were horizontal, and three (4B 61, 77, 108) were upright. One of the upright jars (4B 61) was capped with a circle of fine clay 11 cm. thick.

There were four funnel-bottom jars (see Pl. 75:2 and Vol. I, Pl. 157:8), one from SE III or II and three from SE II (d. 68–75, base d. 11–20, h. 61–74.5 cm.). One jar (4B 66) was horizontal and three (4B 60, 91, 134) were upright. Burial 4B 60 can be seen on Plate 25 C.

BOWL BURIALS

There were two examples of bowl burials (see Pl. 56:7), one (4B 75) from SE III or II and one (4B 90) from SE II (d. 37–40, base d. 20, h. 25.5–30 cm.). One of the bowls (4B 75) had a fine, unbaked-clay lid with a handle (Pl. 56:9).

SLIPPER COFFINS

All of the slipper-coffin burials belonged to the Parthian cemetery, and in several instances they were placed above or cut into earlier slipper-coffin burials; a total of 61 were found. There were glazed and unglazed coffins which differed only in their surface treatment. The coffins were 190–215 cm. long, tapered from 55–60 cm. at the head to 20–25 cm. at the foot, and were 25–40 cm. high (see Pl. 57:5). There were a few coffins (4B 6, 23, 37, 97) for younger people that measured 115–33 cm. long. The top openings were round to oval, 50–80 cm. long and 40–55 cm. wide; the rims varied from 3 to 8 cm. in width and sometimes broadened on top of the coffin. The holes in the foot end were 11–13 cm. in diameter.

Eight of the slipper coffins (3B 81, 82, 94 and 4B 31, 33, 36, 38, 112) were glazed (see Pls. 75:5, 7, 76:1–3). Two coffins (3B 81 and 4B 31) were decorated with a rope design, which divided the top into four panels, each containing a nude female figure (see Pl. 75:5, 7); on another coffin (4B 36) the basic design was treated somewhat differently (Pl. 76:2, 3). The four panels of another coffin (3B 94) contained a central rope design of concentric rings (Pl. 75:8). In one burial (4B 38) the top opening was covered with a buff-slipped, reddish-ware, convex lid, which was divided crosswise into halves; the lid was decorated with two grooves around the rim and a single wavy line lengthwise (see Pl. 76:1). The opening of another slipper coffin nearby (4B 36) was covered with two pointed jars, each containing parts of adult skeletons (see Pl. 76:1). Baked bricks and jar fragments were piled over the opening of another slipper coffin (4B 31).

Fifty-three examples, including two unnumbered coffins in SE 81 I 2, were not glazed (see Pl. 75:9, 10). Several simple design elements were used to decorate the rim around the top opening: incised hatching (3B 65, 101 and 4B 143; see Pl. 57:5), incised zigzag (3B 99), dot-filled zigzag (4B 25), and incised semicircles (3B 66) and full circles (3B 100). Rope designs were used to divide the surface of one coffin (3B 66) into panels; its central panel contained a clothed female figure (Pl. 75:9, 10). Another coffin (4B 34) had an oval lid, 54 × 73 cm., with rope edging and two grooves crossing on the diameters. Three burials (3B 88 and 4B 35, 144) had sherds over the top opening, and in another (4B 6), the opening was covered by baked bricks, 35 × 35 × 7 cm.

LIST OF BURIALS AND THEIR CONTENTS

The burials are listed in numerical order (except for a few unnumbered ones listed at the end), with the levels to which they are attributed and the loci and levels in which they were found. The burials are shown on the excavation plans of the levels in which they were found. The orientation of the skeletons, unless otherwise noted, is from sacrum to atlas. Personal ornaments and gifts, if any, are listed after the description of the burial.

3B 40.   SE I intrusive into SE 79 I 2 (not shown on plan); earth burial; adult contracted on left side, oriented southeast

	3N 211	Jar (Pl. 51:3)
	3P 199	Jar (see Vol. I, type 58)
	3P 206	Bowl (see Vol. I, type 49)
	3N 214	Necklace of 375 beads of frit and carnelian, in jar 3N 211
	3N 204	Bronze rod in sheet bronze sleeve; l. 17.6, d. 0.3 cm.; bronze sleeve l. 10.6, d. 0.8 cm.
	Discard	Finger ring
	3N 202*a*	Bronze cylinder; l. 10.6, d. 1.5 cm.
	3N 202*b*	Plano-convex stone whorl; d. 2.3, th. 0.85 cm.
	3N 224	Plano-convex grayish stone whorl; d. 2.3, th. 0.85 cm.
	Discard	Piece of lead
3B 47.	SE I intrusive into SE 79 I 2 (not shown on plan); "bathtub" burial; skeleton fragmentary; tub oriented southeast
	3P 216	Jar
	3P 211	Small jar (see Vol. I, type 58)
	3N 210	Thin-ware bowl (see Vol. I, type 67)
	3N 178	Bronze ring with oval bezel; d. 2 cm.
	3D 291*a*	Bronze ring
	3D 291*b*	Bronze pin
	3D 290	Baked-clay spindle whorl
3B 48.	SE I intrusive into SE 79 I 2 (not shown on plan); "bathtub" burial; skeleton fragmentary
	3N 208	Thin-ware bowl (Pl. 50:11)
3B 53.	SE I intrusive into SE I 2 (not shown on plan); "bathtub" burial; adult contracted on right side, oriented northeast
	3N 257	Small glazed bowl (see Vol. I, type 49)
	3P 235	Thin-ware bowl (see Vol. I, type 67)
3B 54.	SE I intrusive into SE I 2 (not shown on plan); earth burial; infant, skeleton disturbed, oriented northeast
	3P 232	Jar (see Vol. I, type 60)
	3P 228	Small jar (Pl. 53:12)
	3P 236	Bowl (see Vol. I, type 66)
	3P 225	Bowl
	3D 298	Beads of shell, paste, and bronze
	3D 297	Two bronze bracelets
3B 55.	SE I intrusive into SE I 2 (not shown on plan); "bathtub" burial; adult, skeleton disturbed
	3P 286	Jar (see the pottery list in Chap. IV, and Vol. I, type 61)
3B 65.	Intrusive into SE 80 *ca.* I 3; slipper coffin (Pl. 57:5); two adolescents in dorsal positions, oriented south
3B 66.	Intrusive into SE 81 *ca.* I 3; slipper coffin (Pl. 75:9, 10); adult in dorsal position, oriented southwest
	3N 397	Bronze tool (Pl. 62:9)
	3N 398	Two lozenge-shaped gold leaf head ornaments; l. 4.7, w. 2.3, th. 0.05 cm.
3B 76.	Intrusive into SE 81 *ca.* I 3; slipper coffin; skeleton in dorsal position; coffin oriented north
	3P 583	Jar, near feet (Pl. 58:2)
3B 77.	Intrusive into SE 81 *ca.* I 3; slipper coffin; adult in dorsal position with hands at pelvis; coffin oriented north
	3N 435	Two bronze rings with oval bezels and one iron ring, on left hand; d. 1.9, 2.2, and 2.0 cm.
	3N 436	Beads of frit, shell, wood, carnelian, and green stone
3B 78.	Intrusive into SE 81 *ca.* I 3; slipper coffin, oriented north

LIST OF BURIALS AND THEIR CONTENTS

	3N 440	Bronze coin; d. 1.3, th. 0.3 cm.
3B 79.	Intrusive into SE 81 *ca.* I 3; slipper coffin, oriented northwest
3B 80.	Intrusive into SE 81 *ca.* I 3; slipper coffin, oriented east
3B 81.	Intrusive into SE 81 *ca.* I 3; glazed slipper coffin (Pl. 75:5, 7), oriented southeast
3B 82.	Intrusive into SE 81 *ca.* I 3; glazed slipper coffin, oriented northeast
3B 83.	Intrusive into SE 80 *ca.* I 1; slipper coffin, oriented northeast
3B 84.	Intrusive into SE 76 *ca.* I 2; slipper coffin, oriented northeast
3B 85.	Intrusive into SE 76 *ca.* I 2; slipper coffin, oriented west
3B 86.	Intrusive into SE 76 *ca.* I 2; slipper coffin, oriented northeast
	3N 477	Stone pendant (l. 2.9, w. 1.5, th. 0.9 cm.) and red stone bead (l. 0.9, w. 0.85 cm.), near right arm
3B 87.	Intrusive into SE 76 *ca.* I 2; slipper coffin, oriented northeast
	3N 437	Bronze pendant (Pl. 62:4); h. 2.3, w. 1.5, th. 1.1 cm.
	3N 438	Assorted beads of carnelian, shell, agate, lapis and glazed frit
	3N 439	Two bronze rings (d. 2.3 cm.) with oval bezels, on finger of skeleton
3B 88.	Intrusive into SE 76 *ca.* I 2; slipper coffin with opening covered with potsherds, oriented northeast
	3N 441	Assorted beads of shell, red stone, and glazed material, near wrist
3B 89.	Intrusive into SE 81 *ca.* I 3; slipper coffin, oriented northwest
3B 90.	Intrusive into SE 76 *ca.* I 3; slipper coffin, oriented west
3B 91.	SE I intrusive into SE 64 II 2; long tub with rounded ends and lid (Pl. 75:3); adult in dorsal position, oriented northeast
	3N 489	Alabaster vase (Pl. 55:5)
	3N 490	Alabaster vase, part of shoulder and rim missing (similar to 3N 492)
	3N 491	Alabaster vase, top only (similar to 3N 492)
	3N 492	Alabaster vase (Pl. 56:3); all vases near head
	3P 584	Pottery dish, near waist (see Vol. I, type 65)
3B 93.	SE I intrusive into SE 67 II 3; earth burial; adolescent contracted on right side with hands at mouth, oriented northeast
	3P 592	Glazed jar (see Vol. I, type 58)
	3P 593	Glazed jar
	3N 499	Glazed jar with three lug handles (Pl. 51:10)
	3P 595	Glazed jar; all four glazed jars near legs
	3P 602	Jar, covered by 3P 604, near head (see Vol. I, type 60)
	3P 603	Jar, near head (Pl. 55:1)
	3P 604	Thin-ware bowl (see Vol. I, type 66)
	3N 487	Beads of frit and stone, near head
3B 94.	Intrusive into SE 75 *ca.* I 3; glazed slipper coffin (Pl. 75:8); two adults, one over the other, oriented northeast
3B 95.	Intrusive into SE 21 *ca.* I 3; slipper coffin, oriented west
3B 96.	Intrusive into SE 80 *ca.* I 3; slipper coffin, oriented southeast
3B 97.	Intrusive into SE 80 *ca.* I 3; slipper coffin; two skeletons, oriented northeast
3B 98.	Intrusive into SE 75 *ca.* I 3; slipper coffin, oriented west
	3N 493	Glass bottle (Pl. 71:19)
	3P 610	Glass bottle
	3P 611	Glass bottle; all three glass bottles near head
	3N 504	Beads of stone, wood, and glazed frit, near neck
3B 99.	Intrusive into SE 75 *ca.* I 3; slipper coffin, oriented southeast
3B 100.	Intrusive into SE 75 *ca.* I 3; slipper coffin, oriented southeast
3B 101.	Intrusive into SE 75 *ca.* I 3; slipper coffin, oriented southwest
3B 102.	Intrusive into SE 75 *ca.* I 3; slipper coffin, oriented northeast
3B 103.	Intrusive into SE 75 *ca.* I 3; slipper coffin, oriented southwest

3B 104.	Intrusive into SE 76 *ca.* I 3; slipper coffin, oriented northeast
3B 105.	SE I intrusive into SE 74 II 2; "bathtub" burial with lid, oriented southwest
4B 1.	Intrusive into SE 24 I 1; upright convex-base jar (Pl. 57:2), opening covered with base of pot; infant
4P 13	Bowl at base of burial jar
4B 2.	Intrusive into SE 24 I 2; pointed jar, potsherd over opening; infant contracted with head toward open end; jar oriented southwest
4B 3.	Intrusive into SE 23 I 2; pointed jar; infant contracted with head toward base; jar oriented northeast
4B 4.	Intrusive into SE 23 I 2; pointed jar, potsherd over opening; infant contracted with head toward open end; jar oriented east
4D 33	Beads; 3 frit spheroids; other shapes in blue glass, agate, carnelian
4B 5.	Intrusive into SE 24 I 1; convex-base jar, potsherd over opening; infant contracted on right side with head toward base; jar oriented northeast
4B 6.	Intrusive into SE 23 I 3; slipper coffin, opening covered with baked bricks; infant; coffin oriented northeast
4N 73	Beads of pottery, bronze, glass, and black stone pendant (Pl. 62:3)
4N 9, 11	Bronze bracelets, one on each wrist (Pl. 62:13) and beads of glass, clay, and shell, at each wrist
4N 10	Two gold earrings (Pl. 62:11)
4B 7.	Intrusive into SE 29 I 1; slipper coffin; juvenile in dorsal position; coffin oriented east
4B 8.	Intrusive into SE 29 I 1; pointed jar (Pl. 57:1), potsherd over opening; infant with head toward open end; jar oriented west
4B 9.	Intrusive into SE 29 I 1; pointed jar; no skeleton; jar oriented north
4B 10.	Intrusive into SE 29 I 1; convex-base jar (Pl. 75:6), opening covered with bowl (Pl. 57:4); infant; jar oriented southeast
4B 11.	Intrusive into SE 29 I 1; pointed jar, potsherd over opening; infant; jar oriented southeast
4B 12.	Intrusive into SE 29 I 1; convex-base jar; infant; jar oriented southeast
4B 13.	Intrusive into SE 29 I 1; pointed jar; infant with head toward open end; jar oriented east
4B 14.	Intrusive into SE 24 I 2; earth burial; adult in dorsal position, missing below waist, oriented west
4D 30	Two bronze rings
4D 31	Beads; mostly white frit cylinders, l. 0.6, d. 0.3 cm.; other shapes in white stone, carnelian, shell
4B 15.	Intrusive into SE 7 I 2; pointed jar, opening covered with upper part of jar (as in Pl. 57:4); infant with head toward open end; jar oriented east
4B 16.	Intrusive into SE 8 I 2; pointed jar, sherd over opening; infant contracted with head toward base; jar oriented south
Discard	Globular bitumen bead and black stone bead
4B 17.	Intrusive into SE 76 *ca.* I 2; pointed jar, potsherd over opening; infant with head toward base; jar oriented southwest
4B 18.	Intrusive into SE 76 *ca.* I 2; two pointed jars; infant contracted on left side, oriented southwest
4B 19.	Intrusive into SE 76 *ca.* I 2; pointed jar, brick over opening; infant with head toward open end; jar oriented northeast
4B 20.	Intrusive into SE 24 I 3; pointed jar; infant crushed; jar oriented southeast
4D 32	Beads, at head; 10 carnelian biconoids, d. 0.6–0.8 cm.; 3 frit disks, d. 0.8 cm.; other shapes in agate, white and green frit
4B 21.	Intrusive into SE 23 I 3; pointed jar, potsherd over opening; infant slightly contracted with head toward open end; jar oriented east

LIST OF BURIALS AND THEIR CONTENTS

4B 22.	Intrusive into SE 23 I 3; slipper coffin; skeleton in dorsal position; coffin oriented east
4B 23.	Intrusive into SE 24 I 2; slipper coffin; juvenile in dorsal position; coffin oriented south
4B 24.	Intrusive into SE 22 I 2; pointed jar (over 4B 25); no skeleton; jar oriented east
4B 25.	Intrusive into SE 22 I 3; slipper coffin; adult male in dorsal position with hands at pelvis; coffin oriented east
4B 26.	Intrusive into SE 14 I 1; pointed jar; no skeleton; jar oriented south
4B 27.	Intrusive into SE 14 I 2; pointed jar, opening covered with a baked brick; infant with head toward open end; jar oriented southwest
	4D 34 Beads, at neck; of various materials and shapes
4B 28.	SE I intrusive into SE 16 I 2; long tub with rounded ends and two-part convex lid covered with an unbaked-brick gable (Pl. 75:4); adult slightly contracted on right side, oriented northwest
4B 29.	SE I intrusive into SE 15 II 1; long tub with rounded ends and a two-part convex lid covered with an unbaked-brick gable; adult in dorsal position, oriented northwest
4B 30.	SE I intrusive into SE 17 II 1; long tub with rounded ends and a two-part convex lid enclosed in an unbaked-brick "box" and covered with an unbaked-brick gable; adult in dorsal position with legs slightly contracted, oriented northwest
	4P 23 Pot (see Vol. I, type 60)
4B 31.	Intrusive into SE 76 *ca.* I 3; glazed slipper coffin, baked bricks and potsherds irregularly placed over opening; adult, skeleton disturbed, apparently secondary interment; coffin oriented south
4B 32.	SE I intrusive into SE 25 I 3; earth burial; adult in dorsal position, oriented northwest
4B 33.	Intrusive into SE 22 I 3; glazed slipper coffin; no skeleton; coffin oriented east
4B 34.	Intrusive into SE 19 I 2; slipper coffin and lid; adult in dorsal position, oriented west
4B 35.	Intrusive into SE 38 II 1; slipper coffin, large sherd of another coffin partly over opening; adult in dorsal position, oriented south
4B 36.	Intrusive into SE 76 *ca.* I 3; glazed slipper coffin, two pointed jars each containing parts of adult skeletons over slipper-coffin opening (Pl. 76:1–3); adult in dorsal position with hands at pelvis, oriented northeast
4B 37.	Intrusive into SE 19 I 2; slipper coffin, disturbed by 4B 34; adult, foot bones only, oriented northwest
4B 38.	Intrusive into SE 76 *ca.* I 3; glazed slipper coffin and two-part lid (Pl. 76:1); adult in dorsal position, oriented north
	4N 15 Two very thin gold leaves (Pl. 62:12) near skull and a gold bead (l. 0.75, d. 0.65 cm.)
4B 39.	SE I intrusive into SE 14 II 1; long tub with rounded ends and convex lid covered with irregularly laid unbaked bricks (tub cut by level I foundations); adult, leg bones only, oriented southeast
4B 40.	Intrusive into SE 38 II 1; pointed jar, large sherd over opening; infant oriented southwest
	4D 75 Beads, at neck
4B 41.	Intrusive into SE 21 I 3; slipper coffin; coffin oriented north
4B 42.	Intrusive into SE 14 I 3; earth burial, baked bricks on southwest partly over skeleton; adult tightly contracted on left side with right hand at face, oriented southeast
4B 43.	Intrusive into SE 21 I 3; bottom part of slipper coffin; no skeleton; coffin oriented northeast
4B 44.	Intrusive into SE 38 II 2; slipper coffin; no skeleton; coffin oriented southeast
4B 45.	Intrusive into SE 38 II 1; pointed jar; adult, skeleton disturbed; jar oriented northeast
4B 46.	Intrusive into SE 76 *ca.* I 3; slipper coffin; juvenile, fragmentary skeleton, coffin oriented northeast
	4D 86 Beads, at central and upper part of coffin; carnelian spheroids, frit disks, brown composition barrels, and others

4B 47.	SE I intrusive into SE 55 *ca.* II 3; long tub with rounded ends and convex half-lid; adult in dorsal position, oriented northeast
	4P 38 Pot (see Vol. I, type 60), outside coffin
4B 48.	SE II intrusive into SE 55 *ca.* II 3; earth burial with unbaked-brick sides and cover; adult in dorsal position with left arm across waist, oriented northeast
	4P 48 Saucer (see Vol. I, type 52), at feet
4B 49.	Intrusive into SE 37 II 1; pointed jar, sherd over opening; infant with head toward open end, oriented northwest
	Discard Bronze bead, at chest
4B 50.	SE II intrusive into SE 51 II 2; earth burial; adult slightly contracted on right side with left hand at face, oriented northeast
4B 51.	SE II intrusive into SE 44 II 2; earth burial; adult, missing below pelvis, on left side with left hand at face, oriented southwest
4B 52.	Intrusive into SE 37 II 1; pointed jar, brick over opening; infant with head toward open end, oriented southwest
	4D 84 Beads; mostly of bronze and brown stone, l. 0.3, square cross section 0.5 cm.
	4D 85 Bracelet
	4D 99 Beads; barrels in stone, frit, glass, l. 0.7–0.9 cm.; bronze spheroids, d. 0.6 cm.; and others
4B 53.	Intrusive into SE 68 II 2; slipper coffin; adult in dorsal position with arms across waist, oriented northwest
	4D 94 Ring, on left hand
4B 54A, B.	SE II intrusive into SE 62 III 1; earth burial, covered with potsherds; two adults, both tightly contracted, possible remains of a third skeleton; *A* oriented northeast, *B* oriented southwest
	With burial *A*:
	4P 82 Glazed pot, at right hand (see Vol. I, type 58)
	4P 77 Pot (see Vol. I, type 60)
	4P 78 Glazed dish (see Vol. I, type 64)
	4N 34 Bronze earring; d. 2.4 cm.
	4N 35 Bronze rod; l. 9.7, d. 0.5 cm.
	4N 36 Three bronze rings, on left hand; d. 2.1–2.6 cm.
	4N 27 Bronze pin; l. 6.0, d. 0.2 cm.
	With burial *B*:
	4P 81 Bowl, near face (see Vol. I, type 67)
	4D 100 Bone ring and beads
4B 55.	SE II intrusive into SE 61 III 1; earth burial; adult, legs and feet missing, on right side with hands at chest, oriented northwest
	4D 98 Beads, at waist
4B 56.	SE II intrusive into SE 42 II 4; earth burial; adult, skeleton fragmentary, oriented northeast
	4N 42 Two gold crescent pendants and miscellaneous beads, at lower jaw (Pl. 74:8)
	4N 39, 40 Two silver bracelets, on forearms (Pl. 74:9)
	4N 37 Two silver earrings (Pl. 74:10)
	4N 41 Finger ring with bezel formed of two silver circlets mounted on bronze platform; d. 2.1 cm.
4B 57.	SE II intrusive into SE 51 II 2; earth burial; adult or juvenile on right side, missing below waist, oriented southwest
4B 58.	SE II intrusive into SE 51 II 2; earth burial; adult in dorsal position with left arm at pelvis, oriented northeast

LIST OF BURIALS AND THEIR CONTENTS

	4P 83	Bowl (see Vol. I, type 52), at head
4B 59.	SE II intrusive into SE 52 II 4; earth burial; adult contracted in dorsal position with left arm across waist, oriented southeast
	4P 97	Pot (see Vol. I, type 60)
	4P 98	Bowl (see Vol. I, type 66)
	4P 99	Saucer (Pl. 50:12); all three at left of pelvis
4B 60.	SE II intrusive into SE 49 II 4; upright funnel-bottom jar (Pl. 75:2); adult tightly contracted on left side with hands at face
	4P 111	Pot (see Vol. I, type 60)
	4P 110	Bowl
	4D 121	Bronze rod
	4D 122	Bronze bracelet
4B 61.	SE II intrusive into SE 47 II 4; upright ring-base jar capped with 11 cm. thick circle of clay (Pl. 75:1); adult tightly contracted on left side
4B 62.	SE II intrusive into SE 55 II 4; earth burial; adult tightly contracted on right side with left hand at face, oriented northeast
	4N 54*a*	Cylinder seal (Pl. 71:2), near lower jaw
	4N 54*b*	Bronze fibula; l. 4.0, w. 2.0 cm.
	4N 54*c*	Biconoid stone bead; l. 1.0, d. 1.0 cm.
	4D 115	Iron pin, at top of head
4B 63.	SE II intrusive into SE 55 III 2; ring-base jar; adult medium contracted, oriented north
	4P 94	Small jar (see Vol. I, type 72)
	4P 95	Large pot (see Vol. I, type 58)
	4P 96	Small pot (see Vol. I, type 58); all three pots near left elbow
	4N 56	Bronze ring with bezel, on left hand; d. 2.0 cm.
	4N 57	Bronze rod; l. 13.0, d. 0.5 cm.
	4D 118	Frit beads
	4N 55	Four bronze bracelets, two below each arm
4B 64.	SE I intrusive into SE 55 III 2; "bathtub" burial; adult tightly contracted on left side with left hand at face; coffin oriented northeast
	4P 100	Glazed pot, below right hand
	4P 104	Pot (see Vol. I, type 60), behind skull
	4P 105	Bowl (see Vol. I, type 67), inverted over 4P 104
	4N 50	Assorted beads, near right forearm
	4N 48	Bronze pin; l. 5.4, d. 0.25 cm.
	4N 47	Iron pin; l. 5.8, d. 0.3 cm.
	4N 53	Bronze rod; l. 14.3, d. 0.3 cm.
	4D 117	Two bronze rings, on right hand
	4N 49	Thin bronze crescent (Pl. 61:5)
4B 65*A*, *B*.	SE II intrusive into SE 60 III 2; upright oval jar; two adults; top skeleton tightly contracted on left side and lower skeleton in same position; jar oriented northeast
	With burial *A*:	
	4P 103	Pot (see Vol. I, type 60)
	4P 102	Bowl (Pl. 50:10), inverted over 4P 103
	4D 116	Iron knife fragments
	4N 52	Two silver earrings, near shoulders (Pl. 61:3)
	With burial *B*:	
	4P 101	Pot (Pl. 52:2, also see Vol. I, type 59)
	4P 106	Small jar (Pl. 55:2)
	4P 107	Dish (Pl. 53:3)
4B 66.	SE II intrusive into SE 55 III 2; funnel-bottom jar; adult tightly contracted on left side, oriented northwest

4B 67. SE II intrusive into SE 44 II 4; earth burial, partly covered with potsherds; infant on right side, oriented southeast
    4P 115   Pot (type 75, as in Pl. 51:1–4), at back of skull

4B 68. SE III intrusive into SE 72 V; oval tub with handles, inverted tub as cover; infant on left side, oriented northwest
    4N 66   Four bronze bracelets; d. 4.0–5.0 cm.

4B 69. SE II intrusive into SE 62 III 2; earth burial; adult slightly contracted on left side with hands at face, oriented northwest
    4P 126   Pot (see Vol. I, type 60)
    4P 127   Dish (see Vol. I, type 64)
    Discard   Bead

4B 70. SE II intrusive into SE 62 III 2; earth burial, lower part of skeleton placed on oval tub; adult on right side, oriented northeast

4B 71. SE II intrusive into SE 77 III; earth burial; infant on left side, lower leg bones missing

4B 72. SE III intrusive into SE 72 V; earth burial; adult on left side, skeleton fragmentary
    4P 130   Small glazed pot (see Vol. I, type 72)
    4P 131   Glazed pot (see Vol. I, type 58)
    4P 132   Pot (see Vol. I, type 60)
    4P 133   Bowl (see Vol. I, type 66), over mouth of 4P 132

4B 73. SE III intrusive into SE 72 V; earth burial; adult in a dorsal position, oriented northeast
    4P 137   Pot (see Vol. I, type 60)
    4P 138   Dish (see Vol. I, type 67)

4B 74. SE II intrusive into SE 73 V; oval tub with handles (Pl. 56:6); infant on right side, oriented northeast
    4P 134   Small pot (see the pottery list in Chap. IV), at feet
    Discard   Beads

4B 75. SE III or II intrusive into SE 73 V; bowl burial with unbaked clay lid (Pl. 56:9); infant, skeleton fragmentary
    4D 123   Beads; 4 white frit spheroids, d. 0.4 cm.; 12 yellow frit disks, d. 0.8, th. 0.4 cm.

4B 76. SE II intrusive into SE 73 V; upright oval jar; adult tightly contracted, probably buried in a sitting position
    4P 135   Glazed dish (see Vol. I, type 64)
    4P 136   Bowl (see Vol. I, type 52)
    4N 74   Scaraboid (Pl. 71:3), with beads

4B 77. SE II intrusive into NT 25 I 2; upright ring-base jar; juvenile(?) in sitting position
    4P 163   Large jar (Pl. 54:10)
    4N 133   Glass vase (Pl. 56:8), at left leg

4B 78. SE II intrusive into NT 18 I 1; earth burial; adult slightly contracted on right side, oriented northeast
    4P 143   Handled jug (Pl. 55:6)
    4P 144   Fine-ware bowl (see Vol. I, type 66)

4B 79. SE II intrusive into SE 77 III; round tub; infant tightly contracted on left side, oriented southwest

4B 80. SE II intrusive into SE 77 III; inverted oval tub; infant contracted on left side, oriented northwest

4B 81. SE II intrusive into NT 15 I 3; oval tub; infant contracted on right side, oriented northeast
    4P 164   Pot
    4D 165   Beads, at neck

4B 82. SE III intrusive into NT 17 I 1; earth burial covered with potsherds; adult contracted on right side, oriented northeast

LIST OF BURIALS AND THEIR CONTENTS

4B 83.   SE II intrusive into SE 77 III; earth burial; adult contracted on right side, oriented northeast
- 4P 150   Glazed jug (Pl. 54:6), at head
- 4P 151   Pot (see Vol. I, type 60)

4B 84.   SE III or II intrusive into NT 31 II 1; earth burial; adult contracted on left side with right hand at face, oriented southeast
- 4P 205   Small jar (see Vol. I, type 72)
- 4D 232   Bronze kohl stick
- 4D 233   Iron fragment, at face
- Discard   Bronze pin with hook end, at face

4B 85.   SE II intrusive into SE 77 III; earth burial; adult on left side, oriented northeast
- 4P 154   Glazed pot (see Vol. I, type 58), at head
- 4P 155   Pot (see Vol. I, type 60), at feet
- 4P 153   Bowl (see Vol. I, type 67), over mouth of 4P 155
- 4P 152   Bowl (see Vol. I, type 49), at knees
- 4D 167   Beads

4B 86.   SE II intrusive into NT 16 I 3; earth burial, covered with potsherds; infant slightly contracted on left side, oriented northeast
- 4P 157   Green glazed handled pot (see Vol. I, type 60)
- 4P 156   Reddish bowl (see Vol. I, type 66)
- 4P 158   Saucer (see Pl. 50:12)
- 4D 177   Beads
- 4D 178   Bronze earring and bronze ring, at head

4B 87.   SE II intrusive into NT 16 I 3; earth burial with baked bricks on southeast side leaning over skeleton; infant, skeleton disturbed; grave oriented northeast
- 4P 190   Double-handled jar (see Vol. I, type 60)

4B 88.   SE II intrusive into NT 26 II 1; inverted oval tub; adult contracted on left side, evidence of disintegrated cloth
- 4P 145   Bowl (see Vol. I, type 67)
- 4P 146–49   Glazed bowls (see Vol. I, type 72); all pottery around tub
- 4N 80   Bronze rod; l. 12.6, d. 0.45 cm.
- 4D 164   Two bronze rings, at waist

4B 89.   SE II intrusive into SE 77 III; upright convex-base jar, lower part of jar only; infant, skeleton fragmentary, oriented northeast
- 4D 174   Beads

4B 90.   SE II intrusive into NT 25 I 1; bowl burial (Pl. 56:7); infant, skeleton disintegrated
- 4D 169   Bronze bracelet

4B 91.   SE II intrusive into NT 16 I 2; upright funnel-bottom jar; adult in sitting position
- 4N 178   Glazed decorated jar (see Vol. I, type 57)
- 4N 130   Cylinder seal (Pl. 71:12) and 64 beads of carnelian, quartz, and frit
- 4D 225   Bracelet, d. 6.0, cross section d. 0.3 cm.; and shell ring, d. 2.5, w. 0.4–1.0, th. 0.2 cm.

4B 92.   SE II intrusive into SE 73 V; earth burial; adult on left side, lower part missing, oriented northwest

4B 93.   SE II intrusive into NT 25 I 1; ring-base jar; adult tightly contracted on right side; jar oriented northwest
- 4P 204   Small pot (Pl. 51:15 and see Vol. I, type 59), at legs

4B 94.   SE II intrusive into NT 16 I 1; earth burial; adult contracted on right side, oriented southeast
- 4P 168   Pot (see Vol. I, type 60), at head
- 4P 169   Dish, at waist

4B 95.	SE III or II intrusive into NT 23 I 2; oval tub; infant contracted on right side, oriented southwest
4P 171	Glazed pot (see Vol. I, type 58), at hands
4P 165	Pot (see Vol. I, type 60), outside tub
4D 176	Beads, near neck; many white to green disks, l. 0.3, d. 0.3 cm.; 20 brown-surfaced white, chalky composition barrels, l. 1.0, d. 0.3 cm.; 3 lapis, 3 carnelian, 1 green composition, in various shapes
4D 175	Bronze anklet, on right leg
4B 96.	Intrusive into SE 76 *ca.* I 3; slipper coffin; adult, skeleton disturbed, oriented southeast
Discard	Bead
4B 97.	Intrusive into SE 76 *ca.* I 3; slipper coffin; juvenile in dorsal position, oriented southwest
4B 98.	Intrusive into SE 76 *ca.* I 3; slipper coffin; adult in dorsal position, oriented northwest
4B 99.	Intrusive into SE 76 *ca.* I 3; slipper coffin; no skeleton; coffin oriented northeast
4B 100.	Intrusive into SE 76 *ca.* I 3; slipper coffin; no skeleton; coffin oriented southwest
4B 101.	SE II intrusive into SE 68 II 4; earth burial, covered with a few potsherds; infant contracted on right side, oriented northeast
4B 102.	SE II intrusive into SE 71 II 3; earth burial; juvenile slightly contracted on left side, oriented northeast
4P 202	Bowl (see Vol. I, type 66), at feet
4P 203	Pot (see Vol. I, type 60), at feet
4B 103.	SE III intrusive into NT 31 II 1; "bathtub" burial; adult contracted on right side, oriented southeast
4N 116	Bronze bowl (see Vol. I, Pl. 108:17), back of pelvis
4N 117	Bronze bracelet (Pl. 61:4), at right arm
4B 104.	SE III or II intrusive into NT 52 II 1; "bathtub" burial, many fragments of palm wood inside tub suggest a wood cover; adult contracted on left side, oriented northeast
4P 209	Small jar (Pl. 51:16 and see Vol. I, type 72), in front of body
4P 210	Pointed jar (Pl. 51:13 and see Vol. I, type 59), in front of body
4N 98	Frit cylinder seal with pale green glaze, l. 1.9, d. 1.0 cm. (similar to seal in Vol. I, Pl. 113:8), at chest
4N 102	Bronze fibula, l. 3.0, h. 1.9 cm., at chest
4N 103	Bronze nail, max. l. 7.5, cross section d. 0.4 cm., at legs
4N 96, 97	Beads, near neck; 110 beads of assorted shapes in agate, carnelian, amethyst, and striated green stone, and blue paste
4N 104	Four bronze rings, on left hand; d. 1.9–2.0 cm.
4B 105.	SE II intrusive into NT 17 I 2; oval tub; adult contracted on right side, oriented northeast
4P 195, 196	Jars, at head
4P 197	Jar (Pl. 54:7), at feet
4D 227	Beads, at neck
4B 106.	SE III intrusive into NT 18 I 3; earth burial covered with half a broken jar; adult contracted on right side, oriented northeast
4P 179	Jar, at feet
4P 177	Pot (see Vol. I, type 60), at feet
4P 180	Dish, covering mouth of 4P 177
Discard	Beads
4D 234	Bronze ring, at wrist
4D 228	Bronze rod, at neck
4B 107.	SE III or II intrusive into NT 32 II 1; earth burial; adult contracted on left side with right hand at face, oriented south
4B 108.	SE III intrusive into NT 16 I 3; upright ring-base jar; adult, probably in sitting position

LIST OF BURIALS AND THEIR CONTENTS

4B 109.   SE III or II intrusive into NT 33 II 1; oval jar; juvenile or adult contracted on right side, oriented northeast
- 4P 217   Jar (see Vol. I, type 60), outside burial jar
- 4P 218   Bowl (see Vol. I, type 67), covering mouth of 4P 217
- 4P 198   Dish (see Vol. I, type 64), at head
- 4D 220   Bronze clamp, at chest
- 4D 230   Knife with wood handle (Pl. 60:9), below arms

4B 110.   SE III or II intrusive into NT 46 II 1; "bathtub" burial, adult contracted on right side, oriented northeast
- 4N 177   Glazed jar (see Vol. I, type 57), at elbow
- 4D 333   Bronze bracelet on left arm
- 4N 121   Bronze fibula, at shoulder; l. 5.0, h. 2.6, w. 0.7 cm.

4B 111.   SE III or II intrusive into NT 17 I 3; "bathtub" burial with inverted tub for cover; adult contracted on right side, oriented northeast
- 4P 206   Small glazed jar (see Vol. I, type 72), at head
- 4P 207   Jar (see Vol. I, type 58), in front of arms
- 4P 208   Pot (see Vol. I, type 60), at knees
- 4P 213   Dish (see Vol. I, type 64), in front of arms

4B 112.   Intrusive into SE 76 *ca.* I 3; glazed slipper coffin; no skeleton; coffin oriented southwest

4B 113.   SE III intrusive into SE 77 III; oval jar; juvenile or adult, skeleton fragmentary, oriented northeast
- 4P 183   Pot
- 4P 184   Dish, covering mouth of pot 4P 183
- 4P 185   Small jar
- 4P 186   Glazed jug with handles (Pl. 54:8)
- 4P 182   Glazed dish
- 4N 112   Beads of carnelian, chalcedony, and green stone
- Discard   Bronze earring
- Discard   Bronze rod
- Discard   Small bronze pins
- Discard   Shell

4B 114.   SE III or II intrusive into NT 15 I 3; "bathtub" burial; juvenile or adult, skeleton fragmentary, oriented northeast
- 4P 189   Small jar at pelvis
- 4D 224   Two bronze rings

4B 115.   SE III or II intrusive into NT 12 I 2; oval tub; infant contracted on left side, oriented southeast
- 4P 175   Pot (see Vol. I, type 60), at feet
- 4P 176   Bowl (see Vol. I, type 67), covering mouth of 4P 175
- 4D 318   Beads, at neck; carnelian and frit in various shapes; 2 scaraboids, l. 0.7, w. 0.6, h. 0.4 cm.
- 4N 120   Two bronze anklets, one on each leg; d. 5.9–6.0 cm.

4B 116.   SE III or II intrusive into NT 9 II 2; "bathtub" burial; adult, skeleton fragmentary; tub oriented northeast

4B 117.   SE III or II intrusive into NT 32 II 1; "bathtub" burial; adult contracted on left side, oriented southeast
- 4P 194   Jar (see Vol. I, type 60), behind body
- 4P 187   Small glazed jar, at feet
- 4P 188   Glazed vase, at feet
- 4P 193   Glazed dish (see Vol. I, type 64), behind body
- 4N 139   Fifteen beads of shell, carnelian, and amethyst including four scaraboids (Pl. 71:7–10), at neck

4B 118.   SE III intrusive into NT 31 II 1; upright convex-base jar, lower part of jar only; infant

66 THE BURIALS

		contracted on left side, oriented northeast
	4P 191	Pot (see Vol. I, type 60), at feet
	4P 192	Bowl (see Vol. I, type 67), covering 4P 191
	Discard	Beads, at neck
4B 119.		SE III intrusive into NT 32 II 1; "bathtub" burial; no skeleton; tub oriented southeast
	4N 179	Glazed decorated jar (see Vol. I, type 59)
	4N 180	Glazed decorated jar (see Vol. I, type 57)
	4N 115	Fragmentary bronze bowl (Pl. 56:5)
	4N 142	Beads of quartz, carnelian, and frit; 150 barrel beads, l. 0.7–2.0, d. 0.5–0.9 cm.; other beads in spherical, biconoid, and disk shapes
4B 120.		SE III or II intrusive into NT 7 I 3; earth burial; adult contracted on right side, oriented northeast
	4N 149	Iron dagger (Pl. 60:10), behind shoulder
	4N 150	Iron arrowheads (Pl. 60:8), behind shoulder
	4N 151	Bronze ring, on right hand; d. 2.2 cm.
	4N 152	Bronze ring on left hand; d. 2.1 cm.
4B 121.		Intrusive into SE 76 *ca.* I 3; slipper coffin; adult, skeleton disturbed; coffin oriented northwest
4B 122.		Intrusive into SE 76 *ca.* I 3; slipper coffin; adult, skeleton disturbed; coffin oriented northwest
	4P 223	Fragment of large glazed dish at mouth of coffin
	4P 224	Fragment of small glazed dish at mouth of coffin
4B 123.		SE III intrusive into SE 71 III 2; earth burial with unbaked-brick sides; adult in dorsal position with arms across chest, legs contracted, oriented northeast
	4P 227	Pot (see Vol. I, type 60), at feet
	4P 228	Thin-ware bowl (see Vol. I, type 66), covering mouth of 4P 227
4B 124.		SE III intrusive into SE 71 III 2; "bathtub" burial; adult contracted on right side, oriented northeast
	4P 229	Jar (see Vol. I, type 60), behind body
	4P 231	Thin-ware bowl (see Vol. I, type 66), at head
	4P 230	Dish (Pl. 53:1), at knees
	Discard	Bronze ring, on right hand
4B 125.		SE III intrusive into SE 71 III 2; "bathtub" burial; adult contracted on left side, oriented northeast
	4P 222	Jar (Pl. 54:3), at knees
	4N 113	Bronze bowl (see Vol. I, Pl. 108:17), at right hand
4B 126.		SE III intrusive into NT 149 II 2; earth burial with an oval of unbaked bricks on edge around skeleton; adult contracted on right side, oriented northwest
4B 127.		Intrusive into SE 76 *ca.* I 2; slipper coffin; adult in dorsal position, oriented northeast
4B 128.		SE III or II intrusive into NT 149 III; "bathtub" burial; adult, skeleton disturbed; tub oriented southeast
	4D 336*a, b*	Bronze shaft ring on pithy wood (Pl. 61:6) and bronze stave top (Pl. 61:7), at pelvis
	Discard	Bronze fragments
4B 129.		SE III intrusive into SE 71 III 2; inverted "bathtub" burial; adult, skeleton fragmentary; tub oriented northeast
	4P 237	Glazed pot (see Vol. I, type 60)
	4N 114	Bronze bowl (see Vol. I, Pl. 108:17), covering mouth of 4P 237
4B 130.		SE III intrusive into SE 71 III 2; earth burial; adult, skeleton disturbed, oriented southeast
	4P 238	Jar (see Vol. I, type 72), at head
	4P 239	Thin-ware dish, covering the mouth of 4P 238 (see Vol. I, type 66)
4B 131.		SE III intrusive into SE 71 III 2; earth burial; adult, skeleton disturbed

LIST OF BURIALS AND THEIR CONTENTS

	4P 236	Pot (see Vol. I, type 60)
4B 132.	\multicolumn{2}{l}{SE II intrusive into SE 69 II 4; earth burial; adult on right side, skull and arm bones only, oriented southeast}
	4P 232	Small glazed jar (see Vol. I, type 72)
	4P 233	Glazed jar (see Vol. I, type 58)
	4P 234	Jar with ear lugs (see Vol. I, Pl. 105:9)
	4P 235	Bowl (see Vol. I, type 49)
	4D 334	Iron tweezers; l. 4.8, w. 2.7, th. 0.2 cm.
	4D 335	Three bronze tubes, all wood-filled; l. 9.1, d. 1.9, th. 0.15 cm.; all near head
4B 133.	\multicolumn{2}{l}{SE III or II intrusive into SE 68 III 1; oval tub with baked brick at broken end; no skeleton; tub oriented southeast}
4B 134.	\multicolumn{2}{l}{SE III or II intrusive into NT 155 III; upright funnel-bottom jar; adult in sitting position}
4B 135.	\multicolumn{2}{l}{Intrusive into SE 81 *ca.* I 3; slipper coffin; adult in dorsal position, oriented southwest}
	4N 109*a*	Shell ring; d. 2.25 cm.
	4N 109*b*	Silver ring with carnelian bezel (Pl. 62:10)
	Discard	Two rings on finger of left hand
4B 136.	\multicolumn{2}{l}{SE III or II intrusive into NT 34 II 2; "bathtub" burial; adult contracted on right side, oriented northeast}
	4N 181	Jar
4B 137.	\multicolumn{2}{l}{SE III or II intrusive into NT 30 III; "bathtub" burial; adult, skeleton disturbed, tub oriented southeast}
	4P 252	Pot (see Vol. I, type 60)
	4P 253	Glazed dish (see Vol. I, type 64)
	4P 254	Glazed jar with ear lugs (see Vol. I, type 72)
	4P 255	Glazed jar (see Vol. I, type 58)
	4P 256	Dish (Pl. 52:13)
	4D 320	Iron knife
4B 138.	\multicolumn{2}{l}{SE III intrusive into SE 82 VI; "bathtub" burial; adult contracted on right side, left hand at face, oriented northeast}
	4P 248	Pot (see Vol. I, type 60), at back of head
	4P 249	Bowl (see Vol. I, type 67), covering mouth of 4P 248
	4P 250, 251	Small glazed jars (see Vol. I, type 72), at feet
	4D 332	Bronze pin, at head
4B 139.	\multicolumn{2}{l}{SE III intrusive into SE 82 VI; "bathtub" burial; adult contracted on left side, oriented northeast}
	Discard	Bronze ring
	4D 324	Iron knife
4B 140.	\multicolumn{2}{l}{SE II intrusive into SE 68 III; earth burial; infant contracted on right side, oriented southeast}
	Discard	Beads, at neck
4B 141.	\multicolumn{2}{l}{Intrusive into SE 76 *ca.* I 3; slipper coffin; adult in dorsal position, oriented northwest}
	Discard	One shell
4B 142.	\multicolumn{2}{l}{Intrusive into SE 76 *ca.* I 3; slipper coffin; adult in dorsal position, oriented northeast}
4B 143.	\multicolumn{2}{l}{Intrusive into SE 76 *ca.* I 3; slipper coffin; adult in dorsal position, oriented northwest}
4B 144.	\multicolumn{2}{l}{Intrusive into SE 81 *ca.* I 3; slipper coffin, sherds of another coffin partly over opening; adult in dorsal position, oriented southwest}
4B 145.	\multicolumn{2}{l}{SE III or II intrusive into NT 148 II 2; "bathtub" burial; adult or juvenile contracted on left side; tub oriented southeast}
	4P 247	Jar, at knees
	4N 83	Bronze bracelet; d. 6.5 cm.
4B 146.	\multicolumn{2}{l}{SE III or II intrusive into NT 74 III; "bathtub" burial; adult contracted on right side,}

		oriented northeast
	Discard	Glazed jar (see Vol. I, type 58), at knees
	Discard	Dish (see Vol. I, type 52), at feet
	4D 337	Round-end bronze rod (l. 12.6, d. 0.3 cm.) imbedded in leadlike mass in incised decorated bone tube (d. 2.3 cm., l. unknown)
	Discard	Bronze earring, at head
	4D 340*a*	Beads; mostly disks of carnelian, bronze; other shapes in lapis, agate, carnelian
	4D 340*b*	Bone pin; preserved l. 5.5, d. 0.8 cm.
	4D 340*c*	Bronze fibula; l. 2.7, h. 1.9, th. 0.5 cm.
4B 147.		SE III or II intrusive into NT 67 IV 1; earth burial; juvenile in dorsal position, oriented northwest

The following burials were not given numbers:

SE I intrusive into SE 79 II; jar burial; child
3P 288   Thin-ware bowl (Pl. 50:8)
Intrusive into SE 81 *ca.* I 2; slipper coffin
Intrusive into SE 81 *ca.* I 2; slipper coffin
Intrusive into SE 38 II; convex-base jar (Pl. 57:6); infant
Intrusive into SE 50 II 2
4P 70   Bowl (Pl. 53:5)
4P 71   Bowl (Pl. 53:6)
4P 72   Bowl (Pl. 53:7)
4P 73   Bowl (Pl. 51:1)
4P 74   Pot
4P 75   Bowl (Pl. 51:4)

VI

HISTORY OF THE NORTH TEMPLE

By DONALD E. MCCOWN

DESPITE the incompleteness of the available evidence, some deductions can be made concerning the history of the area. It can be divided into three distinct phases: in the first the temple was part of a residential quarter; in the second the resulting mound was converted into a platform, which probably served as a base for an enlarged temple; and in the third phase the area was a residential one without religious buildings.

The area was first occupied in the Protoliterate period, but the excavation was too small to show the type of structures built there. There are indications that the temple was not a part of the area until the middle or later part of Early Dynastic I. Its existence is certain from that time into the Akkadian period, and the area can be thought of as a typical city quarter of private houses grouped around its temple. Unfortunately, the god to whom the temple was dedicated is not known.

Sometime after the Akkadian period the mound formed by the earlier city quarter was converted into a platform. This suggests that the role of the temple had increased significantly and that the character of the area had become religious. The evidence for the date of this change is not precise, but the pottery found in the large triple drain at the eastern corner of the earlier temple and at the base of the platform wall (see Chap. IV) leaves little doubt that the platform was constructed during the Third Dynasty of Ur. The platform and its niched, baked-brick facing are the best evidence that this is a religious spot, continuing an earlier tradition. No walls or floors of the buildings on top of the platform were preserved, but it is most likely that the platform was a base for a large temple. There is no sign of activity during the Isin-Larsa period; perhaps the Third Dynasty temple continued unchanged, or Kassite activity may have removed all traces of an Isin-Larsa building. During the Old Babylonian period, however, a large well was constructed down through the courtyard of the Early Dynastic temple. In the Kassite period, and most probably after 1400 B.C., a new facing of mud brick was given the platform wall, and there is evidence that the Old Babylonian well was still in use. Sometime after the refacing of the platform, substantial houses were built immediately to the southwest of the platform, and an exclusive religious use of the area may be questioned.

Most probably the site was unoccupied from late Kassite times down to the very end of the Assyrian period. Then and in Hellenistic times the site seems to have been a residential area without religious buildings.

VII

THE CUNEIFORM INSCRIPTIONS

By ROBERT D. BIGGS

THE INSCRIPTIONS recovered from the North Temple (and SE, the sounding in which the temple was discovered) span a time of over two thousand years from the Fara period to the Seleucid era. Only the Old Babylonian period is completely unrepresented. The Fara period (around 2600 B.C.) is represented by several clay tablets and by a statue. The statue (see Pls. 67:3 and 68:1, 2) was among several found in a cache, apparently buried when the cella of the temple was extended in Level II.[1] The inscription on the statue (given here as No. 1), which the excavators hoped would be a votive inscription giving the name of the deity to whom the temple was dedicated, is virtually illegible. The inscription is in fact a land-sale contract so worn that few details of the transaction can be recovered.[2]

The latest texts are Seleucid. Several of the tablets found in SE Level I, such as No. 45, are almost certainly Seleucid, though others found in this level were obviously not in their original context.

Exercise tablets make up the largest category of texts. Most are already known from numerous other exemplars and consequently are only described here. It should be noted in particular that No. 42 is from a Middle Babylonian level. One should therefore bear in mind that some of the many hundreds of Babylonian exercise tablets, especially those from the old University of Pennsylvania excavations where virtually nothing is known of their stratification, may be Middle Babylonian rather than Neo-Babylonian.

Unfortunately, the texts (including the stratified votive texts) provide no convincing evidence for the identification of the temple. In spite of a number of mentions of Ešumeša, the temple of Ninurta,[3] and a field called "Field of Ninurta,"[4] it would be unwarranted to propose that the North Temple is the famous temple of Ninurta, which is more likely to have been near the Ekur.[5]

Most of the texts presented here in copy (see pp. 78 - 92)[6] are in the Iraq Museum, where I spent a month in the summer of 1972 copying them.[7] Because the texts are so varied in content

---

[1] The statue was illustrated on the cover of *Archaeology*, Vol. 5 (Summer, 1952) and was mentioned by Donald McCown on p. 75; a view of the statue was published by André Parrot in his *Sumer* (Paris, 1960) Fig. 132, where its provenience is erroneously given as the Diyala region.

[2] I should like to express my special gratitude to Dr. Fauzi Rachid for making the extraordinary arrangements that permitted me to study the inscription (the statue is fixed in a permanent display and cannot be moved). In spite of two days' careful work, many traces remain uncertain, and it is not clear in some instances where the limits of the inscription are.

[3] Nos. 21, 22 (Middle Babylonian) and 24 (Neo-Babylonian).

[4] No. 15 (Ur III).

[5] R. D. Biggs, "A Letter from Kassite Nippur," *Journal of Cuneiform Studies* XIX (1965) 100.

[6] The texts from the third season are published with the permission of Åke Sjöberg, of the University Museum, University of Pennsylvania; those from the fourth season are published with the permission of John A. Brinkman, chairman of the Baghdad School of the American Schools of Oriental Research, which has rights to the publication of the inscriptions.

[7] I wish to thank Dr. Isa Salman, Director General of Antiquities, for permitting me to have access to them. Dr. Fauzi Rachid, Director of the Iraq Museum, and Dr. Bahijah Khalil greatly facilitated my work, and I wish to express my gratitude here.

and date and are generally in poor condition, it was a particularly frustrating group to deal with. There are casts of a good many of the texts at the Oriental Institute, and these have allowed me to improve on some of my somewhat hasty original copies. In a few instances where no cast was available and a copy seemed to require substantial rechecking, I have thought it best to omit the copy and to give only a description. In other instances where the questionable points seemed relatively insignificant (as in No. 7), the copy has been included.[8]

All copies are reproduced at the same size as the originals, with the exception of seal impressions, which are reproduced at twice their original size, and No. 1, an inscription on a statue, which is reproduced at half its original size.

In the interest of economy ḫ has been set as h throughout.

No. 1 (3N 402). NT 99 III 1. Land-sale contract approximately of the Fara period inscribed across the shoulders of a statue (see Pls. 67:3, 68:1, 2). Except for some personal names and amounts of land and copper, the text is too worn to read. Part of column iv is uninscribed.

The only other land-sale contract inscribed on a statue is approximately from the time of Eannatum of Lagash (published by E. de Sarzec, *Découvertes en Chaldée* [Paris, 1884–1912] partie épigraphique, Pls. LV and LIVa, edited most recently by D. O. Edzard, *Sumerische Rechtsurkunden des III. Jahrtausends* [Bayerische Akademie der Wissenschaften, Philos.-hist. Kl., "Abhandlungen," NF, Vol. 67 (Munich, 1968)] pp. 181–84, as No. 115).

No. 2 (4NT 55). NT 45 III 1. Pre-Sargonic (approximately Fara period) account concerning grain, livestock, and KINDA and various amounts of copper and bronze.

No. 3 (4NT 62+63). NT 54 III. Fragments of a Pre-Sargonic text (approximately Fara period) concerning sheep and goats. There are traces of two lightly scratched signs in column ii of the obverse. There is no trace of SAL (for expected SAL + ÁŠ + GÀR) at the top of column ii.

No. 4 (4NT 61). NT 29 II 2. Fragment of a small, almost globular, administrative text concerning barley. Reverse uninscribed. The sign in the bottom line probably corresponds to LAK 492 (A. Deimel, *Die Inschriften von Fara* I: *Liste der archaischen Keilschriftzeichen* ["Wissenschaftliche Veröffentlichungen der Deutschen Orient-Gesellschaft," Vol. 40 (Leipzig, 1922)]; see my article, "The Abū Ṣalābīkh Tablets: A Preliminary Survey," *Journal of Cuneiform Studies* XX [1966] 87, n. 103, and *Inscriptions from Tell Abū Ṣalābīkh* [OIP XCIX (Chicago, 1974)] p. 111).

No. 5 (4NT 66). NT 61 IV 2. Fragment of a late Pre-Sargonic or early Old Akkadian account recording amounts of a commodity (probably barley, although the name is not preserved) with the names of individuals, some with their occupations given. The tablet probably had six or seven columns on the obverse originally. The reverse has only 46+[x] še-gur preserved. For the reading of the name A-ul$_4$-gal in col. iii, l. 5, see *OIP* XCIX 69–70.

No. 6 (4NT 64). NT 76 IV. Very poorly written tablet, probably a school exercise, approximately from the Fara period. It consists at least in part of personal names.

No. 7 (4NT 24). SE II 1. Administrative document(?), probably Old Akkadian. The tablet is poorly written and is damaged by wormholes.

No. 8 (4NT 53). NT 3 II 1. Old Akkadian contract written in an awkward hand.

No. 9 (4NT 26). NT 5 I 1. Small fragment of an Old Akkadian contract.

---

[8] I am grateful to my colleagues John A. Brinkman, Miguel Civil, I. J. Gelb, Johannes Renger, and Robert M. Whiting, Jr., for giving me the benefit of their advice on particular texts or genres. I am particularly indebted to Miguel Civil, who is responsible for identifying many of the lexical fragments, especially Syllabary A and Syllabary B.

No. 10 (4NT 56). NT 48 II 2. Found in a jar in a corner of the room. Old Akkadian account dealing in part with textiles or clothing (line 1: 1 TÚG *na-ba-ru-um*). The date formula mentions Naram-Sin's daughter (name destroyed), presumably Enmenanna, known to have been an en-priestess of Nanna (see E. Sollberger, "Sur la chronologie des rois d'Ur et quelques problèmes connexes," *Archiv für Orientforschung* XVII [1954-56] 27).

No. 11 (4NT 59). NT 48 II 1. Fragment of the reverse(?) of an Old Akkadian legal text (the oath begins in line 8). The obverse(?) is destroyed.

No. 12 (4NT 60). NT 48 II 1. Old Akkadian administrative document. The sign TA, copied below LI in line 6 of the obverse, may in fact belong to the top line of the reverse.

No. 13 (4NT 31). NT 8 I 2. Old Akkadian contract for the sale of a house. Copied from a cast.

No. 14 (4NT 65). NT, stratification uncertain. Small chip of an Ur III account. Other side destroyed.

No. 15 (4NT 57). SE IV or III. Ur III account of plowing oxen. Dated to the first year of Amar-Sin.

No. 16 (4NT 58). SE IV or III. Ur III account concerning barley. Date not preserved. The sign following KI in line 3 of the obverse is probably sì.

No. 17 (4NT 51). Intrusive into NT 22. Ur III account concerning barley and flour. Dated to the fourth year of Amar-Sin.

No. 18 (4NT 175). Intrusive into NT IV. Ur III list of animals as offerings to the cultic torch and the goddess Nin-sún. Reverse destroyed except for traces at the ends of some lines.

No. 19 (3NT 139). SE V 3. Receipt for loan of barley. Dated to Ibbi-Sin, year 1. The inscription on the seal reads Lú-^{d}EN.ZU / dumu Ur-an-si$_4$-an-na. This text will be included by David I. Owen in a forthcoming volume of Ur III Nippur texts as No. 152. It appears that GUD(?) following the name Na-bí-^{d}EN.ZU was intended to be erased. I am indebted to William Peterson for the drawing of the seal impression.

No. 20 (4NT 22). SE, stratification uncertain. Receipt for birds. Dated to Ibbi-Sin, year 2. The seal inscription reads Šeš-kal-la / SILÀ.ŠU.DU$_8$ gal / Lú-^{d}En-líl-lá / dub-[sar]. Copied from a cast (reading of the seal inscription is based partly on T. Jacobsen's description in the field catalogue). The seal impression was drawn by William Peterson.

No. 21 (4NT 25). SE 24 I. Middle Babylonian record of ÉŠ.GÀR in amounts of grain in Ešumeša, the temple of Ninurta. Note that the day is repeated after the year.

No. 22 (4NT 10). SE 23 I 3. Middle Babylonian record of ÉŠ.GÀR in amounts of grain in Ešumeša. See No. 21 and the description of 4NT 5. Note that the date begins with MU SAG.

No. 23 (4NT 7). SE I 3. Middle Babylonian loan contract. Dated to Kaštiliaš, year uncertain. Parts of several fingernail impressions are preserved.

No. 24 (4NT 23). SE 62 III 2. Neo-Babylonian contract for sale of a brewer's prebend in the Ninurta temple, Ešumeša. The time covered by the contract is not given, but probably one should assume it was for a year. There are ten sets of three fingernail impressions, some on each edge of the tablet. Dated to the first year of Nebuchadnezzar II. The text is given here in transliteration.

The person whose name is written *Im-ma-a-tum* in line 9 is the same as the one whose name is written *Ina*-KUR (i.e., Ina-māti) in line 4, an observation I owe to Hermann Hunger, to whom

I am indebted for several corrections in my transliteration.

1. ṭup-pi GIŠ.ŠUB.BA LÚ.BAPPIR-ú-t[u]
2. šá É-šu-me-šá₄ pa-pah ᵈNin-urta ki-i
3. EN LÚ.BAPPIR.MEŠ šá É-šu-me-šá₄ ᵐᵈMAŠ-ba-na
4. A ᵐIna-KUR ina ŠUⁱⁱ ᵐBA-šá-a A ᵐId-di-ia a-na
5. 3 MA.[NA] 5 GÍN KÙ.BABBAR KÙ.PAD.DU ga-mir-tum
6. i-šam [ŠÁM] gam-ru-tu ù 5 GÍN KÙ.BABBAR šá UMBIN-šú
7. šá ki-i KA DIRI SUM-nu PAB.PAB 3 MA.NA 10 GÍN KÙ.BABBAR
8. KÙ.PAD.DU ki-i ka-sap TIL-tú ᵐᵈMAŠ-ba-na
9. A ᵐIm-ma-a-tum it-ti ᵐBA-šá-a A ᵐId-di-ia
10. KI.LAM im-be-e-ma i-šam ŠÁM GIŠ.ŠUB.BA-šú
11. gam-ru-tu (erasure) na-din ma-hir a-pil
12. za-ki ru-gu-um-ma-a ul i-ši ul i-tur-ru-ma
13. a-na a-ha-meš ul i-rag-⟨gu⟩-mu ma-ti-ma ina EGIR.MEŠ
14. UD-mu ina ŠEŠ.MEŠ DUMU.MEŠ IM.RI.A ni-su-tum
15. u sa-lat šá É ᵐBA-šá-a A ᵐId-di-ia šá E₁₁-ma
16. a-na UGU GIŠ.ŠUB.BA MU.MEŠ i-dab-bu-ub
17. ú-šad-ba-bu BAL-ú ú-paq-qa-ru
18. ù pa-qir-ra-nu ú-šab-šu-ú um-ma
19. GIŠ.ŠUB.BA MU.MEŠ ul SUM-nu-ma KÙ.BABBAR ul ma-hir
20. i-qab-bu-ú KÙ.BABBAR im-hu-ru GIŠ.ŠUB.BA
21. ki-i ub-ba-lu a-di 12.TA.ÀM i-ta-[na]-pal
22. šá da-ba-ba an-na-a BAL-ú

---

23. niš ᵈEn-líl u ᵈNin-líl DINGIR.MEŠ ba-ni-šú-nu it-mu-ú
24. niš ᵈNin-urta ù ᵈNusku PA.KAŠ₄ šu-lum-šú-nu it-mu-ú
25. niš ᵈAG-NÍG.DU-ŠEŠ LUGAL-šú-nu it-mu-ú

---

26. ina ka-nak IM.DUB MU.MEŠ

---

27. IGI ᵐᵈUTU-SÙH-SUR	A ᵐᵈMAŠ-ú-ṣal-la LÚ.BAPPIR ᵈ50
28. ᵐBa-ni-ia	A ᵐA-a LÚ.BAPPIR ᵈMAŠ
29. ᵐRi-mut	A ᵐᵈMAŠ-ú-ṣal-la
30. ᵐNUMUN-DU	A ᵐDÙ-ᵈEn-líl
31. ᵐᵈ50-MU-MU	A ᵐBA-šá-a na-di-na-nu is-qu
32. ᵐTab-ni-e-a	A ᵐᵈMAŠ-ŠEŠ-MU
33. ᵐᵈUTU-ŠEŠ-MU	A ᵐBa-ni-ia
34. ᵐᵈMAŠ-NUMUN-DU	A ᵐᵈMAŠ-ú-bal-liṭ LÚ.BAPPIR ᵈEn-líl
35. ᵐᵈMAŠ-DÙ	A ᵐAr-ra-bi

---

36. u LÚ.ŠID šá-ṭir IM.DUB ᵐᵈMAŠ-pa-qid-su-nu
37. A ᵐᵈEn-líl-NUMUN-DÙ NIBRUᵏⁱ ITI APIN x
38. UD.23.KAM MU.1.KAM ᵐᵈAG-NÍG.DU-ŠE[Š]
39. LUGAL TIN.TIR.KI ṣu-pur ᵐBA-šá-a A ᵐI[d-di-ia]
40. ku-um IM.DUB-šú šu-ud-da-t[a]

No. 25 (4NT 48). Intrusive into NT 46 II (in burial shaft of 4B 110). Fragment of a Neo-Babylonian contract for the sale of an empty lot (*bīt kišubbû*). The obverse is mostly illegible and is omitted here. The reverse has a curse formula, oath, and names of witnesses. Datable to the reign of Cambyses (see the oath in line 6 of the reverse). The reverse can be read as follows:

1. [šá da-ba-ba an-n]a-a BAL-ú ᵈA-num
2. [ᵈEn-líl u ᵈ][É]-a ar-rat ZI-tì-šú li-ru-ur(text: ur-ru)-ma
3. [la i-gam]-m[i-i]u ZI-tì-su
4. [niš ᵈEn-lí]l u ᵈNin-líl ⌈DINGIR.MEŠ⌉ ⟨i⟩-la-nu-šú-nu za-kirₓ(KAR)
5. [niš ᵈMAŠ u ᵈPA.K]U ra-bi-iṣ šu-lum-šú-nu za-kirₓ(KAR)
6. [niš ᵐKam-bu]-zi-iá LUGAL E.KI u KUR.KUR LUGAL EN-šú-nu za-kirₓ(KAR)

---

7. [ina ka-nak] NA₄.KIŠIB MU.MEŠ
8. [IGI] ᵈUTU-NUMUN-⌈DÙ⌉ A-šú šá ᵈKASKAL-ha-a-a A LÚ.ŠU.HA
9. [x x x x x A] ᵐᵈUTU-ŠEŠ-MU ᵐᵈMAŠ-na-din-MU A-šú šá ᵐTa-qiš-ᵈx x
rest traces

No. 26 (3NT 891). SE ca. II 4. Neo-Babylonian account concerning barley. Dated to the fifteenth year of Nebuchadnezzar II. MU.AN.NA in a year date also occurs in O. Krückmann, *Neubabylonische Rechts- und Verwaltungstexte* ("Texte und Materialien der Frau Professor Hilprecht Collection of Babylonian Antiquities im Eigentum der Universität Jena," II/III [Leipzig, 1933]) No. 104.

No. 27 (4NT 4). SE 42 II 3. Undated Neo-Babylonian note(?) or letter order with an impression of a stamp seal. The impression was drawn by Ann Searight.

No. 28 (4NT 19). SE 44 II 4. Neo-Babylonian contract concerning a status as *hatānu*. Dated to Assurbanipal, year 22.

No. 29 (4NT 17). SE 67 II 4. Small fragment of a Neo-Babylonian account(?). Reverse uninscribed.

No. 30 (4NT 54). SE III. Neo-Babylonian account concerned with dates.

No. 31 (4NT 8). SE dump. Neo-Babylonian copy of an incantation to Ninurta. Reverse uninscribed.

No. 32 (4NT 20). SE 58 III 1. Small Neo-Babylonian fragment of a ritual involving figurines. Probably the reverse.

No. 33 (4NT 40). Intrusive into NT 9 I 3. Fragment of a large Neo-Babylonian tablet (at least two columns). Ritual(?).

No. 34 (4NT 42). Intrusive into NT 9 I 3. Neo-Babylonian literary extracts. The first extract was published by W. G. Lambert, "Fire Incantations," *Archiv für Orientforschung* XXIII (1970) Pl. 10 (see p. 39). The second and third extracts are unidentified. The reverse is mostly destroyed but has a further literary extract and a colophon in which Nippur is mentioned. The reverse and the part previously published are not copied here.

No. 35 (4NT 43). Intrusive into NT 9 I 3. Fragment of a Neo-Babylonian tablet with literary extracts. The first is unidentified; the second is an incantation against paralysis (*šimmatu*), duplicated by O. R. Gurney and P. Hulin, *The Sultantepe Tablets* II (London, 1964) No. 136 ii 37 ff. and Sm. 104+523 (British Museum, unpublished); the third extract is probably from an incantation about fire. The preserved part of the reverse is uninscribed.

No. 36 (4NT 44). Intrusive into NT 9 I 3. Fragment of a Neo-Babylonian copy of a literary text in Sumerian. Unidentified. The reverse is uninscribed.

No. 37 (4NT 32). Intrusive into NT 25 I 1 (in burial shaft 4B 93). Fragment of a Neo-Babylonian tablet with literary extracts, very difficult to read. Lines 1–4 may be from Lugale II 14 f. (suggestion of M. Civil). Lines 5–11 correspond to the Sumerian text Angim, lines 36 ff., and will be included by Jerrold S. Cooper in his edition of Angim. The lines on the lower edge are unidentified. The reverse is destroyed.

No. 38 (4NT 33). Intrusive into NT 9 I 3. Fragment of a Neo-Babylonian tablet with literary extracts. The reverse corresponds to lines 34–39 of the Sumerian version of Angim (see No. 37). The obverse is unidentified.

No. 39 (4NT 46). Intrusive into NT 46 II (in burial shaft 4B 110). Fragment of a Neo-Babylonian exercise tablet. Column ii consists of personal names beginning with Ninurta and Nergal. The other side has traces only.

No. 40 (4NT 49). Intrusive into NT 46 II (in burial shaft 4B 110). Fragment of a Neo-Babylonian exercise tablet. The obverse has an unidentified literary extract; the reverse is a fragment of Lu Excerpt II, from which line 173a of the edition (M. Civil, ed., *Materials for the Sumerian Lexicon* XII [Rome, 1969] 109) can be restored as *ur-ru-ṣu*.

No. 41 (4NT 52). SE IV or III. Perhaps an exercise tablet; genre (possibly omens?) and date uncertain. Reverse uninscribed.

No. 42 (3NT 195). SE V 3. Fragment of an exercise tablet. Middle Babylonian (according to the excavators' dating of the level). One side has unidentified literary extracts (a phrase ending šu-sikil-la-kam in line 4 and the expression ù-tu-ud-da in the bottom extract are legible). The other side has an excerpt from Hh. XIII (lines 143–45, perhaps 146–47, with variants to the published text). The tablet turns to the side rather than top to bottom.

No. 43 (4NT 12). SE I. Fragment of a Neo-Babylonian exercise tablet containing part of Hh. XXII. Edited by E. Reiner, *Materials for the Sumerian Lexicon* XI (Rome, 1974) 28–29, as Source G. The other side is destroyed.

No. 44 (4NT 21). SE 58 III 1. Fragment of a well-written Neo-Babylonian exercise tablet. The obverse has an unidentified literary extract, the reverse possibly Hh. III 7–8.

No. 45 (4NT 14). SE 22 I 3. Fragment of a Neo-Babylonian exercise tablet. The obverse (not copied) has S^a (signs only): col. ii, ll. 95–107; col. iii, ll. 120–35; col. iv, ll. 146–59. The reverse has part of a god list on the right; the left column is unidentified.

No. 46 (4NT 73). NT 120 VII. Fragment of an inscription of Lugalkinišedudu on the rim of a thick alabaster bowl, corresponding to H. V. Hilprecht, *Babylonian Expedition of the University of Pennsylvania*, Series A: *Cuneiform Texts* I (Philadelphia, 1896) No. 86:6–8.

No. 47 (4NT 69). NT 33 II 2. Final line of a Pre-Sargonic inscription on a cream-colored thin-walled bowl: rig_7, "presented ex-voto."

No. 48 (4NT 68). Surface, western part of the mound. Fragment of an Old Akkadian or Ur III votive inscription on an alabaster vessel; the divine name is probably to be restored as [^{d}Nin-din-u]g_5-ga.

No. 49 (4NT 15). Surface, near SE. Fragmentary Ur III votive inscription with royal epithets on the body of an alabaster vessel.

No. 50 (4NT 30). Surface. Chip of black stone, completely flat and quite smooth. Probably from a stone tablet or a stele. Old Babylonian(?).

No. 51 (4NT 1). SE I 2. Inscription in Akkadian on a bowl of greenish-black stone with streaks of light green. It is 1.5 cm. thick at the rim and 2.2 cm. thick at the thickest preserved part. Note the drill marks in column i, not necessarily made at the time the bowl was inscribed. Column ii may be part of a curse formula. Middle Babylonian(?).

No. 52 (4NT 2). SE II. Inscription in Akkadian on a thin chip of black stone. Prices are given, suggesting a transaction concerning land or some commodity. The curvature of the last two lines suggests that it is not from a bowl. Perhaps a *kudurru* fragment (suggestion of J. A. Brinkman). Middle Babylonian(?).

No. 53 (3N 509). NT dump. Fragment of a Pre-Sargonic votive inscription on a cream-colored bowl.

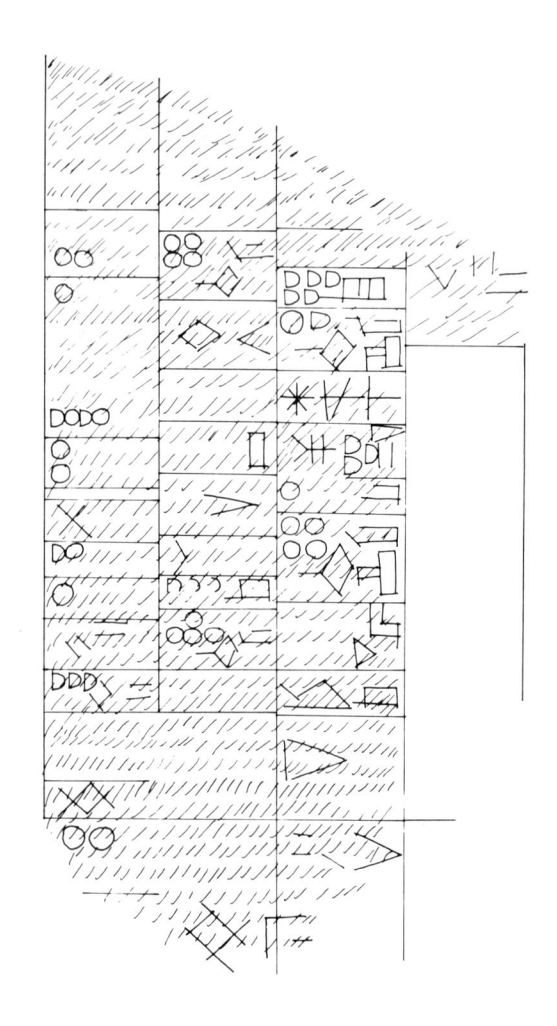

No. 1

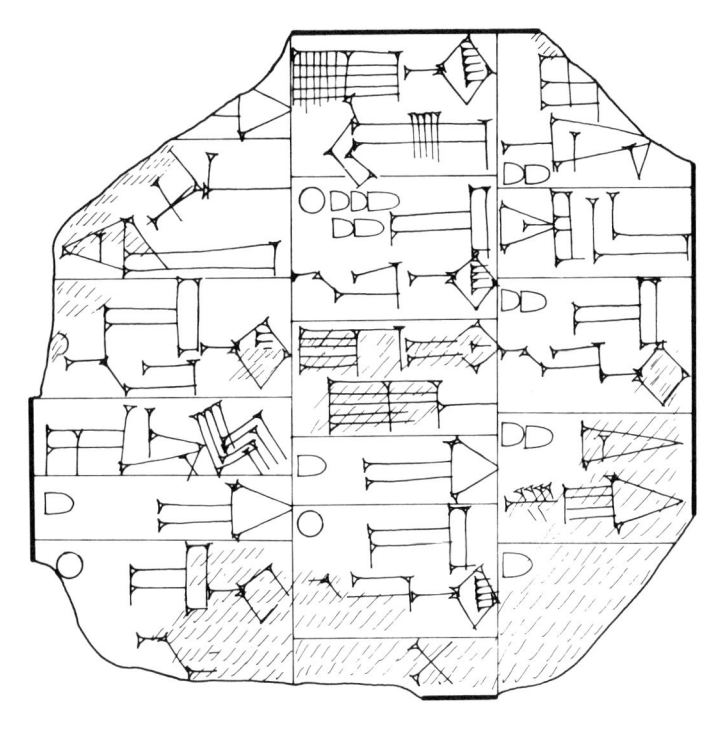

obverse

No. 2

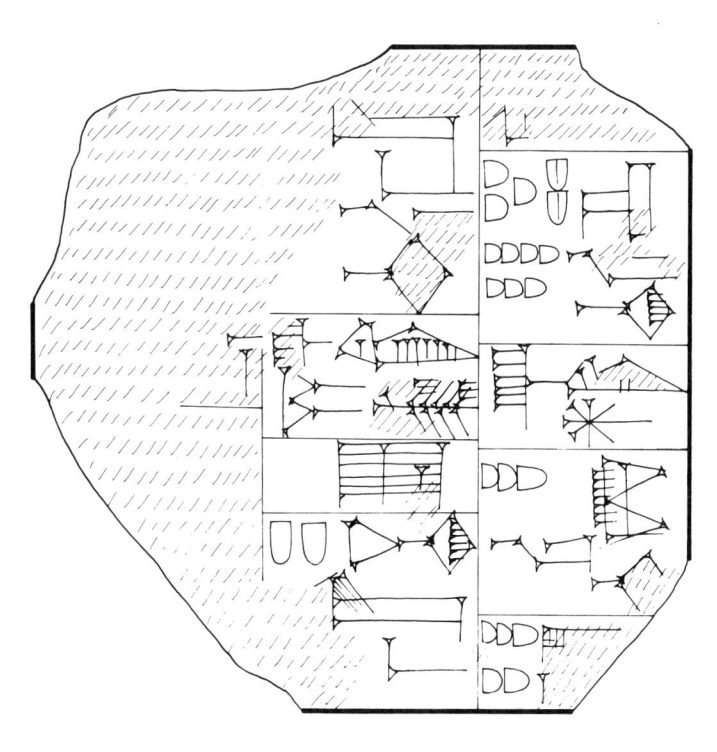

reverse

No. 2

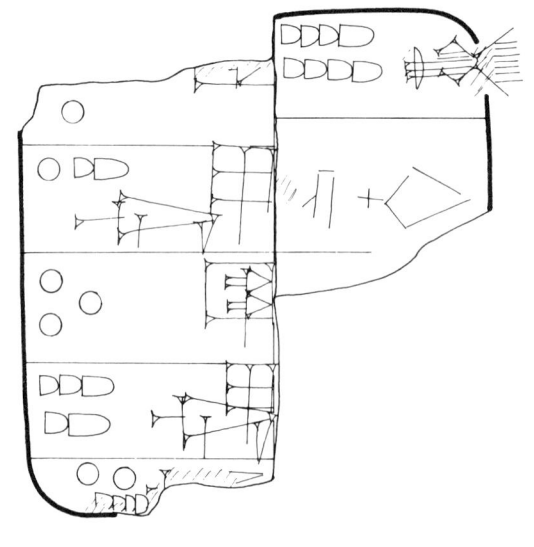

obverse

No. 3

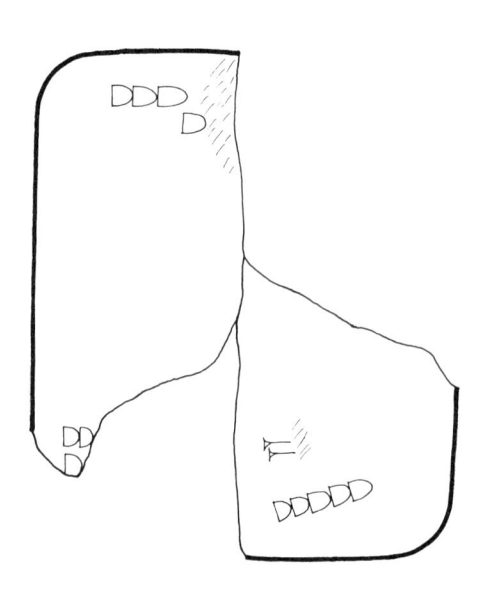

reverse

No. 3

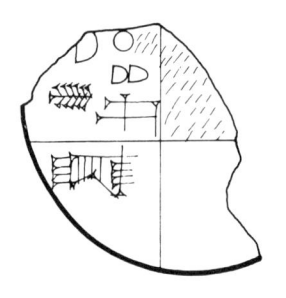

No. 4

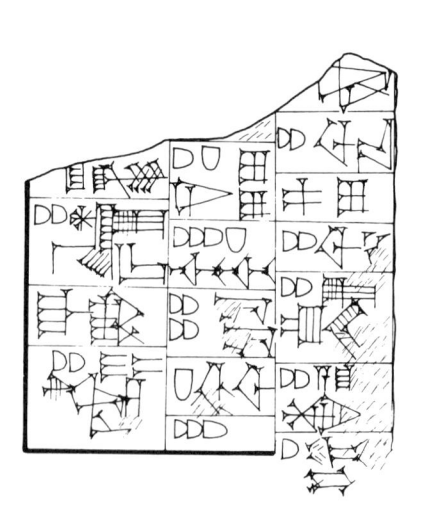

No. 5

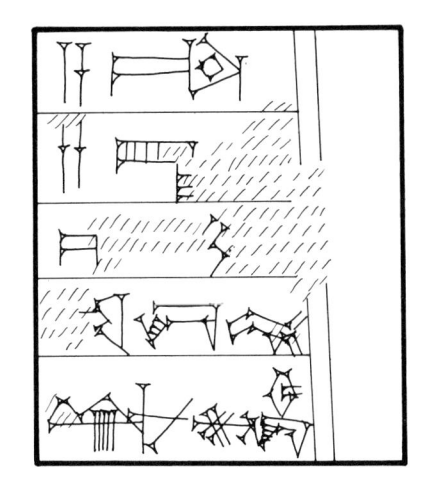

obverse

No. 6

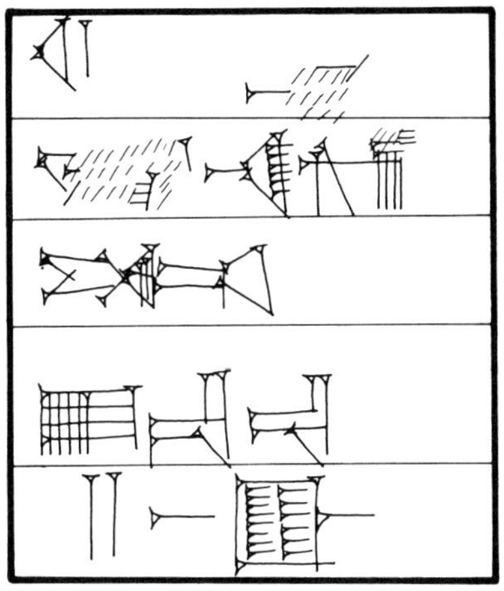

reverse

No. 6

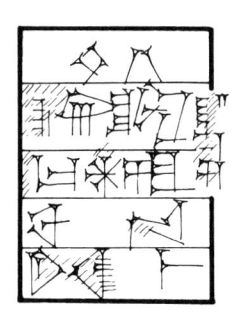

obverse

No. 7

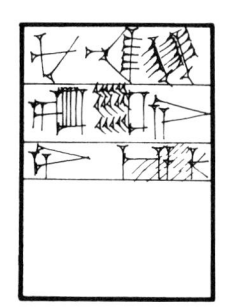

reverse

No. 7

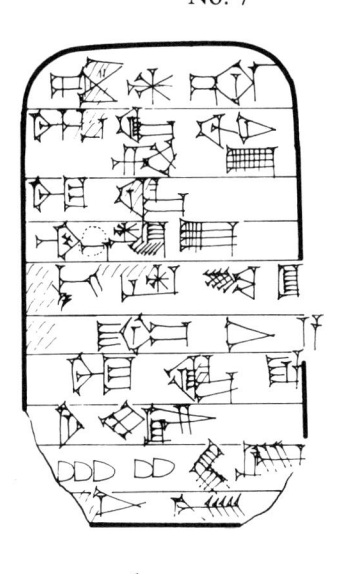

obverse

No. 8

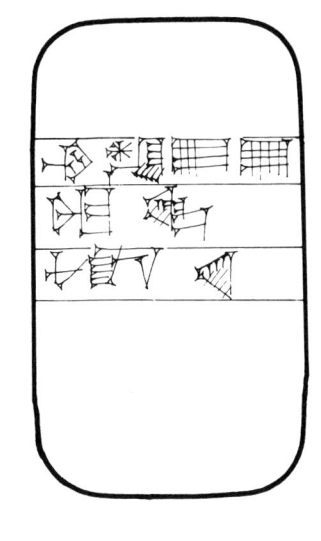

reverse

No. 8

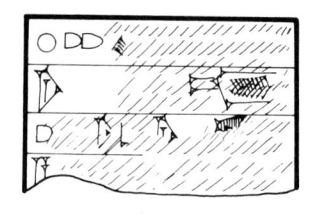

obverse
No. 9

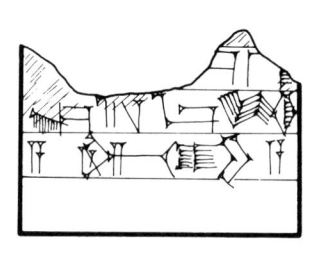

reverse
No. 9

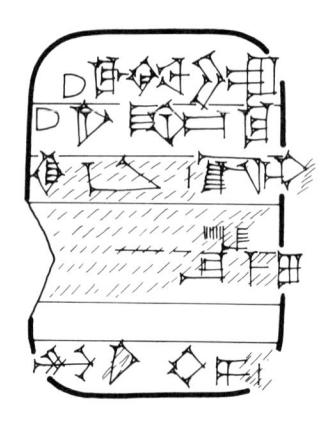

obverse
No. 10

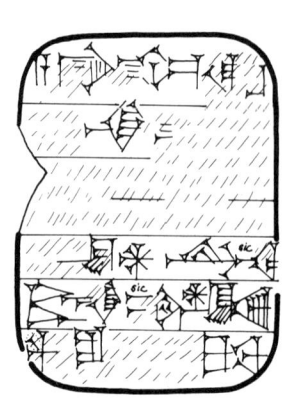

reverse
No. 10

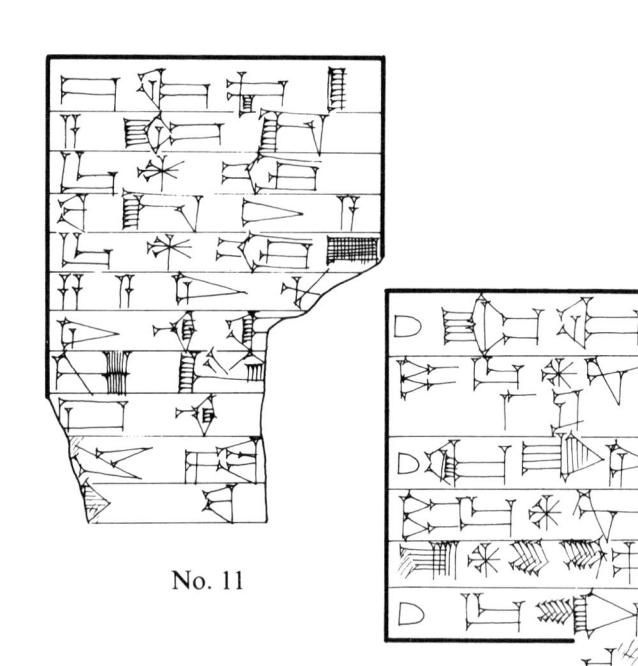

No. 11

obverse
No. 12

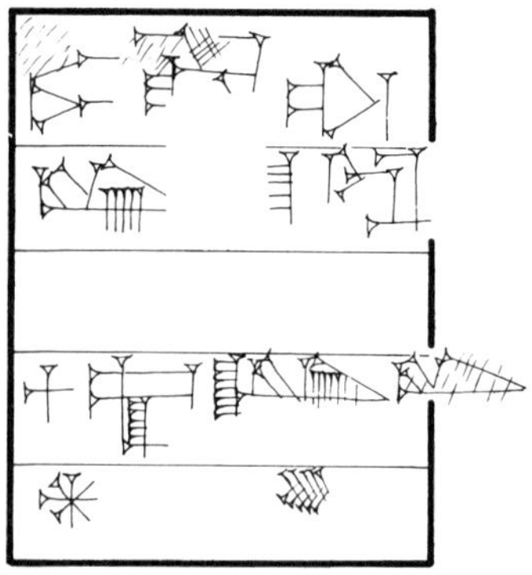

reverse
No. 12

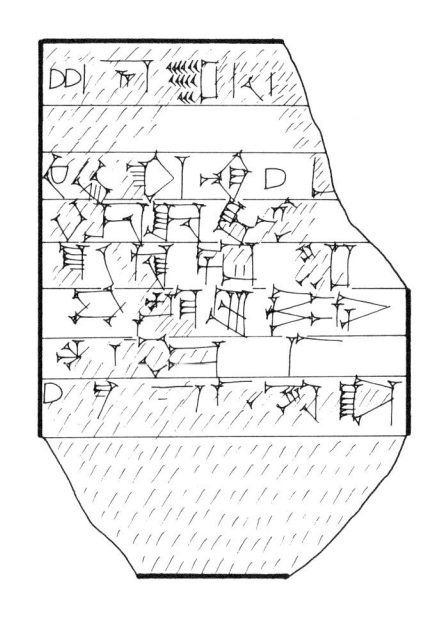

obverse

No. 13

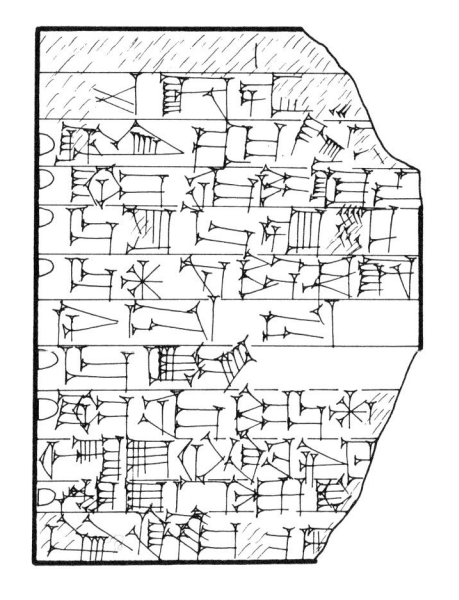

reverse

No. 13

edge

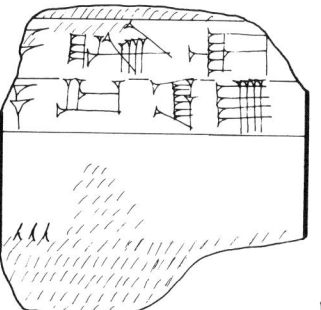

No. 14

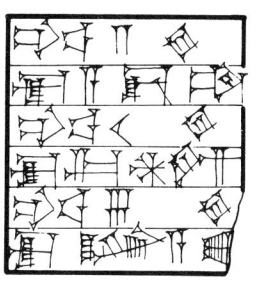

obverse

No. 15

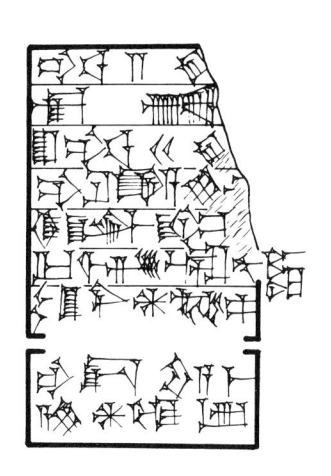

reverse

No. 15

edge

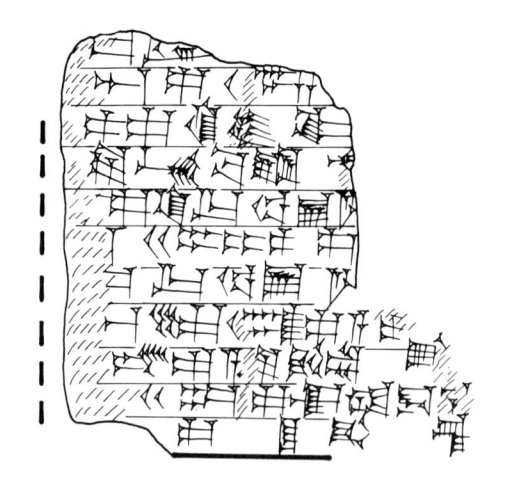

obverse

No. 16

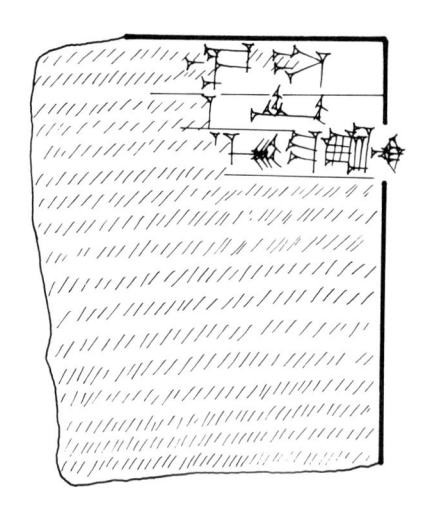

reverse

No. 16

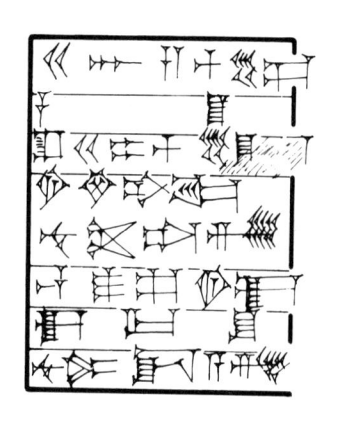

obverse

No. 17

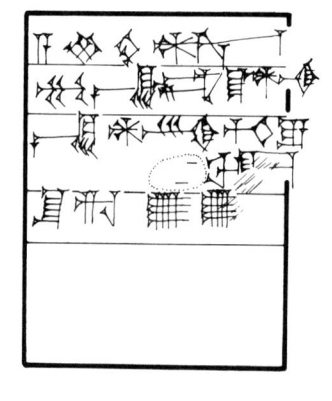

reverse

No. 17

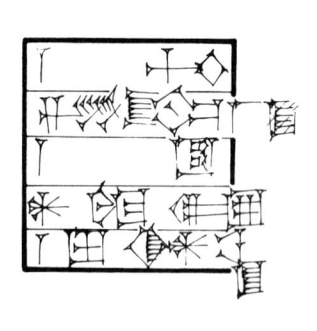

No. 18

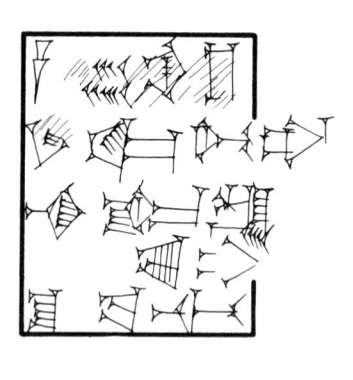

obverse

No. 19

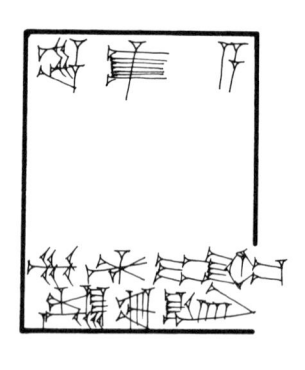

reverse

No. 19

84

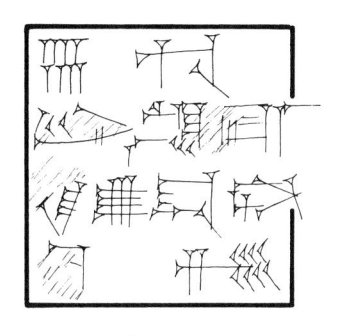

obverse

No. 20

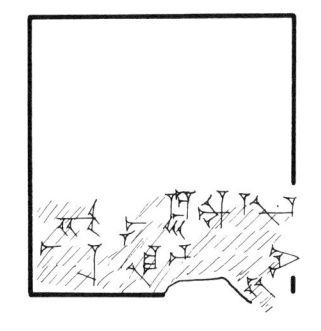

reverse

No. 20

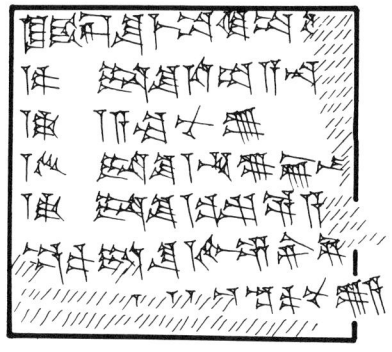

obverse

No. 21

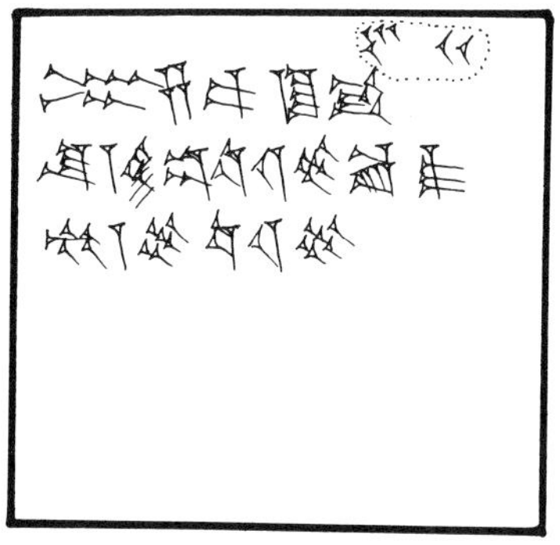

reverse

No. 21

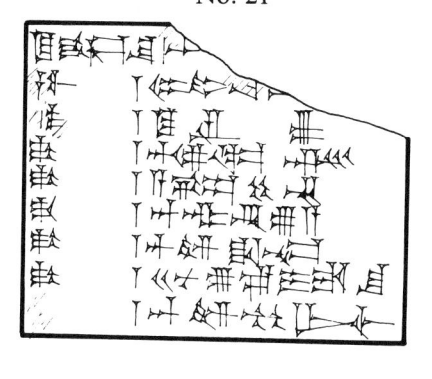

obverse

No. 22

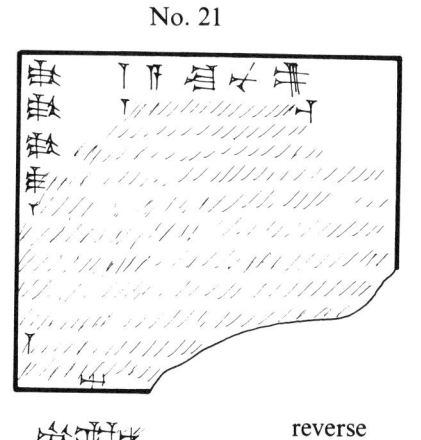

reverse

No. 22

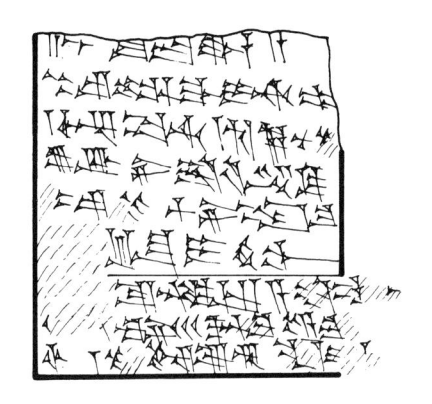

obverse
No. 23

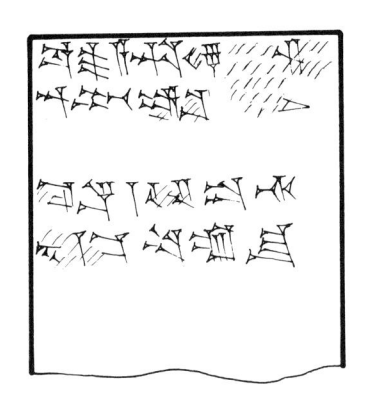

reverse
No. 23

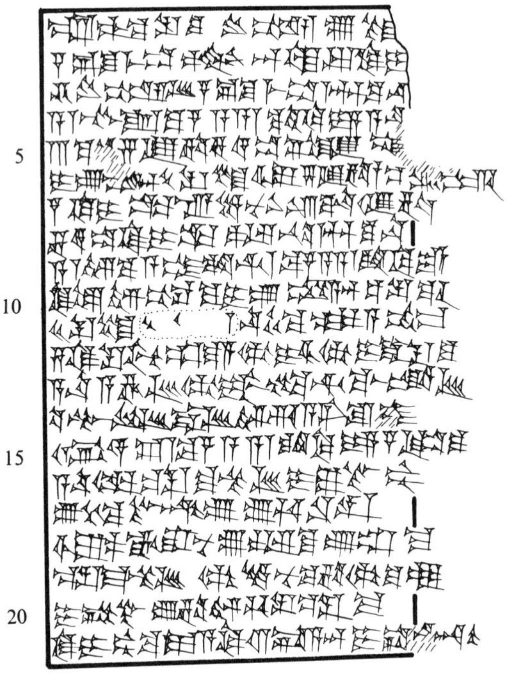

obverse
No. 24

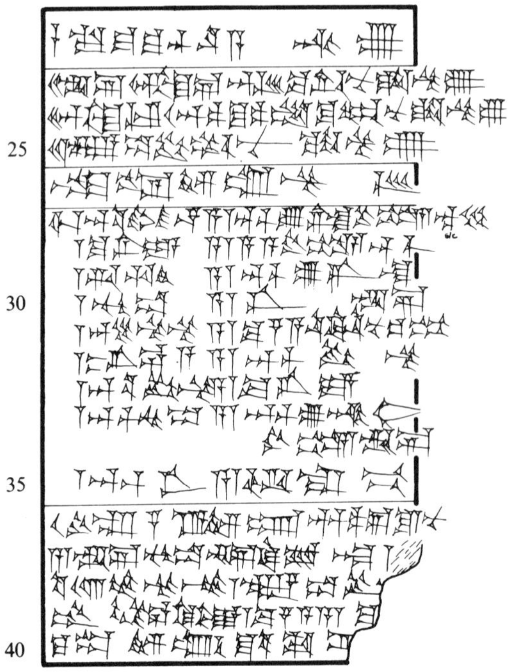

reverse
No. 24

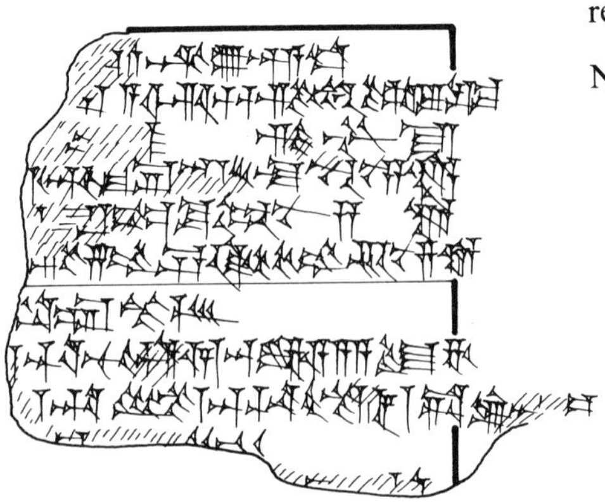

No. 25

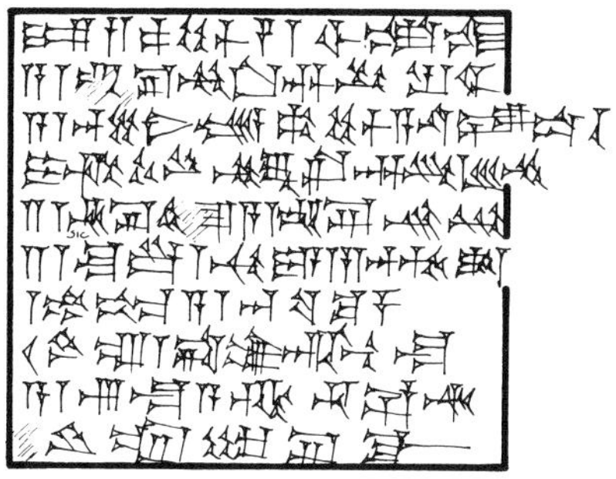

obverse

No. 26

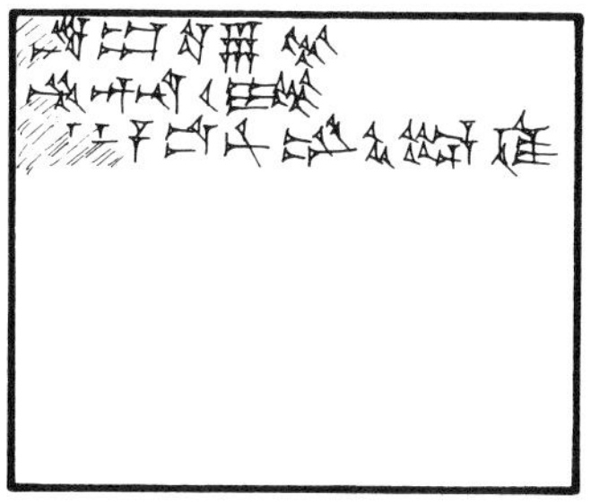

reverse

No. 26

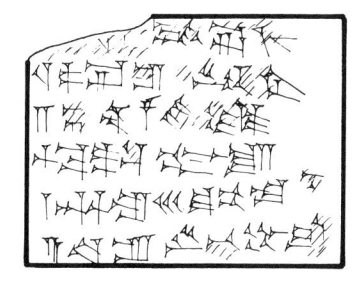

obverse

No. 27

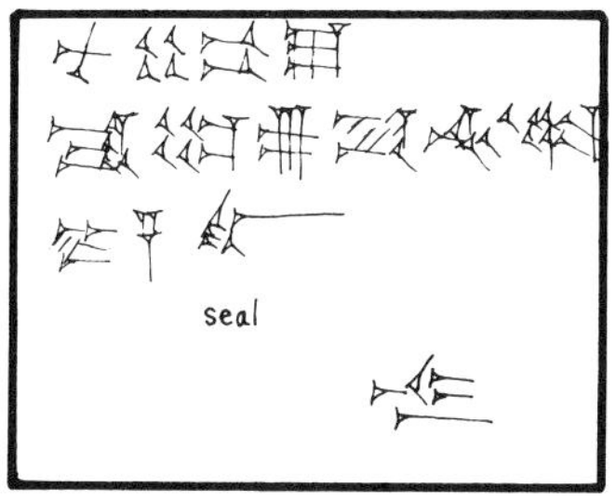

reverse

No. 27

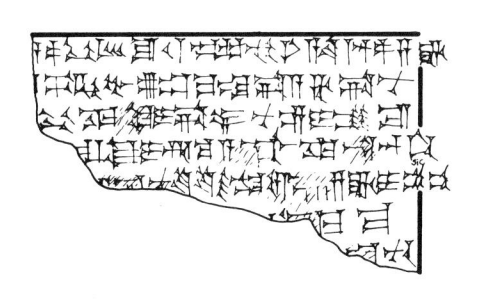

obverse

No. 28

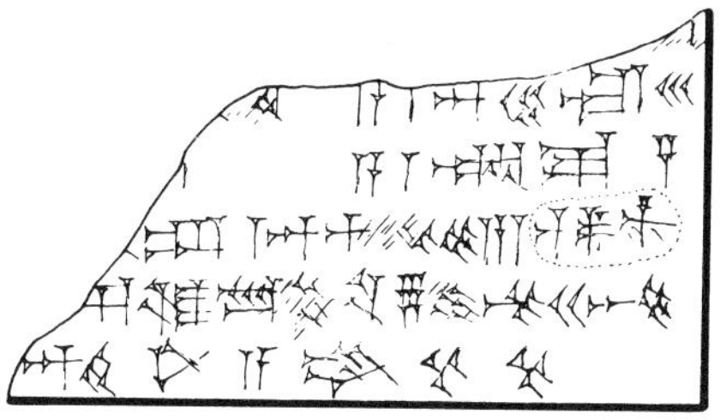

reverse

No. 28

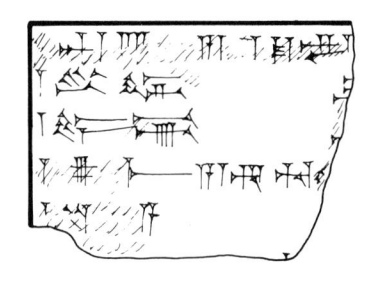

No. 29

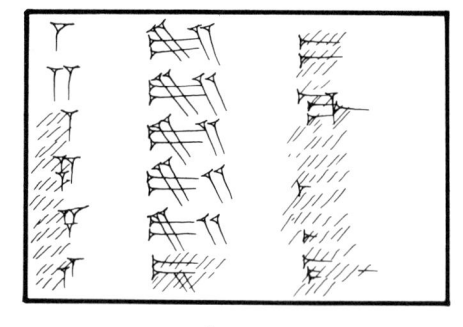

obverse
No. 30

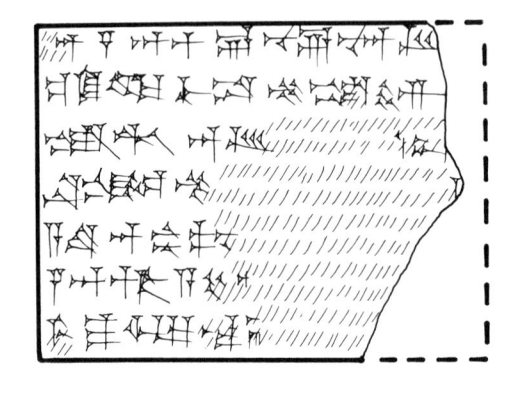

No. 31

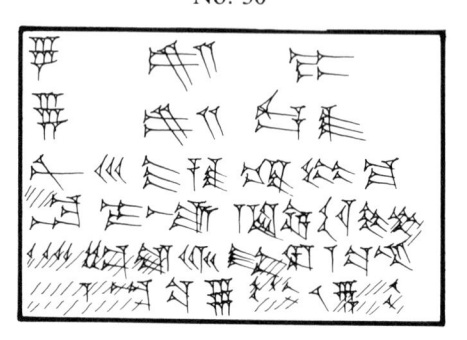

reverse
No. 30

No. 32

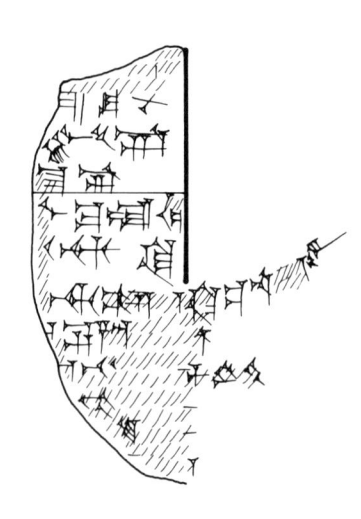

obverse
No. 33

reverse
No. 33

88

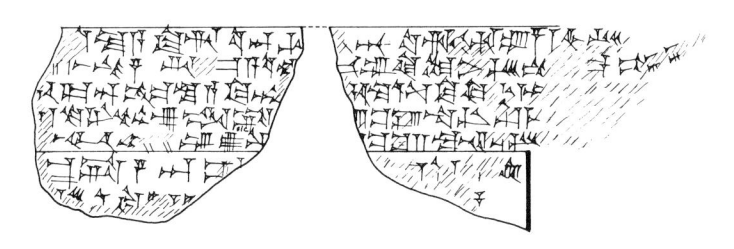

No. 34

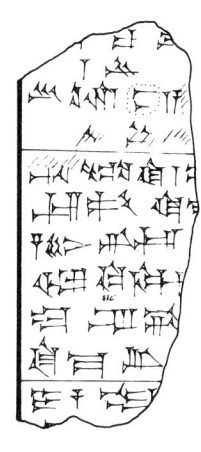

No. 35

No. 36

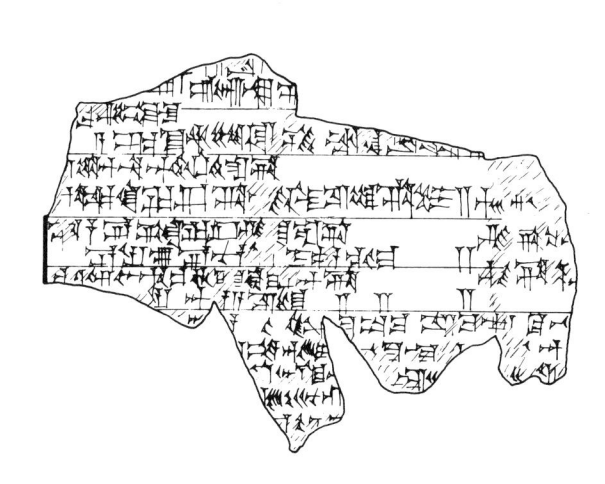

No. 37

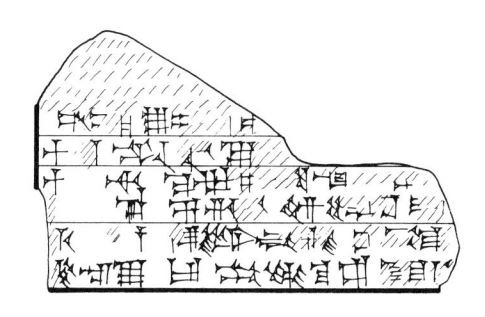

obverse
No. 38

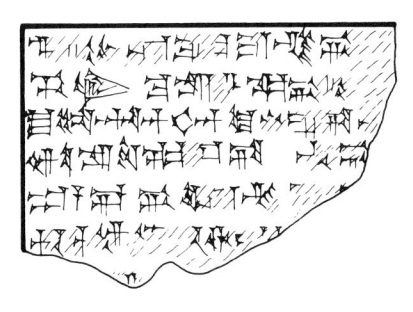

reverse
No. 38

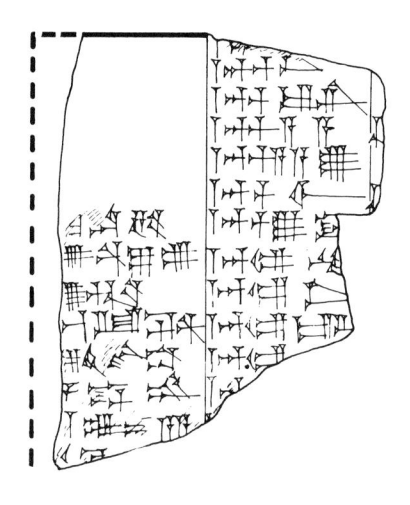

No. 39

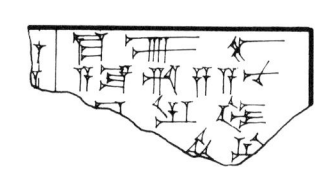

obverse
No. 40

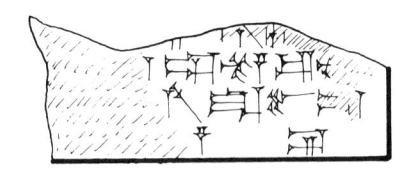

reverse
No. 40

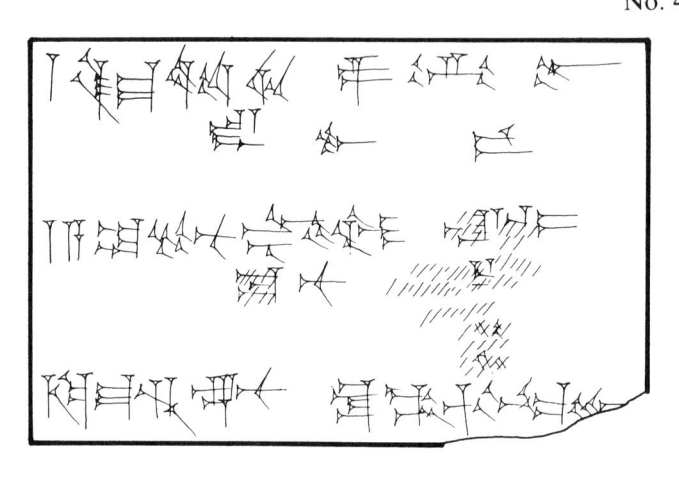

No. 41

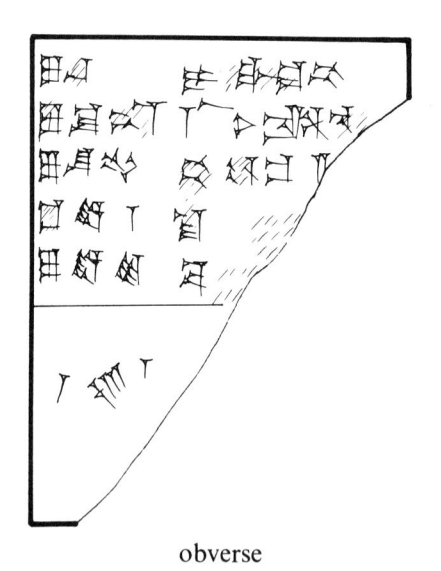

obverse
No. 42

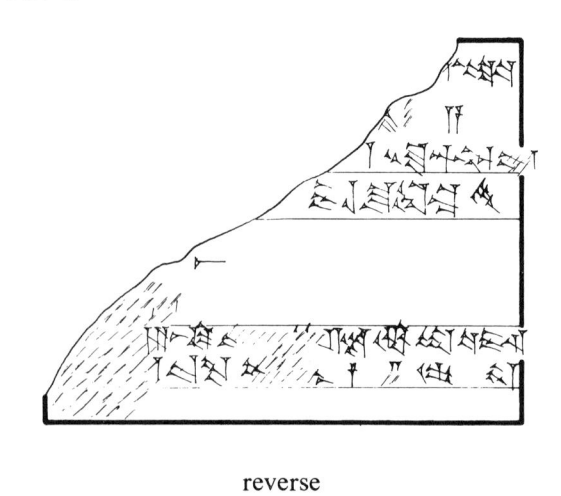

reverse
No. 42

No. 43

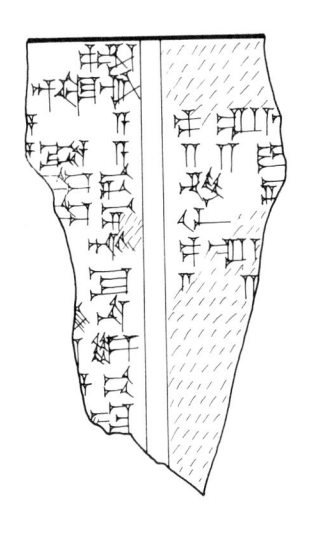

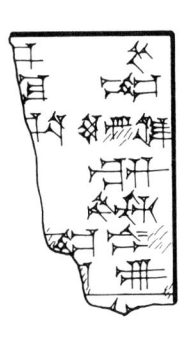

obverse
No. 44

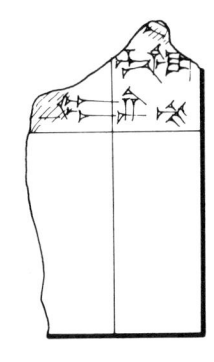

reverse
No. 44

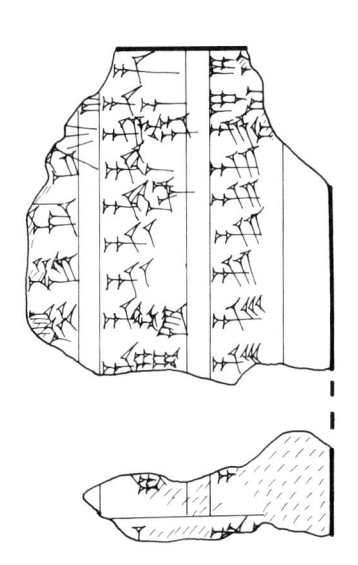

No. 45

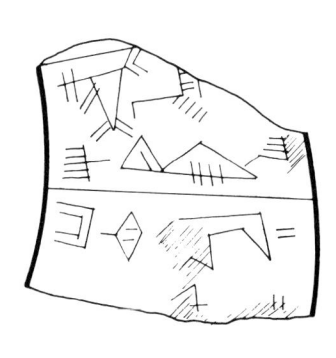

No. 46

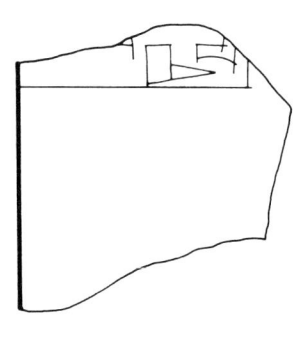

No. 47

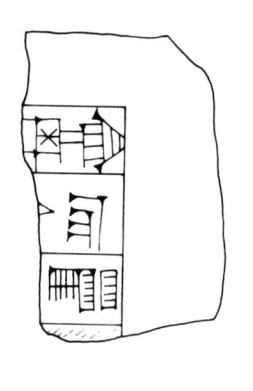

No. 48

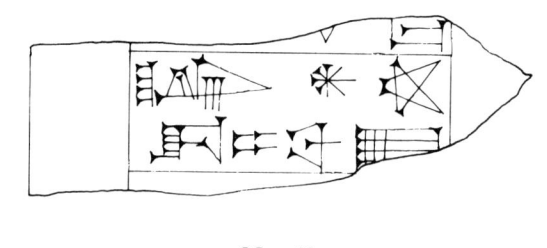

No. 49

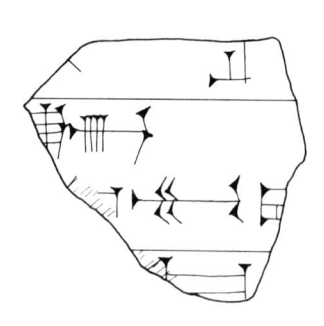

No. 50

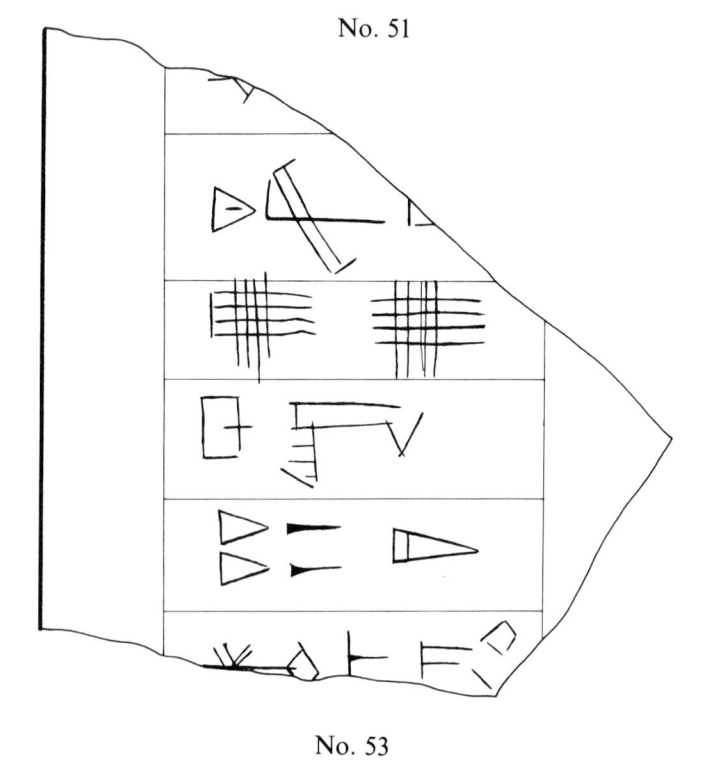

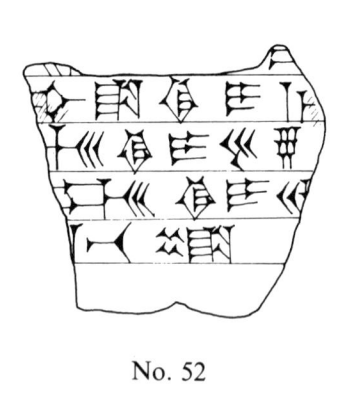

No. 51

No. 52

No. 53

As mentioned above, a number of the texts from the North Temple and Sounding E have not been copied for this volume. The following list gives a brief description of each of these texts along with information on stratification.

3NT 140. SE 3 V 2. Top half of a Middle Babylonian document.

3NT 141. SE 3 V 2. Contract dated to Kadašman-Enlil, year 7.

3NT 142-49. SE 3 V 2. Eight Middle Babylonian contracts ranging in date from Kadašman-Enlil, year 6, to Šagarakti-Šuriaš, year 1. Nos. 3NT 142-49 were found together in one jar. It is likely that 3NT 141 belongs to this group of tablets, since it involves some of the same persons as 3NT 142 (dated Kadašman-Enlil, year 7). To be published separately elsewhere along with 3NT 140.

3NT 848. SE dump. Fragmentary Ur III text, with only ki Ur-^{d}En-ki-ta / Lugal-á-zi-da / šu-ba-ti legible.

3P 508. NT IV 1.

3D 597. NT III 2. Small fragment of a stone bowl with only the sign AN and traces of another sign preserved in the inscription.

3D 606. NT 65 IV 1. Small fragment of a stone bowl with parts of two lines of writing.

4NT 3. SE 20 I. Later copy of a document dated to the second year of Marduk-balassu-iqbi. To be published elsewhere by J. A. Brinkman; it is mentioned in his *A Political History of Post-Kassite Babylonia* ("Analecta Orientalia," Vol. 43 [Rome, 1968]) pp. 351 ff., as No. 26.2.2.

4NT 5. SE I 2. Washed out fragment of a Middle Babylonian text with personal names, similar to Nos. 21 and 22. The reverse is uninscribed.

4NT 6. SE I 2. Poorly preserved fragment of a Middle Babylonian account dated to Kudur-Enlil, year 7 or 8.

4NT 9. SE I 3. Poorly preserved Middle Babylonian administrative document dated to Kaštiliaš IV, year 3.

4NT 11*a*. SE 43 II 3. School exercise. Upper right corner, only one side preserved. S^a (signs only): col. i, ll. 27-42; col. ii, ll. 131-35 followed by a ruling, then ll. 1-11; col. iii, ll. 97-111.

4NT 11*b*. SE 43 II 3. School exercise. Small fragment preserving the upper edge. S^a (signs only): col. i, ll. 1-6; col. ii traces.

4NT 11*c*. SE 43 II 3. School exercise. Small fragment of a lower right corner. S^a (signs only): col. i, ll. 152-63 (with three forms of DIN; line 161 not preserved); col. ii, ll. 176-88; rev., col. i, ll. 189-203; col. ii, ll. 216-21, with two unusual forms of UG(?) preceding.

4NT 13. SE dump. Small fragment with ends of lines, including a date (year broken) of Nabonidus.

4NT 16. SE 44 II 3. School exercise. Fragment of left edge. S^a (signs only): obv., ll. 356-64; traces on rev.

4NT 18*a*. SE 58 III 1. School exercise. Fragment of upper right corner. S^a (signs only): obv., col. i traces; col. ii, ll. 5-10; rev., col. i, ll. 7-13; col. ii, ll. 23-28.

4NT 18*b*. SE 58 III 1. School exercise. Fragment of lower left corner. S^a (signs only): ll. 38-40 on both obverse and reverse.

4NT 27. SE 68 II 4. Lexical. Originally the tablet probably had the entire text of Hh. II. Obv., ll. 5-17; rev., col. i, ll. 254-61 (omitting 255 and 258; var. egir for i-zi in l. 261); col. ii, ll. 331-43. In line 340 the fragment has *mu-še-lu-ú* instead of *za-ru-u*.

4NT 28. SE 58 III 2. School exercise. Fragment of lower left corner. S^b I 60-64 (signs only).

4NT 29. SE 58 III 2. School exercise; very fragmentary. Unidentified, but possibly mathematical.

4NT 34. Intrusive into NT 9 I 3. Narrow fragment (*ca.* 2.3 cm.) of a Neo-Babylonian literary(?) text, poorly written and virtually illegible.

4NT 35. Intrusive into NT 9 I 3. Small fragment of a Neo-Babylonian letter(?).

4NT 36. Intrusive into NT 9 I 3. School exercise. Very small tablet, two columns on obverse, three on reverse; part of the right and bottom edges are preserved. S^b (signs only): obv., col. i traces; col. ii, ll. 225-33; rev., col. i, ll. 234-40; col. ii, ll. 244-52; col. iii, ll. 258 ff. (with signs inside KA sometimes unclear).

4NT 37. Intrusive into NT 9 I 3. Neo-Babylonian account fragment with 7 lines containing personal names, with total 15 UDU.NITA.

4NT 38. Intrusive into NT 9 I 3. S^a (signs only): obv.(?), col. i traces; col. ii, ll. 36-43; rev.(?), col. i, ll. 118-24 followed by a ruling, then ll. 1-4; col. ii traces.

4NT 39. Intrusive into NT 9 I 3. School exercise. Fragment of left side. Hh. II 359-62 (only Sumerian column preserved) followed by ruling and then Hh. III 209 f.

4NT 41. Intrusive into NT 9 I 3. Incantation. Published by W. G. Lambert, in *Archiv für Orientforschung* XXIII, Pl. 10 (see p. 39).

4NT 45. Intrusive into NT 9 I 3. School exercise. Fragment of upper left corner with five lines on obverse followed by a ruling and four on the reverse followed by a ruling. Unidentified.

4NT 47. Intrusive into NT 46 II (in burial shaft of 4B 110). School exercise. Lower edge is preserved. Column i of the obverse has traces at ends of lines; column ii has the Sumerian column of Hh. I 343-46. Traces on reverse.

4NT 50. SE III. Neo-Babylonian fragment with several damaged lines of an account.

4NT 67. NT 61 IV 2. Fragment of a stone bowl. Of the inscription only ⌈a⌉-mu-ru is preserved. See Pl. 47:11.

4NT 70. NT dump. Fragment of a stone bowl with one legible sign (AMA).

4NT 71. NT 32 II. Fragment of a Pre-Sargonic cream-colored stone bowl. Of the inscription only the line [a-m]u-ru is preserved.

4NT 72. NT 67 III 2. Fragment of a thin whitish stone bowl. Of the inscription only DU[B] is preserved.

4NT 259. NT 120 VI 2. Fragment of a Fara-type document. Obverse has traces of awkward writing, mostly destroyed. Reverse destroyed.

4NT 268. NT 1 I 2. Old Akkadian seal impression with inscription Íl nu-èš. See Pl. 64:4. For the term nu-èš, see J. Renger, "Untersuchungen zum Priestertum der altbabylonischen Zeit," *Zeitschrift für Assyriologie*, Vol. 59 (1969) pp. 138-43.

4NT 269. NT 43 II 1. Old Akkadian seal impression with inscription Íl bur-šu-[ma] lugal (reading partly restored from another impression of the same seal). See Pl. 64:3. For the term bur-šu-ma, see J. Renger, in *Zeitschrift für Assyriologie*, Vol. 59, p. 201.

4NT 270. NT 43 II 1. Fragment with the same seal impression as 4NT 268. See Pl. 64:1 (the inscription is not clearly visible).

4NT 273. NT well shaft, near the water level. Fragmentary brick of Adad-šuma-uṣur. Duplicate of Hilprecht, *Babylonian Expedition* I, No. 81.

INDEX OF CATALOGUE NUMBERS

In the "reference" column, "No." refers to text on pages 71–77 in Chapter VII and to the corresponding copies on pages 78–92. For example, "(No. 1) 82, 78" refers to that text on page 72 and to the corresponding copy on page 78. In the "allocation" column, A stands for Andover Newton Theological School, AS for the American Schools of Oriental Research, B for Iraq Museum, Baghdad, C for Oriental Institute Museum, Chicago, D for "Discarded," H for Harvard University, J for Johns Hopkins University, P for University Museum, Philadelphia, Pr for Princeton University, T for University of Toronto, and Y for Yale University. Objects which have an allocation but no museum number either have been kept for study but not accessioned or have been given an accession number not known at this time. The location of objects for which no allocation is given is at present unknown.

CAT. NO.	REF.	ALLOCATION	MUS. NO.
3N 158	p. 51	B	
3N 163	p. 50	B	56479
3N 177	p. 50, Pl. 73:1, 2, 4	B	56477
3N 178	p. 56	C	A29414
3N 182	p. 52	C	A29417
3N 183	p. 51	B	
3N 184	p. 50	P	53-11-80
3N 185	p. 50, Pl. 73:5	B	
3N 190	p. 50, Pl. 72:10	C	A29419
3N 196	p. 52, Pl. 61:8	C	A29421
3N 202a	p. 56	C	A29422
3N 202b	p. 56		
3N 204	p. 56	P	53-11-294
3N 208	p. 56, Pl. 50:11	B	56542
3N 210	p. 56	C	A29425
3N 211	p. 56, Pl. 51:3	P	53-11-221
3N 214	p. 56	C	A29426
3N 215	p. 49, Pl. 71:14	B	56499
3N 224	p. 56	B	
3N 225	p. 52	B	
3N 237	p. 50, Pl. 71:16	P	53-11-75
3N 238	p. 49, Pl. 71:15	C	A29435
3N 257	p. 56	C	A29438
3N 274	p. 32, Pl. 59:2	B	56508
3N 275	p. 32, Pl. 70:8	P	53-11-3
3N 296	p. 51	B	
3N 323	p. 33	B	
3N 328	p. 32, Pl. 67:4	C	A29456
3N 349	p. 52	B	
3N 365	p. 49, Pl. 56:4	P	53-11-286
3N 392	p. 32, Pl. 60:6	B	56574
3N 397	p. 56, Pl. 62:9	P	53-11-317
3N 398	p. 56	B	56523
		P	53-11-323
3N 401	p. 32, Pl. 68:3	C	A29469
3N 402	pp. 22, 32, (No. 1) 72, 78, Pls. 67:3, 68:1, 2	B	56506
3N 403	pp. 22, 32, Pl. 70:2, 3	C	A29470
3N 404	pp. 22, 32, Pl. 69:1, 2	P	53-11-1
3N 405	pp. 22, 32, Pl. 67:5	C	A29471
3N 406a	pp. 22, 32, Pl. 70:1	C	A29472
3N 406b	pp. 22, 32, Pl. 68:4	P	53-11-2
3N 409	p. 33	B	
3N 410	p. 33	C	A29473
3N 420	p. 51	P	53-11-300
3N 425	p. 51	B	
3N 426	p. 51, Pl. 62:2	C	A29484
3N 435	p. 56	B	56538
3N 436	p. 56	P	53-11-336
3N 437	p. 57, Pl. 62:4	B	56536
3N 438	p. 57	B	
3N 439	p. 57	P	53-11-311a–b
3N 440	p. 57	P	53-11-318
3N 441	p. 57	C	A29486
3N 471	p. 51	B	56539
3N 473	p. 50, Pl. 72:4	P	53-11-64
3N 474	p. 48	B	2067MS
3N 476	p. 32, Pl. 70:4	P	53-11-5
3N 477	p. 57	P	53-11-347
3N 479	Pl. 57:3	B	56548
3N 480	p. 50, Pl. 71:23	P	53-11-56
3N 481	p. 33, Pl. 70:7	C	A29496
3N 482	p. 50	B	56482
3N 483	p. 52, Pl. 62:8	C	A29497
3N 484	p. 51	C	A29498
3N 485	p. 51	C	A29499
3N 486	p. 51	C	A29500
3N 487	p. 57	B	
3N 489	pp. 48, 57, Pl. 55:5	P	53-11-10
3N 490	pp. 48, 57	B	
3N 491	pp. 48, 57	C	A29501
3N 492	pp. 48, 57, Pl. 56:3	B	56512
3N 493	pp. 49, 57, Pl. 71:19	C	A29502

INDEX OF CATALOGUE NUMBERS

CAT. NO.	REF.	ALLOCATION	MUS. NO.
3N 499	p. 57, Pl. 51:10	P	53-11-223
3N 500	p. 52	B	
3N 504	p. 57	P	53-11-338
3N 505	p. 52, Pl. 74:11	B	56534
3N 506	p. 33	B	56527
3N 508	p. 51	B	
3N 509	pp. 30, (No. 53) 77, 92	C	A29507
3N 510	p. 33, Pl. 70:6	P	53-11-339
3N 511	p. 32, Pl. 69:3–5	P	53-11-7
3N 512	p. 30, Pl. 47:9	B	
3D 290	p. 56	B	
3D 291a	p. 56	C	A29676
3D 291b	p. 56	C	A29677
3D 297	p. 56	C	A29680
3D 298	p. 56	C	A29681
3D 304	p. 50		
3D 563	p. 52, Pl. 60:3	P	53-11-149
3D 585	p. 33, Pl. 59:11	B	
3D 597	p. 93	D	
3D 606	p. 93	D	
3D 690	p. 50, Pl. 72:7	B	
3D 692	p. 50, Pl. 77:5	P	53-11-61
3D 697	p. 50, Pl. 72:14	B	
3D 698	p. 50, Pl. 72:2	P	53-11-62
3P 199	p. 56	B	
3P 206	p. 56	P	53-11-201
3P 211	p. 56		
3P 216	p. 56	C	A29534
3P 225	p. 56		
3P 228	pp. 47, 56, Pl. 53:12	B	
3P 229	p. 46, Pl. 53:9	P	53-11-213
3P 232	p. 56	B	
3P 235	p. 56	P	53-11-205
3P 236	p. 56	B	
3P 255	p. 47, Pl. 55:4		
3P 267	Pl. 50:7	B	
3P 277	Pl. 50:3	B	
3P 278	Pl. 50:5	C	A29544
3P 281	Pl. 49:5	B	
3P 285	Pl. 49:4	P	53-11-250
3P 286	pp. 47, 56	B	
3P 288	p. 68, Pl. 50:8	B	
3P 341	Pl. 50:9	B	
3P 401	p. 30, Pl. 47:10	C	A29568
3P 410	p. 30, Pl. 47:8	P	53-11-11
3P 428	p. 30	B	
3P 508	p. 93	D	
3P 510	Pl. 50:6	C	A29592
3P 528	p. 19, Pl. 3 *C*	C	A29598
3P 529	p. 19, Pls. 3 *C*, 45:4	B	
3P 530	p. 19, Pl. 3 *C*	P	
3P 536	p. 19, Pl. 3 *C*	P	
3P 537	Pl. 45:6	C	A29600

CAT. NO.	REF.	ALLOCATION	MUS. NO.
3P 538	p. 19, Pl. 3 *C*	B	
3P 549	Pl. 58:1	B	
3P 557	p. 19, Pl. 3 *C*	B	
3P 564	Pl. 46:7		
3P 568	Pl. 46:2	C	A29605
3P 583	p. 56, Pl. 58:2	B	
3P 584	p. 57	B	
3P 591	Pl. 45:5	C	A29609
3P 592	p. 57	P	53-11-266
3P 593	p. 57	C	A29610
3P 595	p. 57		
3P 602	p. 57	B	
3P 603	pp. 47, 57, Pl. 55:1	C	A29611
3P 604	p. 57	B	
3P 608	p. 49, Pl. 71:22		
3P 609	p. 49, Pl. 71:21		
3P 610	pp. 49, 57	B	
3P 611	pp. 49, 57	P	53-11-276
3P 613	p. 47, Pl. 55:3	C	A29612
3P 615	Pl. 44:12	C	A29613
3P 616	Pl. 46:8	P	53-11-216
3P 620	p. 30		
3P 621	Pl. 45:1, 3	B	
3P 622	Pl. 46:1		
3P 626	p. 30		
3NT 139	(No. 19) pp. 73, 84	C	A30162
3NT 140	pp. 47, 93	C	A30163
3NT 141	pp. 47, 93	C	A30164
3NT 142 –144	pp. 47 f., 93	C C	A30165–67
3NT 145 –149	pp. 48, 93	P	55-21-263–67
3NT 848	p. 93	B	58759
3NT 195	(No. 42) pp. 76, 90	B	58367
3NT 891	pp. 48, (No. 26) 75, 87	P	55-21-443
4N 3	p. 52	B	
4N 7	p. 51, Pl. 61:2	B	
4N 8	p. 51	B	58310
4N 9	p. 58, Pl. 62:13	H	
4N 10	p. 58, Pl. 62:11	T	955.143.44 A & B
4N 11	p. 58	B	58302
4N 12	p. 52	AS	
4N 13	p. 51, Pl. 62:5, 6, 7	B	58290
4N 14	p. 52	B	
4N 15	p. 59, Pl. 62:12	B	58324, 58325
4N 16	p. 52	H	
4N 17	Pl. 77:1–3	T	955.143.31
4N 18	p. 52, Pl. 60:15	B	58311
4N 19	p. 52	Pr	56.85
4N 20	p. 49	B	58278
4N 21	p. 52	B	
4N 22	p. 51, Pl. 74:7	B	

INDEX OF CATALOGUE NUMBERS

CAT. NO.	REF.	ALLOCATION	MUS. NO.
4N 23	p. 52	B	
4N 25	p. 52, Pl. 62:1	H	
4N 26	p. 49, Pl. 71:1	T	955.143.29
4N 27	p. 60	B	
4N 28	p. 52, Pl. 61:9	AS	
4N 29	p. 52	B	
4N 30	p. 50, Pl. 74:3	B	58281
4N 31	p. 51, Pl. 74:6	B	
4N 33	p. 52	B	
4N 34	p. 60	J	
4N 35	p. 60	T	955.143.37
4N 36	p. 60	Y	
4N 37	p. 60, Pl. 74:10	Pr	
4N 39	p. 60, Pl. 74:9	C	A29913
4N 40	p. 60, Pl. 74:9	B	58329
4N 41	p. 60	AS	
4N 42	p. 60, Pl. 74:8	B	58327
4N 43	p. 50, Pl. 73:3	B	
4N 44	p. 51, Pl. 61:1	B	58326
4N 45	p. 51	B	
4N 46	p. 49	Y	
4N 47	p. 61	T	955.143.36
4N 48	p. 61		
4N 49	p. 61, Pl. 61:5	T	955.143.80
4N 50	p. 61	T	955.143.43
4N 51	p. 47, Pl. 60:16	B	
4N 52	p. 61, Pl. 61:3	B	58304
4N 53	p. 61	Y	
4N 54a	pp. 49, 61, Pl. 71:2	B	58259
4N 54b	p. 61		
4N 54c	p. 61		
4N 55	p. 61	Y	
4N 56	p. 61	Pr	
4N 57	p. 61	B	58312
4N 58	p. 51	H	
4N 59	p. 51	B	58303
4N 60	p. 49, Pl. 71:4	B	58260
4N 61	p. 52, Pl. 61:10	Pr	
4N 62	p. 50, Pl. 72:8	B	
4N 63	p. 50, Pl. 72:6	Y	
4N 64	p. 51, Pl. 73:7	B	
4N 65a	p. 50, Pl. 73:9	Y	
4N 65b	p. 51	Y	
4N 66	p. 62	H	
4N 67	p. 51, Pl. 73:8	T	955.143.2
4N 68	p. 47, Pl. 60:17	B	58286
4N 69	p. 51, Pl. 73:6	C	A29914
4N 70	p. 51	H	
4N 71	p. 49	J	
4N 72	Pl. 76:4, 5	B	
4N 73	p. 58, Pl. 62:3	T	955.143.52
4N 74	pp. 49, 62, Pl. 71:3	T	955.143.42
4N 75	p. 49	Pr	56.84
4N 80	p. 63	B	
4N 81	p. 50, Pl. 72:1	B	58282
4N 82	p. 33	Y	
4N 83	p. 67	J	
4N 86	p. 32, Pl. 70:5	Y	
4N 92	p. 33	T	955.143.51
4N 94	p. 33, Pl. 74:5	B	58319
4N 95	p. 33, Pl. 60:5	B	
4N 96	p. 64		
4N 97	p. 64	B	
4N 98	pp. 49, 64	B	58322
4N 101	p. 33, Pl. 63:10	J	
4N 102	p. 64	J	
4N 103	p. 64	Pr	
4N 104	p. 64	H	
4N 105	p. 31, Pl. 63:12	B	58263
4N 107	p. 33, Pl. 59:9	B	58274
4N 109a	p. 67	B	
4N 109b	p. 67, Pl. 62:10	B	58320
4N 110	p. 32, Pl. 67:1	J	
4N 111	p. 32, Pl. 66:15	H	
4N 112	p. 65	H	
4N 113	pp. 49, 66	C	A29915
4N 114	pp. 49, 66	B	58307
4N 115	pp. 46, 66, Pl. 56:5	Pr	
4N 116	pp. 49, 64	B	58308
4N 117	p. 64, Pl. 61:4	B	
4N 118	p. 33, Pl. 59:6		
4N 119	p. 33		
4N 120	p. 65	B	
4N 121	p. 65	B	58313
4N 122	p. 30, Pl. 71:5	T	955.143.60
4N 123	p. 30, Pl. 71:6	B	58271
4N 124	p. 33	J	
4N 125	p. 33		
4N 126	p. 33	B	58316
4N 127	p. 33	B	
4N 128	p. 33, Pl. 59:12	H	
4N 129	p. 30	B	
4N 130	pp. 49, 61, Pl. 71:12	B	
4N 131	p. 31, Pl. 71:11	B	58295
4N 133	pp. 49, 62, Pl. 56:8	B	
4N 135	p. 49	H	
4N 138	p. 30, Pl. 63:2	B	58264
4N 139a–139d	pp. 49, 65, Pl. 71:7–10	B	58266–68
4N 142	p. 66	B	
4N 145	p. 52, Pl. 60:4	B	58314
4N 146	p. 33, Pl. 60:1	T	
4N 149	p. 66, Pl. 60:10	B	
4N 150	p. 66, Pl. 60:8	Y	
4N 151	p. 66	B	
4N 152	p. 66	Pr	
4N 153	p. 30, Pl. 63:8	H	
4N 155	p. 32, Pl. 66:16	Pr	
4N 157a	p. 31, Pl. 71:13	B	58272
4N 157b	p. 33	B	
4N 158	p. 52	B	58317
4N 163	p. 33, Pl. 60:2	B	

INDEX OF CATALOGUE NUMBERS

CAT. NO.	REF.	ALLOCATION	MUS. NO.	CAT. NO.	REF.	ALLOCATION	MUS. NO.
4N 164	p. 33, Pl. 60:7	J		4D 128	p. 51, Pl. 72:13	B	
4N 165	pp. 33, 62, Pl. 59:5	T	955.143.40	4D 129	p. 31, Pl. 63:11	B	
4N 174	p. 30, Pl. 63:6	B	58265	4D 131	p. 31, Pl. 65:9	C	A29823
4N 177	p. 65	Pr	56.73	4D 136	p. 31, Pl. 65:11	C	A29825
4N 178	p. 63	AS		4D 143	p. 50, Pl. 74:2	H	
4N 179	p. 66	B	58255	4D 146	p. 31, Pl. 65:5	C	A29827
4N 180	p. 66	B	58256	4D 147	p. 31, Pl. 66:6	C	A29828
4N 181	p. 67	B	58243	4D 148	p. 31, Pl. 65:8	B	
4N 184	p. 33, Pl. 59:8			4D 151	p. 31, Pl. 65:4	C	A29830
4N 185	p. 33, Pl. 59:10	B		4D 154	p. 31, Pl. 65:10	C	A29832
4N 186	p. 32, Pl. 59:1			4D 157	p. 31, Pl. 64:5	B	
4N 189	p. 33	Pr		4D 159	p. 32	B	
4N 207	p. 34	B		4D 164	p. 63	B	
4N 208	p. 34	B	58318	4D 165	p. 62	B	
4N 210	p. 33, Pl. 59:3	H		4D 167	p. 63	Y	
4N 213	p. 33, Pl. 59:4	B	58275	4D 169	p. 63	B	
				4D 174	p. 63		
4D 1	p. 52, Pl. 74:12	B		4D 175	p. 64	H	
4D 3	p. 51, Pl. 74:1	B		4D 176	p. 64	Pr	
4D 11	p. 50, Pl. 77:6	B		4D 177	p. 63	J	
4D 17	p. 50, Pl. 71:20	B		4D 178	p. 63	H	
4D 18	p. 50, Pl. 72:12	H, A		4D 181	pp. 31, 67, Pl. 65:13	B	
4D 19	p. 50, Pl. 72:9	T	955.143.7	4D 187	p. 32	B	
4D 23	p. 48	T	955.143.48	4D 192	p. 50, Pl. 72:11	Y	
4D 26	p. 48	T	955.143.46	4D 195	p. 31, Pl. 65:7	B	
4D 27	p. 48	B		4D 199	p. 31, Pl. 63:7	C	A29835
4D 28	p. 48	T	955.143.45	4D 201	p. 51, Pl. 74:4	T	
4D 30	p. 58	Y		4D 202	p. 52, Pl. 60:11–14	B	
4D 31	p. 58	D		4D 204	p. 31, Pl. 64:13	B	
4D 32	p. 58	B		4D 205	p. 31, Pl. 65:1	B	
4D 33	p. 58	AS		4D 208	p. 31, Pl. 66:7	C	A29836
4D 34	p. 59	B		4D 214	p. 31, Pl. 66:13	D	
4D 42	p. 52, Pl. 74:14	T	955.143.27	4D 218	p. 31, Pl. 64:12	C	A29840
4D 43	p. 52, Pl. 74:15	T	955.143.28	4D 220	p. 65	B	
4D 46	p. 48	B		4D 224	p. 65	D	
4D 50	p. 50, Pl. 72:3	J		4D 225	p. 63	B	
4D 51	p. 52, Pl. 74:13	B		4D 226	p. 33		
4D 58	Pl. 77:4	B		4D 227	p. 64	B	
4D 60	p. 50, Pl. 72:5	J		4D 228	p. 64	T	955.143.38
4D 75	p. 59	H		4D 230	p. 65, Pl. 60:9	T	955.143.41 A & B
4D 84	p. 60	B					
4D 85	p. 60	B		4D 232	p. 63	B	
4D 86	p. 59	Pr		4D 233	p. 63	B	
4D 94	p. 60	Pr		4D 234	p. 64		
4D 98	p. 60	H		4D 239	p. 31, Pl. 66:9	C	A29841
4D 99	p. 60	J		4D 240	p. 31, Pl. 66:2	C	A29842
4D 100	p. 60	B		4D 245	p. 31, Pl. 63:9	C	A29844
4D 101	p. 31, Pl. 66:11	Y		4D 248	p. 32	Y	
4D 115	p. 61	AS		4D 249	p. 32, Pl. 70:9	C	A29846
4D 116	p. 61	B		4D 250	p. 31, Pl. 65:2	B	
4D 117	p. 61	B		4D 251	p. 31, Pl. 65:15	C	A29847
4D 118	p. 61	B		4D 252	p. 31, Pl. 66:12	B	
4D 119	p. 31, Pl. 65:6	B		4D 254	p. 31, Pl. 63:14	B	
4D 121	p. 61	B		4D 255	p. 31, Pl. 65:3	C	A29849
4D 122	p. 61	B		4D 257	p. 31, Pl. 63:13	B	
4D 123	p. 62	B		4D 258	p. 31, Pl. 66:1	D	

INDEX OF CATALOGUE NUMBERS

CAT. NO.	REF.	ALLOCATION	MUS. NO.
4D 260	p. 31, Pl. 63:15	C	A29852
4D 264	p. 31, Pl. 66:4	B	
4D 266	p. 31, Pl. 66:5	B	
4D 267	p. 31, Pl. 66:3	C	A29856
4D 273	p. 31, Pl. 65:12	B	
4D 274	p. 31, Pl. 64:6	B	
4D 275	p. 31, Pl. 64:10	C	A29860
4D 278	p. 31, Pl. 64:7	D	
4D 286	p. 31, Pl. 64:11	C	A29864
4D 287	p. 31, Pl. 66:10	B	
4D 297	p. 31, Pl. 66:14	C	A29867
4D 298	p. 31, Pl. 63:3	B	
4D 300	p. 31, Pl. 64:9	C	A29868
4D 303	p. 31, Pl. 64:8	B	
4D 304	p. 31, Pl. 65:14	C	A29869
4D 309	p. 31, Pl. 64:2	B	
4D 315	p. 30, Pl. 63:5	C	A29872
4D 318	p. 65	B	
4D 320	p. 67	Pr	
4D 323	p. 31, Pl. 66:8	B	
4D 324	p. 67	J	
4D 332	p. 67		
4D 333	p. 65	T	955.143.49
4D 334	p. 67	AS	
4D 335	p. 67	H	
4D 336a	p. 66, Pl. 61:6	Y	
4D 336b	p. 66, Pl. 61:7	Y	
4D 337	p. 68	J	
4D 340a–340c	p. 68	B	
4D 348	p. 32	T	955.143.33
4D 374	p. 33, Pl. 59:7	B	
4D 378	pp. 3, 30, Pl. 63:4	B	
4P 1	p. 46	B	
4P 2	Pl. 52:14	B	
4P 5	p. 47, Pl. 54:2	B	
4P 7	p. 45, Pl. 52:8	B	
4P 8	p. 47, Pl. 54:5	C	A29873
4P 10	p. 47, Pl. 56:2	C	A29874
4P 12	p. 46, Pl. 52:3	C	A29875
4P 13	p. 58	A	
4P 15	p. 46, Pl. 52:6	B	
4P 16	p. 46, Pl. 52:9	B	
4P 17	p. 47, Pl. 55:7	B	
4P 18	Pl. 52:1	Pr	56.75
4P 20	p. 46, Pl. 52:16	C	A29878
4P 23	p. 59	Pr	
4P 25	Pl. 52:15	A	
4P 28	p. 46, Pl. 53:11	B	
4P 29	Pl. 57:2	B	
4P 30	p. 46, Pl. 53:4	B	
4P 31	p. 46, Pl. 53:10	B	
4P 32	p. 46, Pl. 53:14	Pr	56.76
4P 33	Pl. 51:11	B	
4P 38	p. 60	A	
4P 41	p. 46	D	
4P 44	p. 45, Pl. 52:11	B	
4P 45	p. 45, Pl. 52:10	B	
4P 47	Pl. 51:2	C	A29881
4P 48	p. 60	B	
4P 49	p. 46, Pl. 53:2	C	A29882
4P 50	p. 46, Pl. 53:13	B	
4P 51	Pl. 51:9	T	955.143.15
4P 52	Pl. 52:4	Pr	56.64
4P 54	p. 47, Pl. 54:1	A	
4P 55	Pl. 57:6	D	
4P 59	p. 47, Pl. 55:10	B	
4P 64	Pl. 51:14	B	
4P 65	p. 46, Pl. 54:4	T	955.143.23
4P 70	pp. 46, 68, Pl. 53:5	T	955.143.17
4P 71	pp. 46, 68, Pl. 53:6	B	
4P 72	pp. 46, 68, Pl. 53:7	C	A29884
4P 73	p. 68, Pl. 51:1	C	A29885
4P 74	p. 68, Pl. 51:7	H	
4P 75	p. 68, Pl. 51:4	H	
4P 76	p. 47	D	
4P 77	p. 60	B	
4P 78	p. 60		
4P 81	p. 60	C	A29886
4P 82	p. 60	C	A29887
4P 83	p. 61	C	A29888
4P 84	p. 46, Pl. 52:7	B	
4P 85	Pl. 51:8	H	
4P 87	Pl. 51:5	B	
4P 94	p. 61	A	
4P 95	p. 61	B	
4P 96	p. 61	J	
4P 97	p. 61	AS	
4P 98	p. 61	D	
4P 99	p. 61	Y	
4P 100	p. 61	B	
4P 101	p. 61, Pl. 52:2	B	
4P 102	p. 61, Pl. 50:10	C	A29889
4P 103	p. 61	B	
4P 104	p. 61	C	A29890
4P 105	p. 61	Y	
4P 106	pp. 47, 61, Pl. 55:2	B	
4P 107	pp. 46, 61, Pl. 53:3	B	
4P 110	p. 61	B	
4P 111	p. 61		
4P 115	p. 62	B	
4P 116	Pl. 50:12	A	
4P 121	Pl. 52:5		
4P 126	p. 62	H	
4P 127	p. 62	Y	
4P 129	p. 46	H	
4P 130	p. 62	B	
4P 131	p. 62	B	
4P 132	p. 62	B	
4P 133	p. 62	T	955.143.12

INDEX OF CATALOGUE NUMBERS

CAT. NO.	REF.	ALLOCATION	MUS. NO.
4P 134	pp. 46, 62	Pr	
4P 135	p. 62	H	
4P 136	p. 62	T	955.143.13
4P 137	p. 62	B	
4P 138	p. 62	Pr	56.80
4P 139	Pl. 56:9	D	
4P 143	pp. 47, 62, Pl. 55:6	Y	
4P 144	p. 62	B	
4P 145	p. 63	B	
4P 146	p. 63	Y	
4P 147	p. 63	B	
4P 148	p. 63	B	
4P 149	p. 63		
4P 150	pp. 46, 63, Pl. 54:6	C	A29893
4P 151	p. 63	A	
4P 152	p. 63	Pr	56.79
4P 153	p. 63	J	
4P 154	p. 63	B	
4P 155	p. 63	B	
4P 156	p. 63	C	A29894
4P 157	p. 63	C	A29895
4P 158	p. 63	T	
4P 159	Pl. 51:12	A	
4P 162	Pl. 51:6	J	
4P 163	pp. 47, 62, Pl. 54:10	D	
4P 164	p. 62	B	
4P 165	p. 64	B	
4P 166	p. 47, Pl. 55:9	C	A29897
4P 167	p. 47, Pl. 56:1	D	
4P 168	p. 63	Pr	
4P 169	pp. 46, 63	Y	
4P 170	p. 29	B	
4P 171	p. 64	B	
4P 172	p. 46, Pl. 53:8	C	A29898
4P 173	p. 47, Pl. 54:9	B	
4P 175	p. 65	B	
4P 176	p. 65	B	
4P 177	p. 64	B	
4P 179	p. 64	J	
4P 180	p. 64	H	
4P 182	p. 65	B	
4P 183	p. 65	B	
4P 184	p. 65	D	
4P 185	p. 65	H	
4P 186	pp. 46, 65, Pl. 54:8	B	
4P 187	p. 65	B	
4P 188	p. 65	A	
4P 189	p. 65	C	A29900
4P 190	p. 63	C	A29901
4P 191	p. 66	T	955.143.10
4P 192	p. 66	B	
4P 193	p. 65	Y	
4P 194	p. 65	B	
4P 195	p. 64	D	
4P 196	p. 64	B	
4P 197	pp. 46, 64, Pl. 54:7	B	
4P 198	p. 65	Pr	56.72
4P 199	p. 46, Pl. 52:12	B	
4P 202	p. 64	B	
4P 203	p. 64	B	
4P 204	p. 61, Pl. 51:15	B	
4P 205	p. 61	B	
4P 206	p. 65	B	
4P 207	p. 65	B	
4P 208	p. 65	B	
4P 209	p. 64, Pl. 51:16	C	A29903
4P 210	p. 64, Pl. 51:13	C	A29904
4P 213	p. 65	B	
4P 217	p. 65	B	
4P 218	p. 65	B	
4P 219	Pl. 47:7	B	
4P 220	p. 47, Pl. 55:8	B	
4P 221	Pl. 47:3	B	
4P 222	pp. 46, 66, Pl. 54:3	B	
4P 223	p. 66	A	
4P 224	p. 66	B	
4P 227	p. 66	C	A29905
4P 228	p. 66	B	
4P 229	p. 66	B	
4P 230	pp. 46, 66, Pl. 53:1	Y	
4P 231	p. 66	B	
4P 232	p. 67	C	A29906
4P 233	p. 67	J	
4P 234	pp. 46, 67	B	
4P 235	p. 67	B	
4P 236	p. 67	B	
4P 237	p. 66	B	
4P 238	p. 66	B	
4P 239	p. 66	B	
4P 240	Pl. 47:5	T	955.143.18
4P 242	Pl. 46:9	B	
4P 247	p. 67	J	
4P 248	p. 67	Y	
4P 249	p. 67	B	
4P 250	p. 67	J	
4P 251	p. 67	T	955.143.16
4P 252	p. 67	J	
4P 253	p. 67	T	
4P 254	p. 67	B	
4P 255	p. 67	Y	
4P 256	pp. 46, 67, Pl. 52:13	Y	
4P 257	Pl. 46:5	J	
4P 260	p. 29	T	955.143.1
4P 261	p. 30, Pl. 48:2	H	
4P 262	Pl. 45:2	B	
4P 264	Pl. 46:4	B	
4P 268	Pl. 44:9	D	
4P 271	p. 29	A	
4P 275	Pl. 47:4	J	
4P 276	p. 30	B	
4P 284	Pl. 44:10		
4P 285	Pl. 44:11	C	A29909

INDEX OF CATALOGUE NUMBERS

CAT. NO.	REF.	ALLOCATION	MUS. NO.
4P 286	Pl. 46:6	T	955.143.24
4P 288	p. 29	Y	
4P 290	Pl. 47:1	C	A29910
4P 291	Pl. 47:2	H	
4P 292	Pl. 44:8	B	
4P 294	Pl. 44:4	B	
4P 295	p. 29, Pl. 47:6	B	
4P 297	p. 9, Pl. 44:7	B	
4P 298	p. 29	B	
4P 299	Pl. 49:1	Y	
4P 300	Pl. 49:2	C	A29911
4P 301	Pl. 49:3	B	
4P 305	Pl. 44:1	B	
4P 307	Pl. 44:2	B	
4P 308	Pl. 44:3		
4P 309	Pl. 44:6	H	
4P 310	Pl. 44:5	B	
4NT 1	pp. 49, (No. 51) 77, 92, Pl. 48:3	B	58933
4NT 2	(No. 52) pp. 77, 92	B	58941
4NT 3	pp. 48, 93	C	A33600
4NT 4	(No. 27) pp. 75, 87	B	58806
4NT 5	p. 93	B	
4NT 6	p. 93	B	58807
4NT 7	(No. 23) pp. 73, 86	B	58808
4NT 8	(No. 31) pp. 75, 88	B	58809
4NT 9	p. 93	B	58810
4NT 10	(No. 22) pp. 73, 85	B	58811
4NT 11a	p. 93	C	A33601
4NT 11b	p. 93	C	A33602
4NT 11c	p. 93	C	A33603
4NT 12	(No. 43) pp. 76, 91	C	A33604
4NT 13	pp. 48, 93	B	
4NT 14	(No. 45) pp. 76, 91	C	A33605
4NT 15	(No. 49) pp. 76, 92	B	58934
4NT 16	p. 93	C	A33606
4NT 17	(No. 29) pp. 75, 88	B	55812
4NT 18a	p. 93	C	A33607
4NT 18b	p. 93	C	A33608
4NT 19	pp. 48, (No. 28) 75, 87	B	58813
4NT 20	(No. 32) pp. 75, 88	B	58814
4NT 21	(No. 44) pp. 76, 91	B	58815
4NT 22	(No. 20) pp. 73, 85	B	55816
4NT 23	pp. 48, (No. 24) 73 f., 86	B	58817
4NT 24	(No. 7) pp. 72, 81	B	58818
4NT 25	(No. 21) pp. 73, 85	B	58819
4NT 26	(No. 9) pp. 72, 82	B	
4NT 27	p. 94	C	A33609
4NT 28	p. 94	C	A33610
4NT 29	p. 94	C	A33611
4NT 30	(No. 50) pp. 76, 92	B	58942
4NT 31	(No. 13) pp. 73, 83	B	58820
4NT 32	(No. 37) pp. 76, 89	B	58821
4NT 33	(No. 38) pp. 76, 89	B	58822
4NT 34	p. 94	B	58823
4NT 35	p. 94	B	58524
4NT 36	p. 94	C	A33612
4NT 37	p. 94	B	58825
4NT 38	p. 94	C	A33613
4NT 39	p. 94	C	A33614
4NT 40	(No. 33) pp. 75, 88	B	58826
4NT 41	p. 94	B	58827
4NT 42	(No. 34) pp. 75, 89	B	58828
4NT 43	(No. 35) pp. 75, 89	B	58829
4NT 44	(No. 36) pp. 75, 89	B	58830
4NT 45	p. 94	C	A33615
4NT 46	(No. 39) pp. 76, 90	B	58831
4NT 47	p. 94	C	A33616
4NT 48	(No. 25) pp. 74 f., 86	B	58832
4NT 49	(No. 40) pp. 76, 90	B	58833
4NT 50	p. 94	B	
4NT 51	pp. 47, (No. 17) 73, 84	B	58834
4NT 52	(No. 41) pp. 76, 90	B	58835
4NT 53	(No. 8) pp. 72, 81	B	58836
4NT 54	(No. 30) pp. 75, 88	B	58837
4NT 55	(No. 2) pp. 72, 79	B	58838
4NT 56	pp. 29, (No. 10) 73, 82	B	58839
4NT 57	(No. 15) pp. 73, 83	B	58840
4NT 58	(No. 16) pp. 73, 84	B	58841
4NT 59	(No. 11) pp. 73, 82	B	58842
4NT 60	(No. 12) pp. 73, 82	B	58843
4NT 61	(No. 4) pp. 72, 80	B	58844
4NT 62, 63	(No. 3) pp. 72, 80	B	58845
4NT 64	(No. 6) pp. 72, 81	B	58846
4NT 65	(No. 14) pp. 73, 83	B	
4NT 66	(No. 5) pp. 72, 80	B	58847
4NT 67	p. 94	B	58935
4NT 68	(No. 48) pp. 76, 92	B	58936
4NT 69	(No. 47) pp. 76, 91	B	58937
4NT 70	p. 94	B	
4NT 71	p. 94	B	58938
4NT 72	p. 94	B	58939
4NT 73	(No. 46) pp. 76, 91	B	58849
4NT 175	pp. 47, (No. 18) 73, 84	B	58880
4NT 259	p. 94	B	58919
4NT 268	p. 94, Pl. 64:4	B	58926
4NT 269	p. 94, Pl. 64:3	B	58927
4NT 270	p. 95, Pl. 64:1	B	58927
4NT 273	pp. 43, 95		

GENERAL INDEX*

ablution places, 8, 9, 10, 11, 12, 13, 15, 17, 18, 21–22
Achaemenian period, 39, 41, 43, 53
Akkadian period, 3, 23–25, 27, 28, 29, 30, 35, 43, 63, 69
altars, 6, 7, 9, 10, 11, 12, 14, 15, 17, 20, 21, 22
Assyrian period, 38, 43, 44, 69

baked bricks, *see* bricks
benches, 5, 8, 9, 10, 11, 12, 13, 14, 15, 16, 18, 20, 22, 23, 40, 41
bins, 6
bitumen, 15, 16, 18, 21; coating, 3, 10, 12, 14, 18, 20, 21; as paving, 11, 14, 15, 16, 17, 19
bowls, 27–28, 44, 45, 53: bevelled-rim, 27; burial, 55; conic, 27, 29; Ur III, 43
bricklaying, 4, 8, 10, 12, 15: flat, 4, 14, 19, 22, 24, 36, 38, 54; herringbone pattern, 4, 19, 20, 22, 24; on edge, 5, 8, 10, 19, 20, 21, 24, 36, 38, 40; radially, 23
bricks, 4, 8, 15, 19, 24, 25, 53, 54, 69: baked, 1, 12, 14, 18, 19, 20, 21, 22, 23, 24, 36–37, 39, 40, 41, 42, 43, 53, 54, 55, 69; bonding of, 8, 25, 36, 37; broken, 4, 12, 14, 36, 37; broken baked, 10, 19, 38; half, 38, 40; hand-fashioned, 22; plano-convex, 1, 4, 20, 25; rectangular, 3, 37; square, 37; unbaked, 3, 4, 5, 7, 8, 9, 10, 11, 12, 13, 14, 15, 16, 17, 18–19, 20, 21, 22, 23, 24, 25, 36, 37, 38, 39, 40, 41, 42, 53, 54
burials: bowl, 55; earth, 53; jar, 54; slipper-coffin, 55; tub, 53, 54

cellae, 6, 7, 8, 9, 11, 12, 13, 14, 15, 17, 18, 19, 20, 21, 22, 23, 24, 76
chalices, 27
coffins, *see* burials
courtyards, 5, 6, 8, 9, 10, 11, 12–13, 14, 17, 18, 19, 20, 21, 22, 23, 24, 25, 38, 39, 40, 63
cuneiform inscriptions, 71
cups, 44, 45
curbs, 5, 9, 11, 14, 15, 18
door pivots, 4, 7, 12, 14, 18, 38
doorways, 5, 6, 7, 8, 9, 10, 11, 12, 14, 17, 18, 19, 20, 21, 22, 24, 38
drain, French, 12
drain pits, 10, 12, 14, 15, 18, 20, 22
drain tiles, 6, 7, 8–9, 18, 21

drains, 7, 9, 12, 16, 18, 21, 22, 35, 36, 40, 41, 42, 43, 69

Early Dynastic period, 3, 8, 9, 17, 23, 27, 28, 29, 30, 35, 43, 69

Fara period, 76
firebox, 16
firepit, 8
fireplaces, 10, 11, 13–14, 19, 23, 24, 42

graves, *see* burials

hearths, 4, 5, 6, 7, 9, 10, 11, 13, 15, 16, 17

inscriptions, *see* cuneiform inscriptions
Isin-Larsa period, 35, 69

jars, 18, 19, 20, 21, 28, 42, 53, 54; *see also* pots

Kassite period, 35, 37, 38, 43, 44, 69
kilns, 40; *see also* ovens
kitchens, 42; temple, 6, 8, 9, 10, 11, 13–14, 18–19, 23

lamp, 44

Middle Babylonian period, 76

Neo-Babylonian period, 35, 39, 40, 43, 53, 76
Nippur, 29, 41, 44

Old Babylonian period, 35, 43, 69, 76
ovens, 14, 16, 19, 20, 23–24, 40; bread, 21, 22, 24; *see also* kilns

Parthian period, 53, 54
pedestals, 10, 13, 14, 19, 20, 21, 22, 40
plaster, 4, 7, 9, 16, 18, 19, 20; clay, 4, 8, 10–11, 12, 14, 15–16, 19; mud, 5, 10, 12, 13, 14, 16, 17, 19, 20, 22, 25, 38, 39, 40, 41
platforms, 7, 8, 9, 14, 15, 16, 18, 35, 36, 37, 43, 69
pots, 9, 28, 43, 44–45; *see also* jars
potsherds, 3, 4, 7, 10, 12, 15, 19, 20, 27, 28, 35, 38–39, 43, 44, 53, 54, 55
Protoliterate period, 3, 27, 69

---

*It should be noted that, but for minor exceptions, the subjects covered by headings in the Table of Contents are not repeated in the Index, nor are the contents of Chapter V, The Burials.

ramps, 9, 10, 11, 13, 18
risers, 6, 7, 15, 20, 42; *see also* stairs *and* steps

saucers, 43, 45
seal impressions, 3
Seleucid period, 35, 41, 43, 44, 53, 76
sherds, *see* potsherds
stairs, 20, 42; *see also* steps
stands, 8, 12, 19–20, 28, 43
steps, 9, 10–11, 13, 15–16, 19, 22; *see also* stairs *and* risers
stone statuettes, 1, 22

tables, 6, 8, 9, 10, 11, 12, 13, 14, 15, 16, 17, 18, 19, 20, 22, 40
tablets, exercise, 76
Third Dynasty of Ur, 28, 35, 36, 37, 38, 43, 69
tombs, 23; *see also* burials

unbaked bricks, *see* bricks

wall stubs, *see* curbs
wells, 12, 13, 35, 36, 43, 69

PLATES

PLATE 1

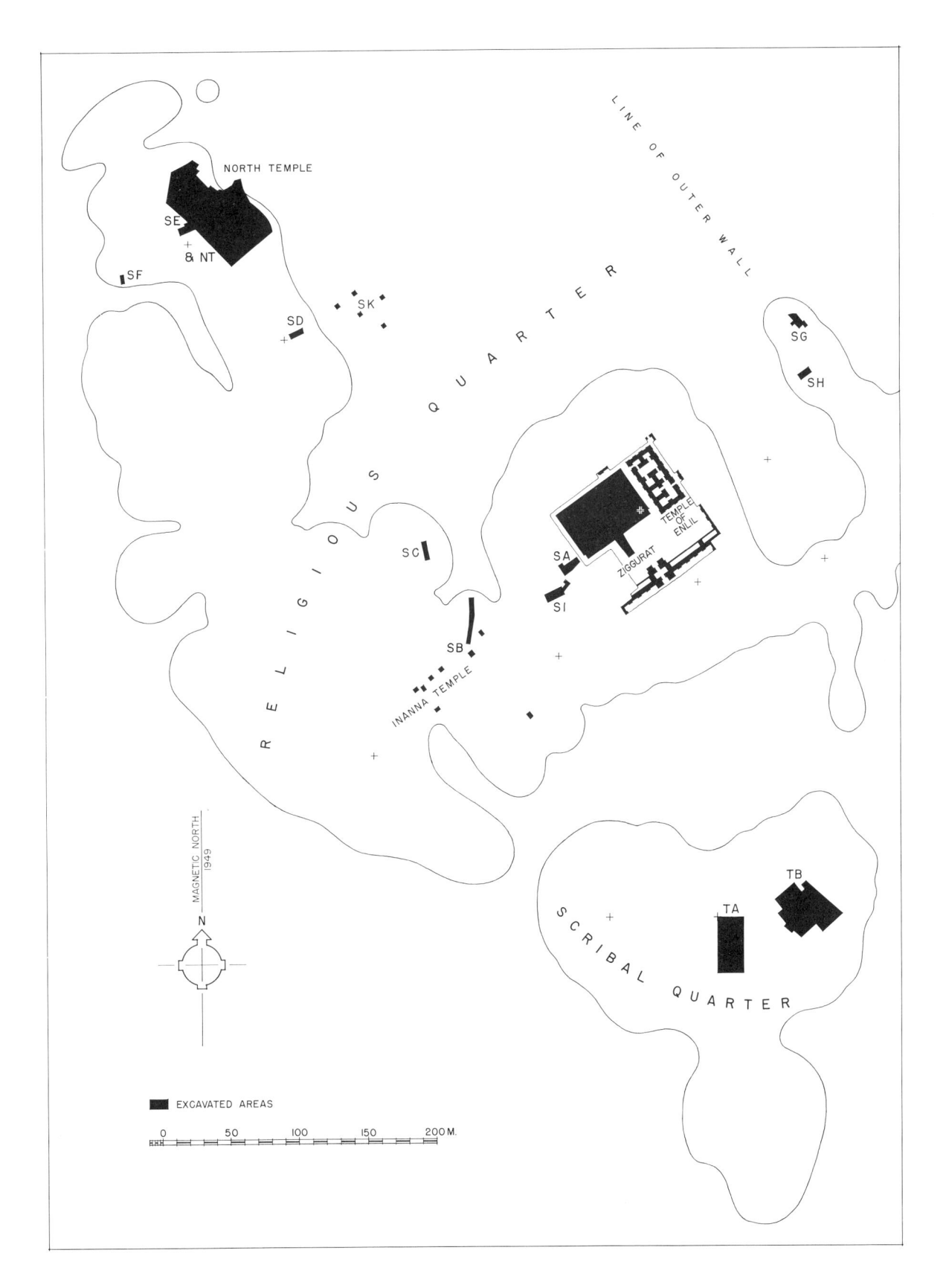

PLAN OF EASTERN NIPPUR SHOWING EXCAVATED AREAS, 1954

PLATE 2

A

B

A. SITE OF SOUNDING E AND THE NORTH TEMPLE, LOOKING SOUTHEAST. *B.* SOUNDING E TRENCH, LOOKING EAST. (In the foreground, the topmost walls belong to locus 78 in SE level I. The wall on the right is immediately above the ruins of a kiln in SE level II, which is above an exterior wall corner of SE level V. The lowest wall at the end of the trench is a buttressed wall in SE level VI. In the left background are the highest walls of the North Temple.)

PLATE 3

A. Findspot of Stone Statuettes in NT Level III, Looking West. (On the right is locus 60 in NT levels IV and III.) *B.* Locus 60, the Cella of the North Temple, at NT Levels IV and III, Looking West. *C.* Pottery *in situ* in the Box Altar, Locus 96, at NT Level IV, Looking East

PLATE 4

A

B

A. View of the Cella Area at NT Level IX, Looking Southeast. (At the bottom of the picture, locus 122 is at NT level IX 1*b;* at the right middle distance, locus 163 is at NT level IX 2; at left and rear, the walls of cella 107 are at NT levels VII and VIII.) *B*. View of the Cella Area at NT Levels IX and VIII, Looking Southeast. (At the bottom of the picture, locus 122 is at NT level IX 1*a;* in the upper part, cella 107 is at NT level VIII 3.)

PLATE 5

A. Cella 107 at NT Level VIII, Looking Southeast. (The altar in the upper right corner of the room belongs to NT level VII.) *B.* Detail of the Hexagonal Platform in Cella 107 at NT Level VIII, Looking North

PLATE 6

A. THE TEMPLE AT NT LEVELS IX TO VII, LOOKING EAST. (At the bottom of the picture loci 121 and 122 are at NT level IX; loci 123 and 124 at NT level VIII; and at the top courtyard 111 at NT level VII.) *B.* THE NORTHEAST PART OF THE TEMPLE, LOOKING SOUTH. (Loci 123 and 124 on the right are at NT level VIII, and locus 131 on the left at NT level VII.)

PLATE 7

A. THE STEPPED ALTAR AT NT LEVEL VII, LOOKING SOUTHEAST. (The hole on the right of the altar is a pot encased by the plasterings on the lower step.) *B.* THE POT ON THE LOWER STEP OF THE ALTAR, LOOKING SOUTH. *C.* THE ENTRANCE TO THE ANTEROOMS OF THE CELLA AT NT LEVEL VIII, LOOKING NORTH. (Locus 131 is on the right and locus 123 on the left.)

PLATE 8

A

B

A. Entrance Corridor to the Temple at NT Level VI, Looking Southwest.
B. Doorway between Entrance Corridor and Temple Courtyard at NT Level V, Looking Northeast

PLATE 9

A. FURNACE FOR MELTING BITUMEN IN LOCUS 116, NT LEVEL V, LOOKING NORTH.
B. CUTAWAY VIEW OF FURNACE, LOOKING NORTHWEST. (The arched firebox is below, with rimmed flat pan above.) *C.* A MODERN BITUMEN FURNACE IN THE VILLAGE OF AFAK

PLATE 10

A

B

THE TEMPLE AT NT LEVEL V. *A.* LOOKING EAST. (The circular drain surround in the lower left is on floor 1 of NT level IV.) *B.* LOOKING SOUTHWEST

PLATE 11

A

B

THE TEMPLE AT NT LEVEL IV. *A*. LOOKING NORTHEAST. (The hearth in room 65 and the ablution place in room 67 are at NT level III.) *B*. LOOKING SOUTHWEST

PLATE 12

A

B

THE TEMPLE AT NT LEVEL V. *A.* AN OFFERING TABLE IN ABLUTION ROOM 110,
LOOKING EAST. *B.* CIRCULAR OFFERING TABLES AND RAMPLIKE CONSTRUCTION
IN COURTYARD 111, LOOKING NORTHEAST

PLATE 13

A

B

THE CIRCULAR OFFERING TABLES IN COURTYARD 111 OF THE TEMPLE AT NT LEVEL V. *A*. TABLE AT LEFT PARTIALLY CUT AWAY TO SHOW SUCCESSIVE PLASTERINGS, LOOKING NORTHWEST. (Each layer cut away represents two or three plasterings instead of one.) *B*. TABLE ON LOWER RIGHT CUT AWAY TO SHOW CORE AND ORIGINAL PLASTERING, LOOKING SOUTHWEST. (The original and final slopes of the ramplike construction can be seen in the background.)

PLATE 14

A

B

CELLA 107 OF THE TEMPLE AT NT LEVEL V 2–1. *A*. SOUTHEAST PART SHOWING STAND AND ENTRANCE DOORWAY ON LEFT AND ALTAR ON RIGHT, LOOKING NORTHEAST. *B*. NORTHWEST PART SHOWING OFFERING TABLE ON RIGHT AND BASIN ON LEFT, LOOKING NORTHEAST. (The semicircular mass against the northeast wall is a sample of the buildup of clay floors left for later examination.)

PLATE 15

A

B

THE CELLA AT NT LEVEL V. *A*. THE ALTAR WITH STEP PARTIALLY CUT AWAY TO SHOW
SUCCESSIVE MUD PLASTERINGS, LOOKING SOUTH. *B*. DETAIL OF CORE
OF FREESTANDING OFFERING TABLE, LOOKING SOUTH

PLATE 16

A. FOUNDATION LAYER FOR BITUMEN OVAL IN CELLA 107 AT FLOOR 4 OF NT LEVEL V, LOOKING EAST. (The curbs in the upper right are at floor 3.) *B*. THE NORTHWEST PART OF CELLA 107 AT NT LEVEL V 4, LOOKING NORTH. (The freestanding offering table and floor 3 hearth are in the center foreground; beyond, an oval bitumen floor is on the left, and a curb at the doorway to room 109 is at the upper center. The semicircular mass [Pl. 14*B*] at the right has been cut back to show the succession of clay floors from NT level V 4 to VI.)

PLATE 17

A

B

NORTHWEST PART OF CELLA 60, LOOKING NORTHEAST. *A.* FOUNDATION LAYER FOR OVAL PLATFORM AT FLOOR 1 OF NT LEVEL IV. *B.* OVAL PLATFORM AT FLOOR 2 OF NT LEVEL III

PLATE 18

A

B

OVENS IN THE TEMPLE KITCHEN. *A*. ROOM 112, AT FLOORS 2 AND 1 OF NT LEVEL V, LOOKING NORTH. *B*. ROOM 65, AT FLOOR 2 OF NT LEVEL IV, LOOKING EAST

PLATE 19

A

B

C

OVENS IN THE TEMPLE KITCHEN. *A*. ROOM 65, AT FLOOR 1 OF NT LEVEL IV, LOOKING NORTH. *B*. ROOM 65, AT FLOOR 1 OF NT LEVEL III, LOOKING NORTHEAST. *C*. ROOM 72, NT LEVEL II, LOOKING NORTH

PLATE 20

A

B

ABLUTION PLACES IN ROOMS 110 AND 67 OF TEMPLE. *A.* AT FLOOR 4 OF NT LEVEL V,
LOOKING EAST. *B.* AT FLOOR 1 OF NT LEVEL IV, LOOKING SOUTHWEST

PLATE 21

A

B

ABLUTION PLACES IN ROOM 67 OF TEMPLE, LOOKING SOUTHWEST. *A.* AT FLOOR 2 OF NT LEVEL III. *B.* AT FLOOR 1 OF NT LEVEL III

PLATE 22

A. View of NT Levels III and II with NT Level IV Temple
in Middle Distance on Left, Looking Southeast. *B.* Oven in Room 49
at Floor 1 of NT Level IV, Looking Northeast.
C. Rooms 48 and 152 at NT Level II, Looking Northeast

PLATE 23

A. View of NT Level I on Left Cut by SE Level V on Right, Looking East. *B.* View of NT Levels III and II with Southwest Wall of SE Level VI Platform on Left, Looking Northwest

PLATE 24

Southwest Wall of SE Level VI Platform. *A.* Looking Southeast. *B.* Detail of Through Joint in Southeast Part of Wall

PLATE 25

Northwest Part of SE Level II. *A.* View Showing Saw-Toothed Wall at Top Left and Intrusive Kilns at Lower Right, Looking Northwest. *B.* Saw-Toothed Wall on West Side of Locus 33 at Floor 1 of SE Level II, Looking West. *C.* Intrusive Kilns in Loci 39 and 40 at SE Level II 4–2. (Jar burial 4B 60 is on the left, and tub burial 4B 64 in the foreground.)

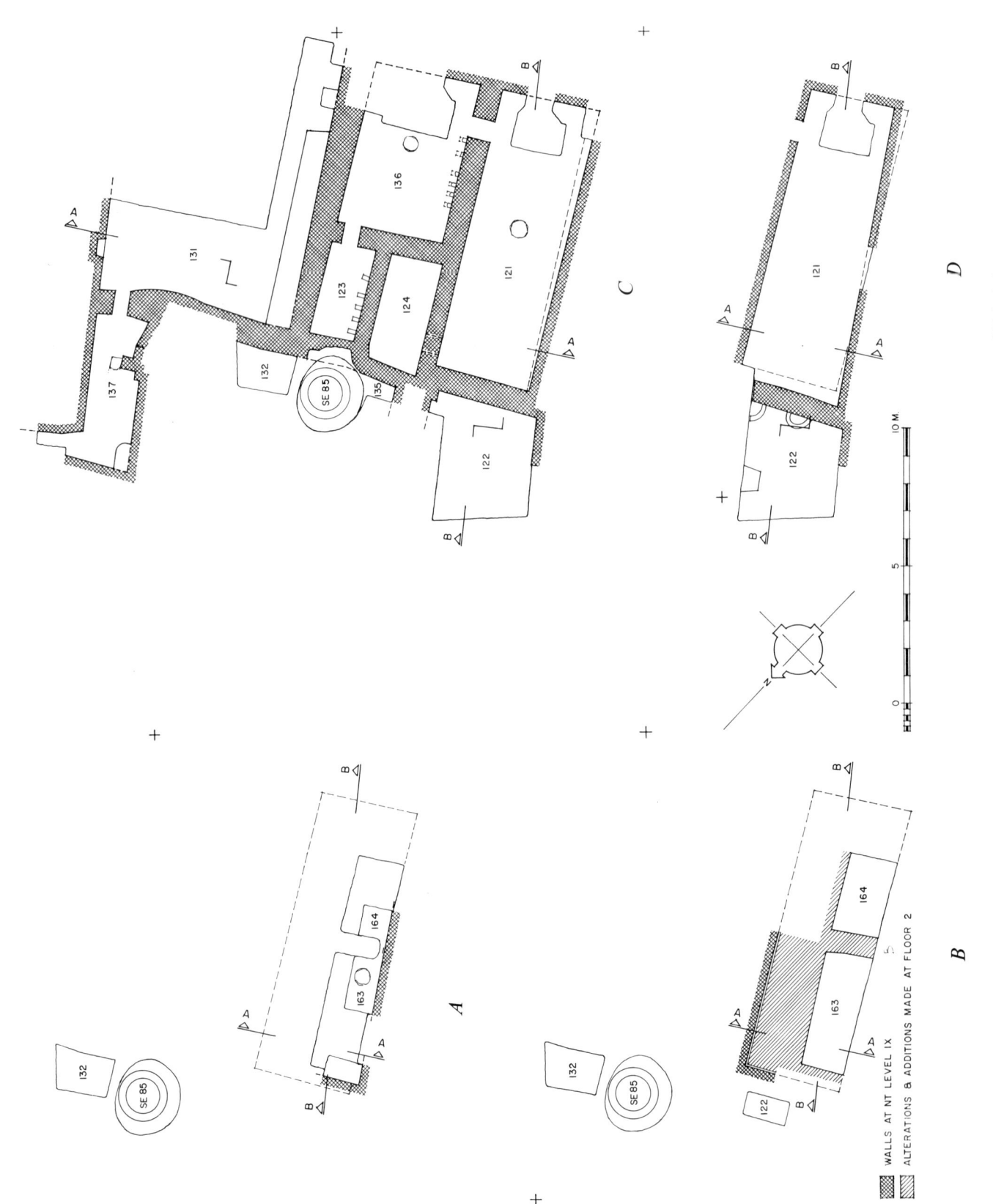

PLANS OF NT LEVELS X (*A*), IX 2 (*B*), IX 1 (*C*), AND ALTERATIONS TO IX 1 (*D*)

PLATE 27

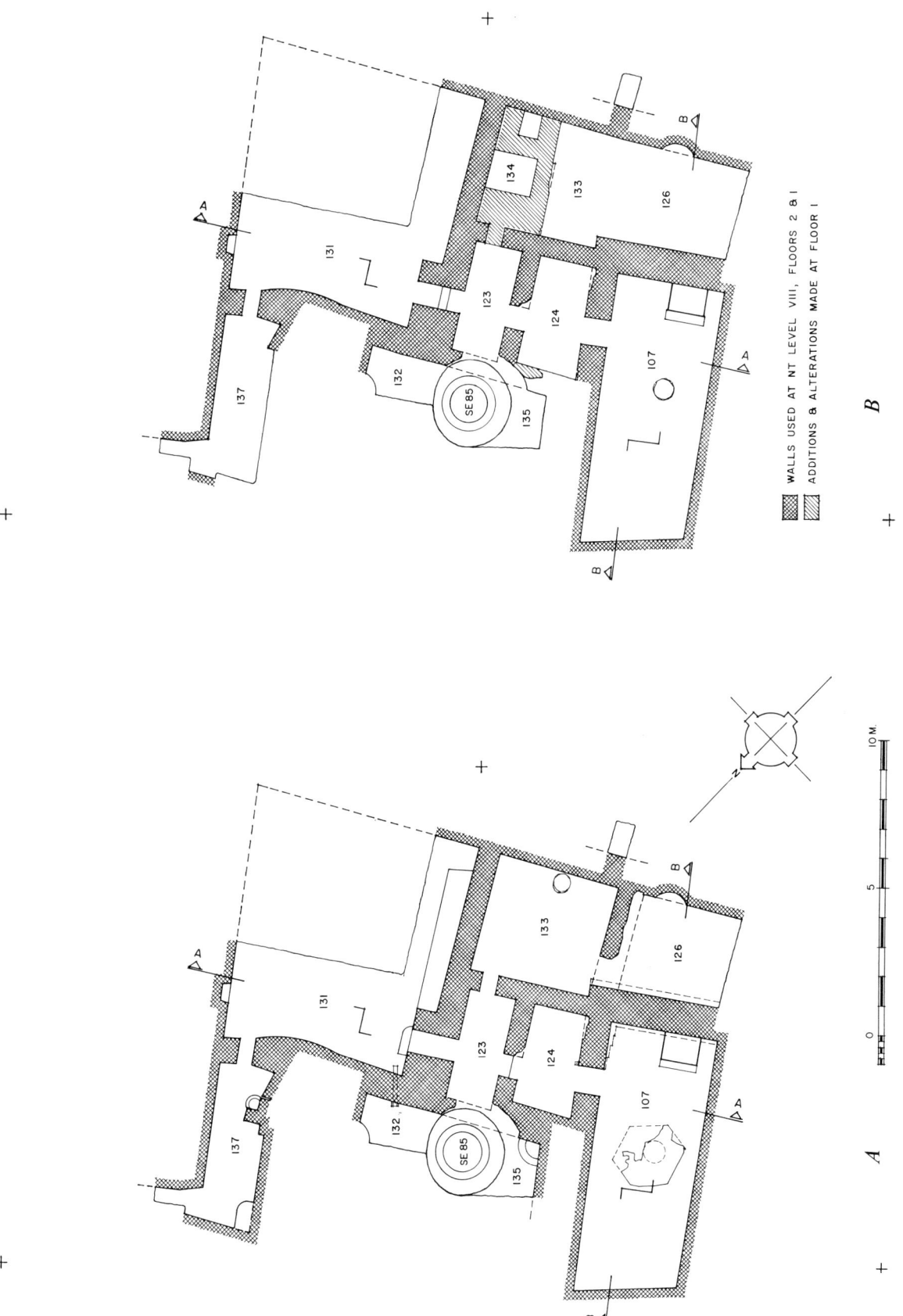

PLANS OF NT LEVEL VIII 2 (*A*) AND 1 (*B*)

PLATE 28

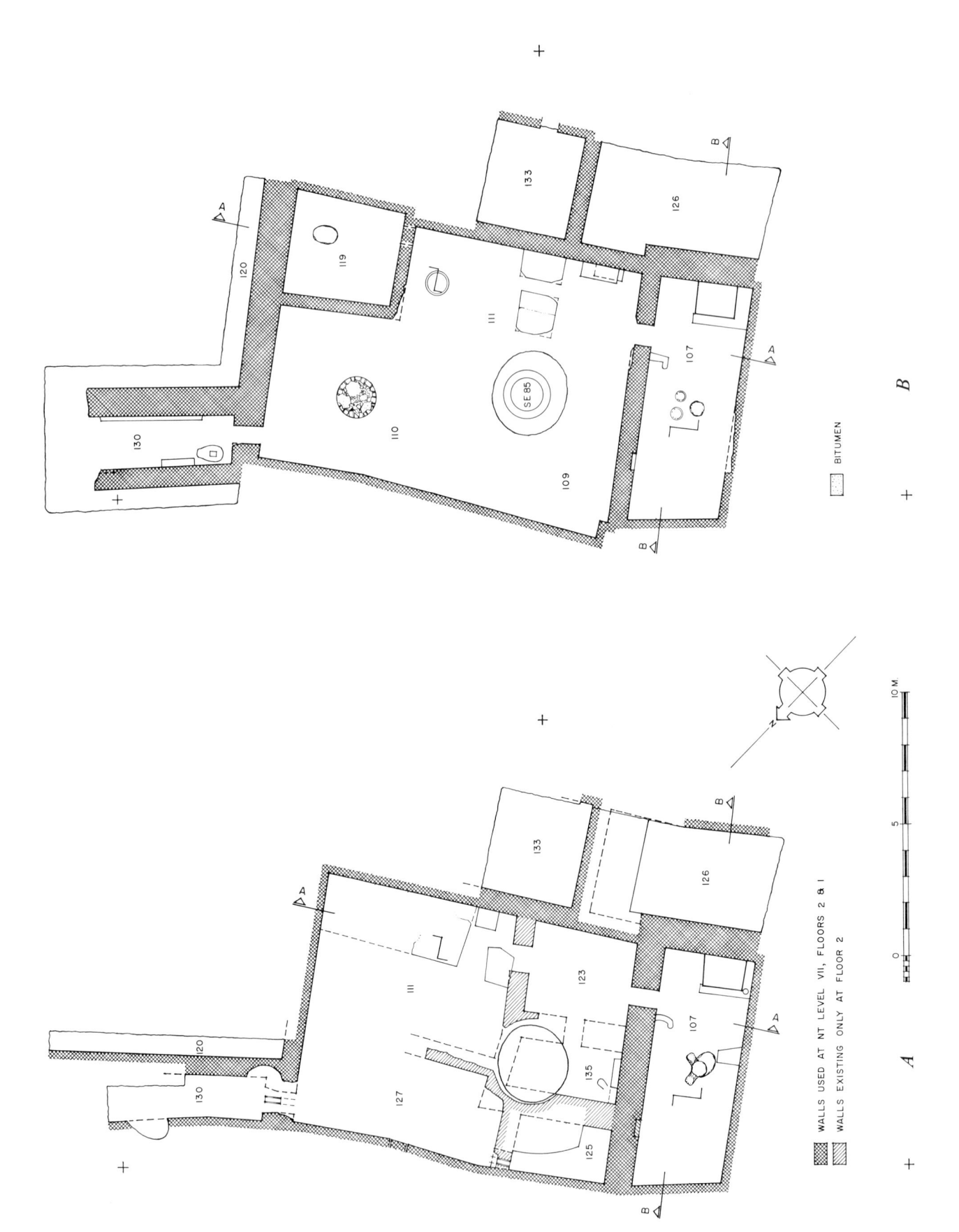

PLANS OF NT LEVELS VII (*A*) AND VI (*B*)

PLATE 29

PLANS OF NT LEVEL V 4–3 (*A*) AND 2–1 (*B*)

PLATE 30

Plans of the Temple at NT Level IV 3–2 (*A*) and 1 (*B*)

PLATE 31

PLAN OF NT LEVEL IV 1

PLATE 32

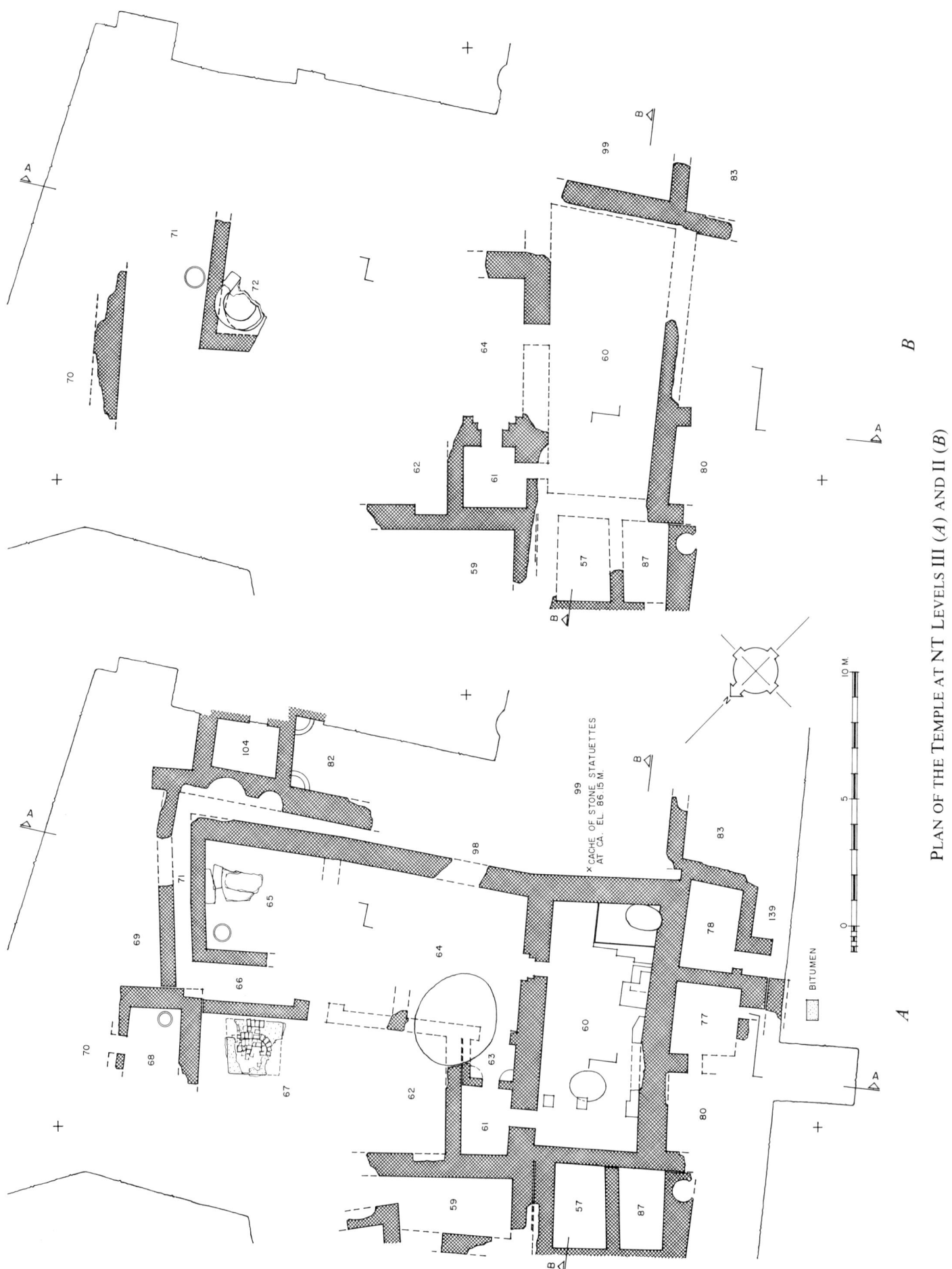

Plan of the Temple at NT Levels III (*A*) and II (*B*)

PLATE 33

PLAN OF NT LEVEL III

PLATE 34

PLAN OF NT LEVEL II

PLATE 35

PLAN OF NT LEVEL I

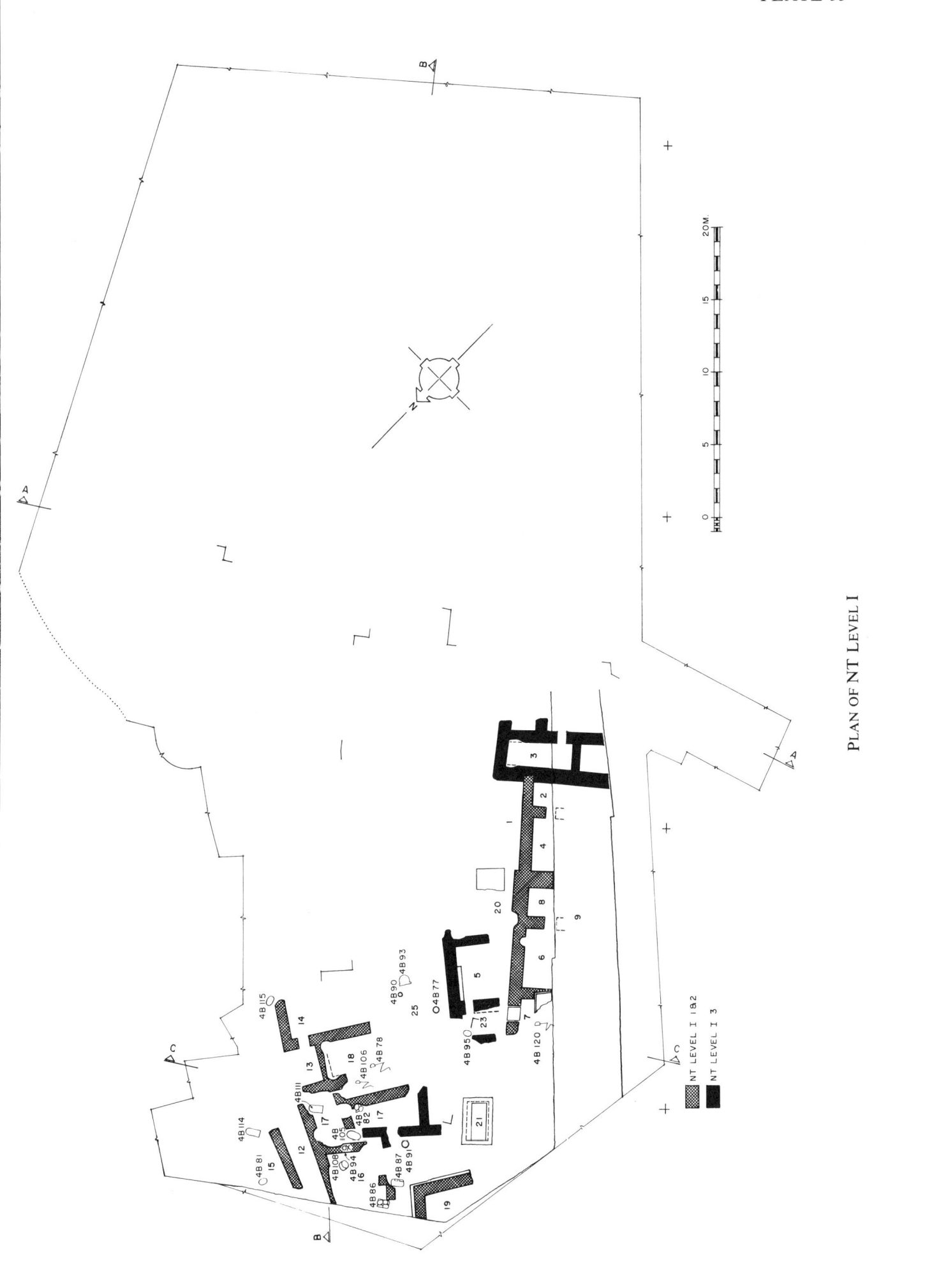

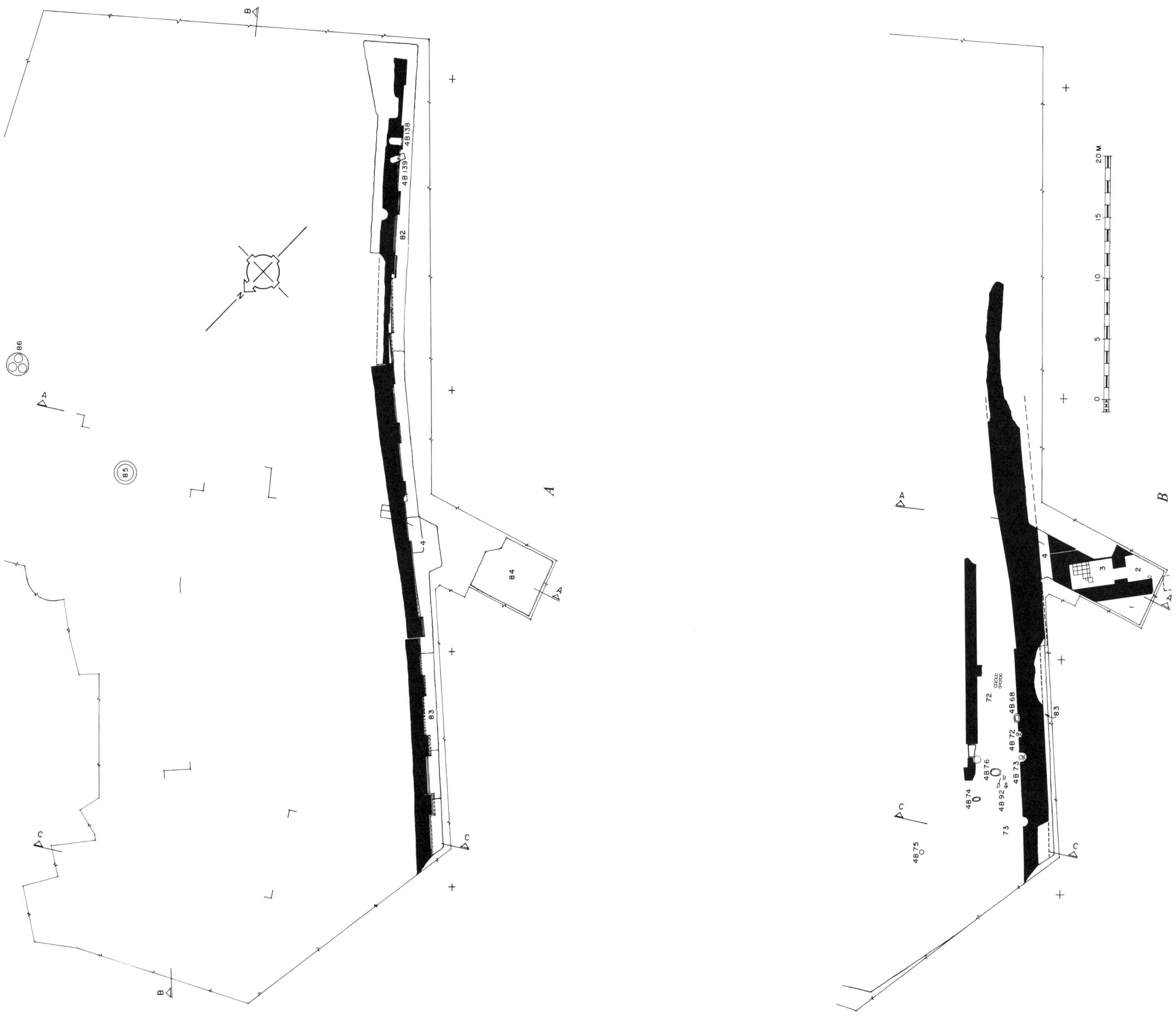

PLATE 36

PLANS OF SE LEVELS VI (*A*) AND V (*B*)

PLATE 37

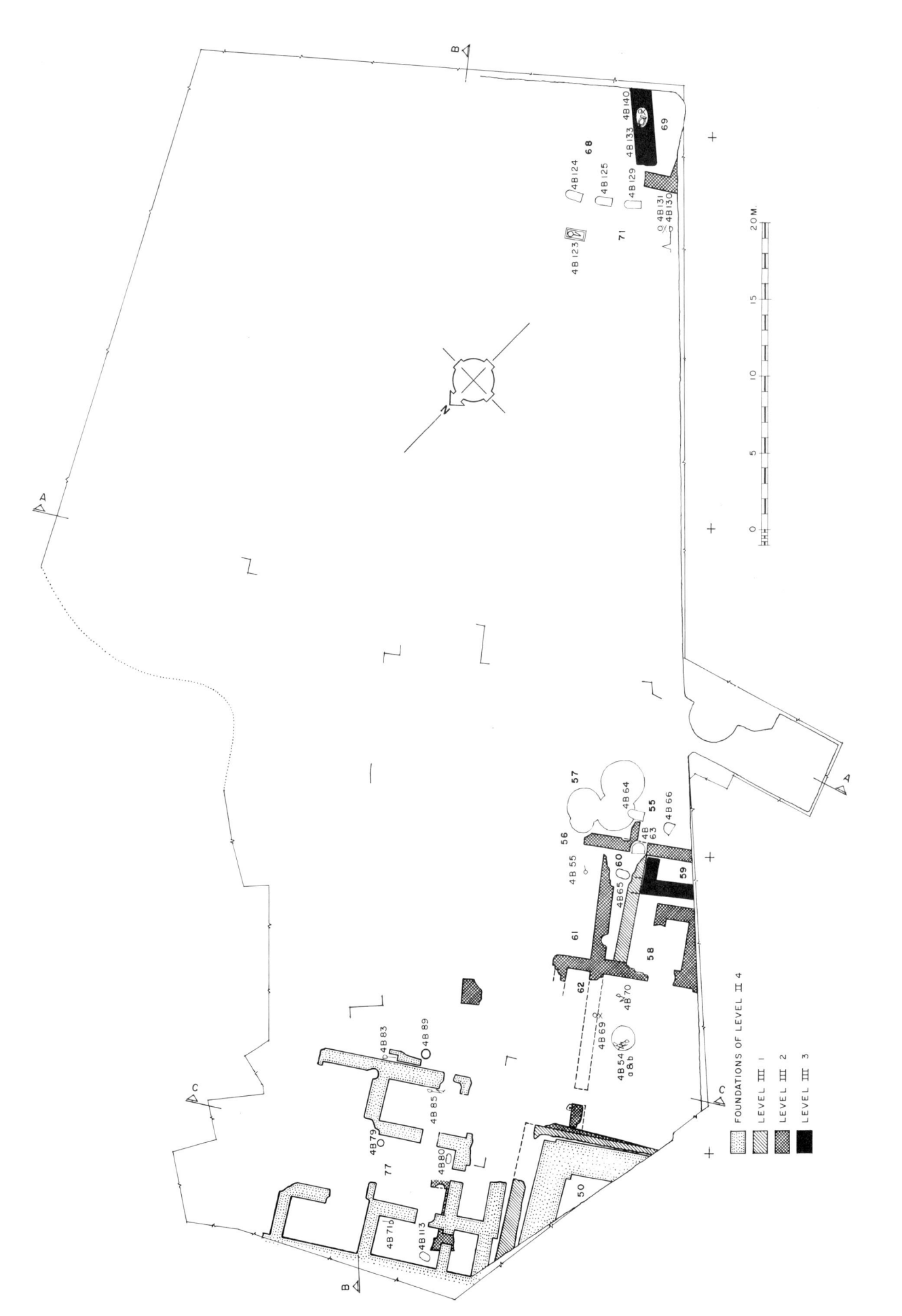

PLAN OF SE LEVEL III

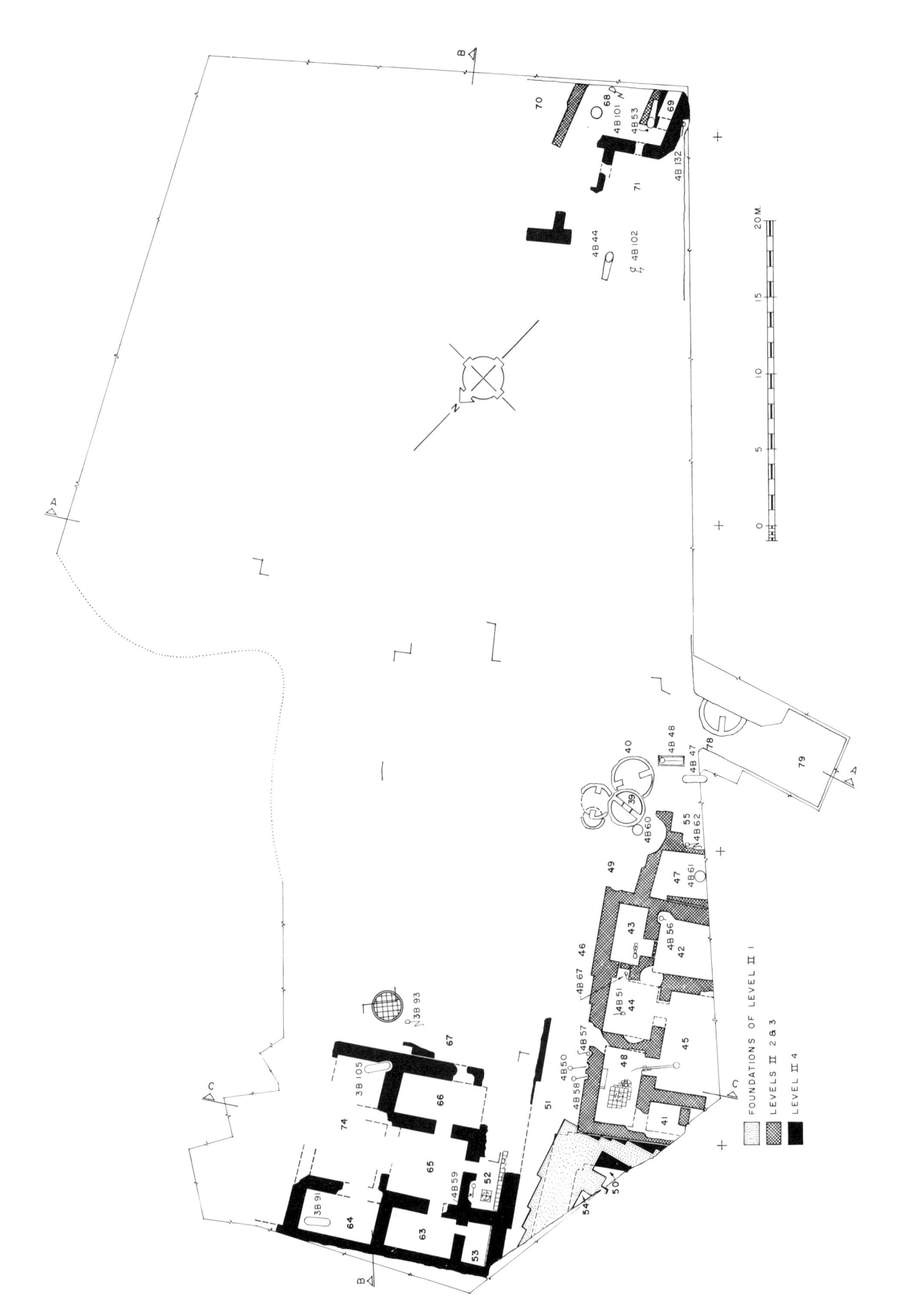

PLATE 38

PLAN OF SE LEVEL II 4–2

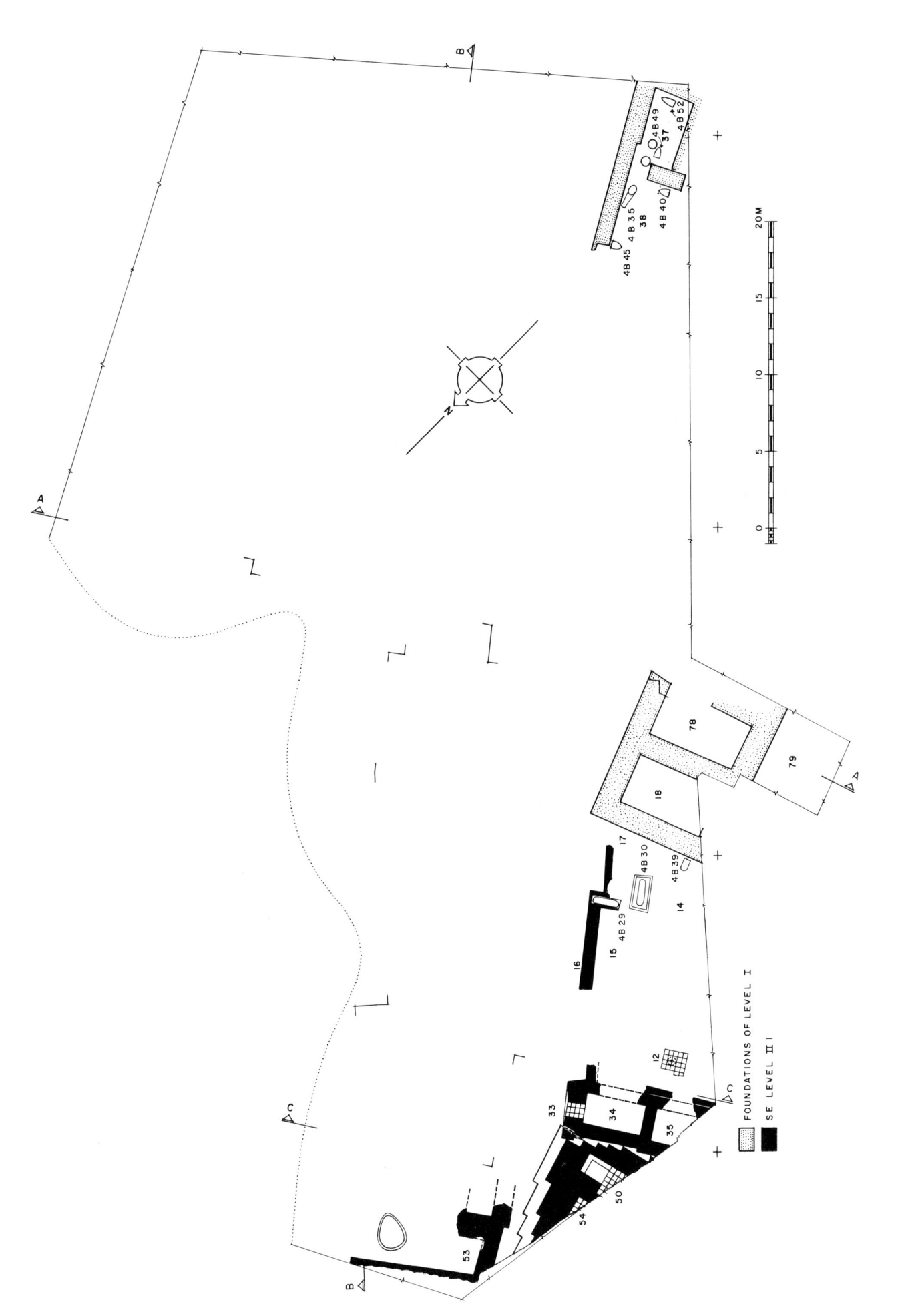

PLATE 39

PLAN OF SE LEVEL II 1

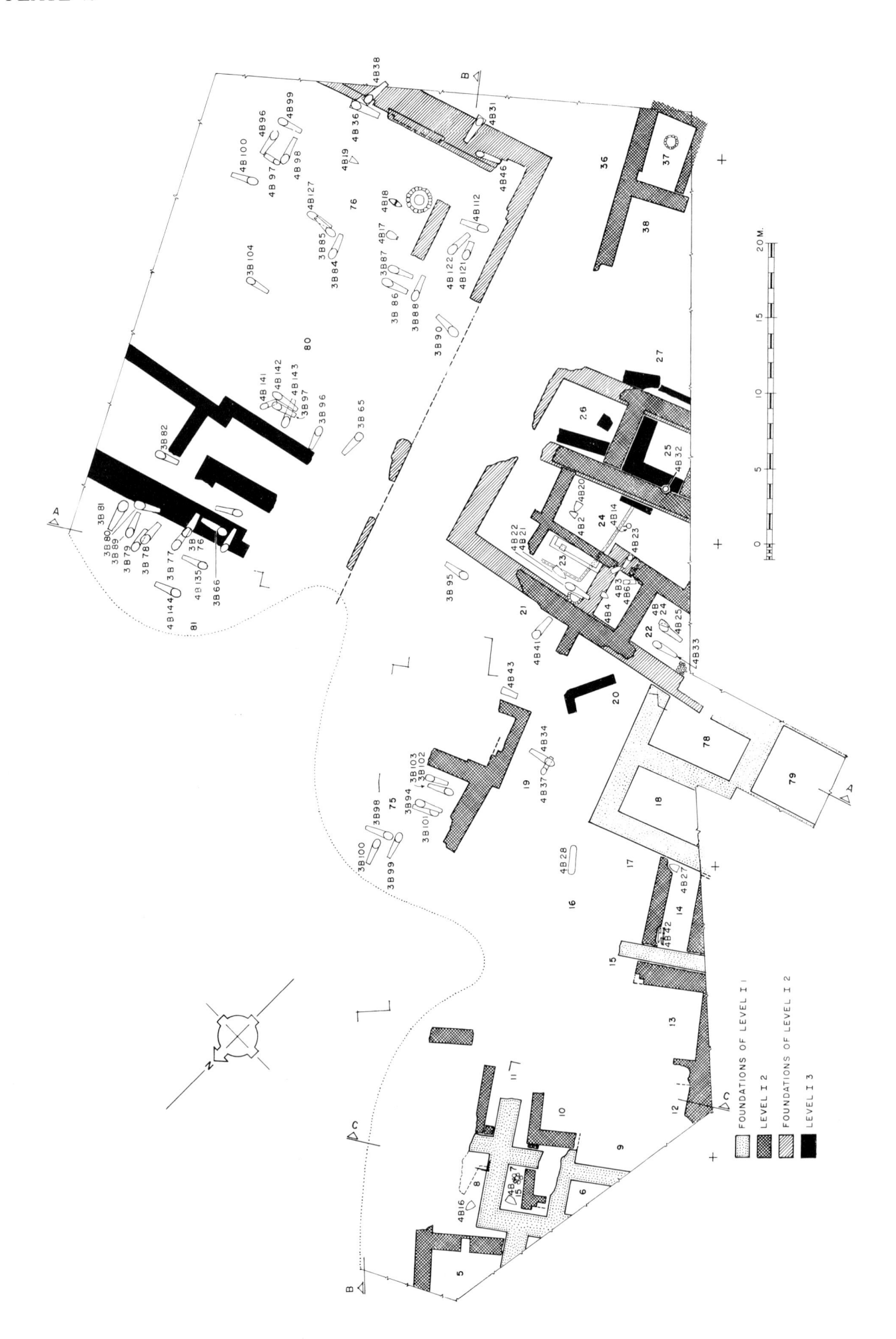

PLATE 40

PLAN OF SE LEVEL I 3–2

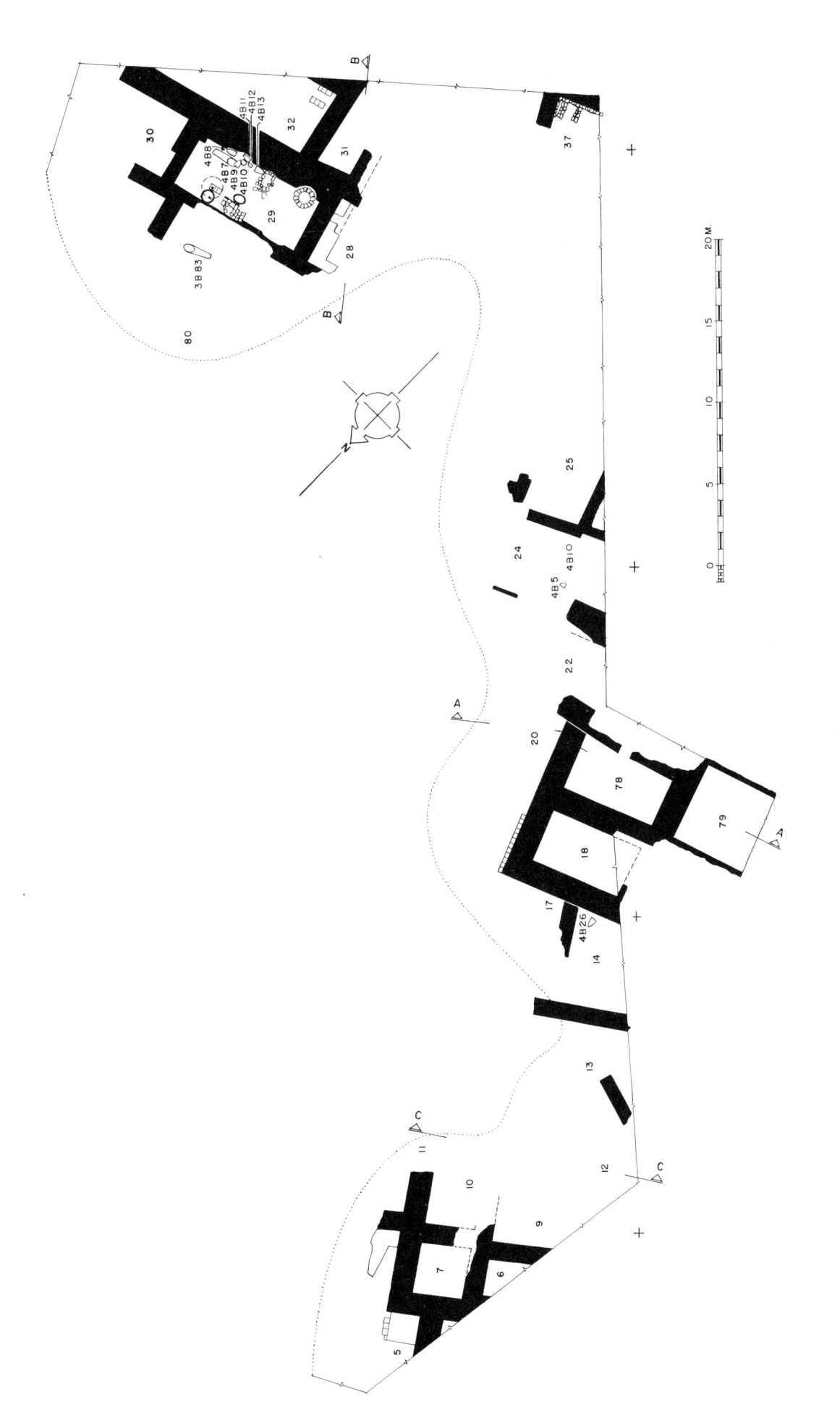

PLATE 41

PLAN OF SE LEVEL I 1

PLATE 42

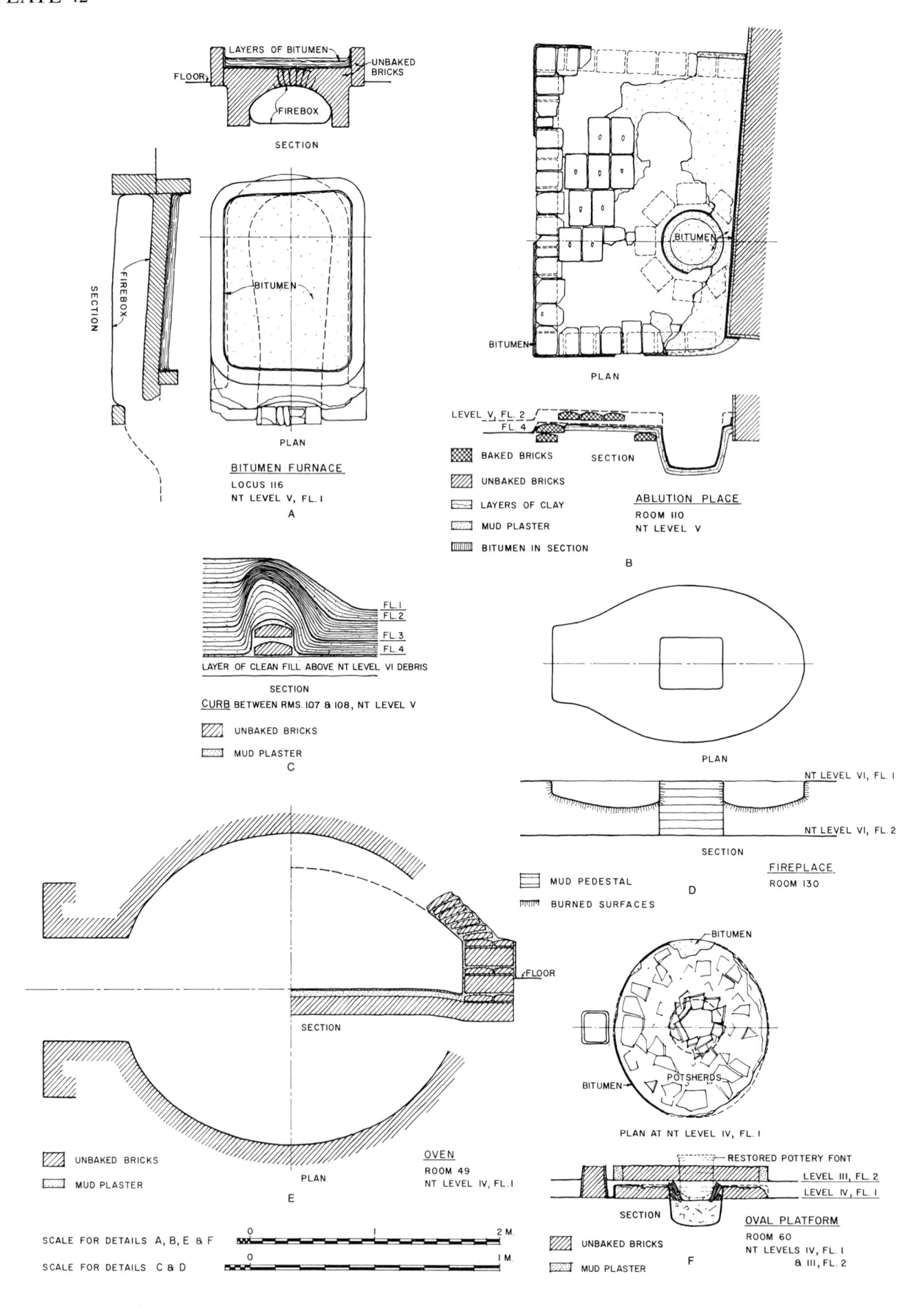

NT Structural Details

PLATE 43

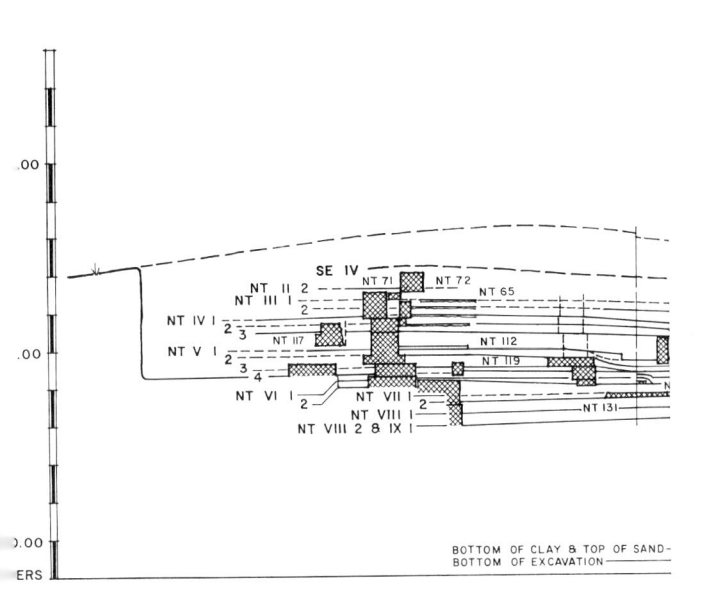

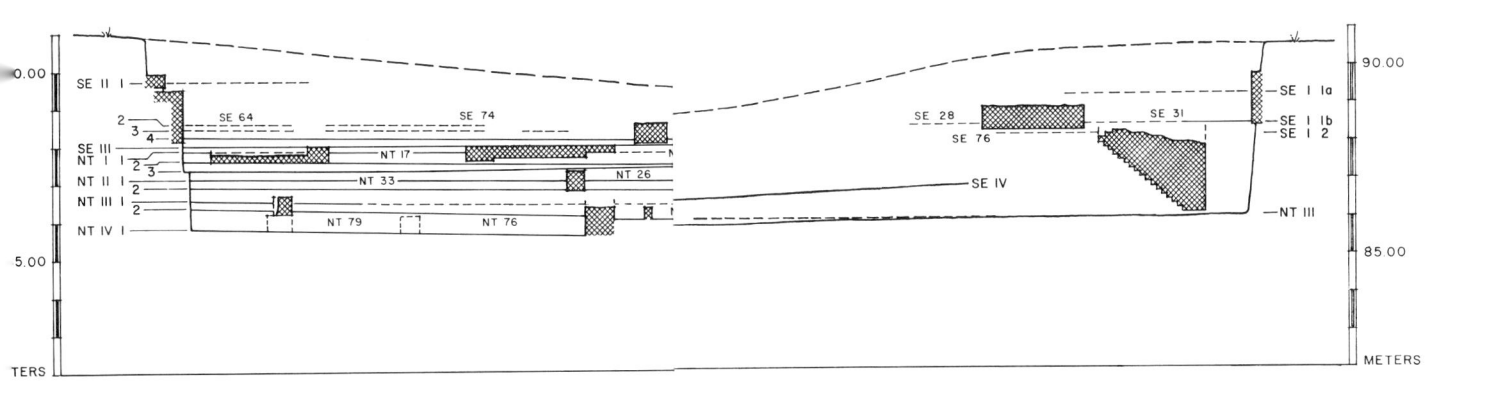

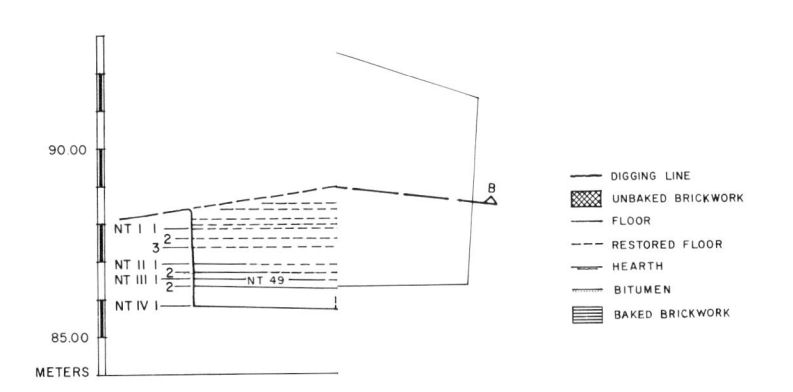

NO.	CAT. NO.	LOCUS	REMARKS
1	4P 305	NT 123 IX	Tan ware, wet-smoothed, fired buff inside and out near rim
2	4P 307	NT 123 IX	Tan ware, buff slip. See *OIP* LXIII, D.535.542, 545.542
3	4P 308	NT 131 IX	Surfaces buff, not well smoothed. With this, another similar vessel with uninterrupted ridge on inner bottom
4	4P 294	NT 121 IX	Tan ware, wet-smoothed; string-cut base
5	4P 310	NT 133 VIII 1	Tan ware, buff slip. See *OIP* LXIII, B.664.520*b, c*
6	4P 309	NT 133 VIII 1	Tan ware, buff slip outside
7	4P 297	NT 107 VII	Tan ware, wet-smoothed; set into altar step
8	4P 292	NT 120 VII	Tan ware, wet-smoothed, fired buff on one side, lower part scraped
9	4P 268	NT 68 IV 1	Dark gray, horizontal, spaced burnish
10	4P 284	NT 107 VII 1	Tan ware, wet-smoothed; string-cut base
11	4P 285	NT IV 1	Tan ware, wet-smoothed, comb-incised zigzags, bitumen-smeared to mend base
12	3P 615	NT IV 2 or 1	Tan ware, buff slip

NO.	CAT. NO.	LOCUS	REMARKS
1	4 P 305	NT 123 IX	Tan ware, wet-smoothed, fired buff inside and out near rim
2	4 P 307	NT 123 IX	Tan ware, buff slip. See *OIP* LXIII, D.535.542, 545.542
3	4 P 308	NT 131 IX	Surfaces buff, not well smoothed. With this, another similar vessel with uninterrupted ridge on inner bottom
4	4 P 294	NT 121 IX	Tan ware, wet-smoothed; string-cut base
5	4 P 310	NT 133 VIII 1	Tan ware, buff slip. See *OIP* LXIII, B.664.520*b, c*
6	4 P 309	NT 133 VIII 1	Tan ware, buff slip outside
7	4 P 297	NT 107 VII	Tan ware, wet-smoothed; set into altar step
8	4 P 292	NT 120 VII	Tan ware, wet-smoothed, fired buff on one side, lower part scraped
9	4 P 268	NT 68 IV 1	Dark gray, horizontal, spaced burnish
10	4 P 284	NT 107 VII 1	Tan ware, wet-smoothed; string-cut base
11	4 P 285	NT IV 1	Tan ware, wet-smoothed, comb-incised zigzags, bitumen-smeared to mend base
12	3 P 615	NT IV 2 or 1	Tan ware, buff slip

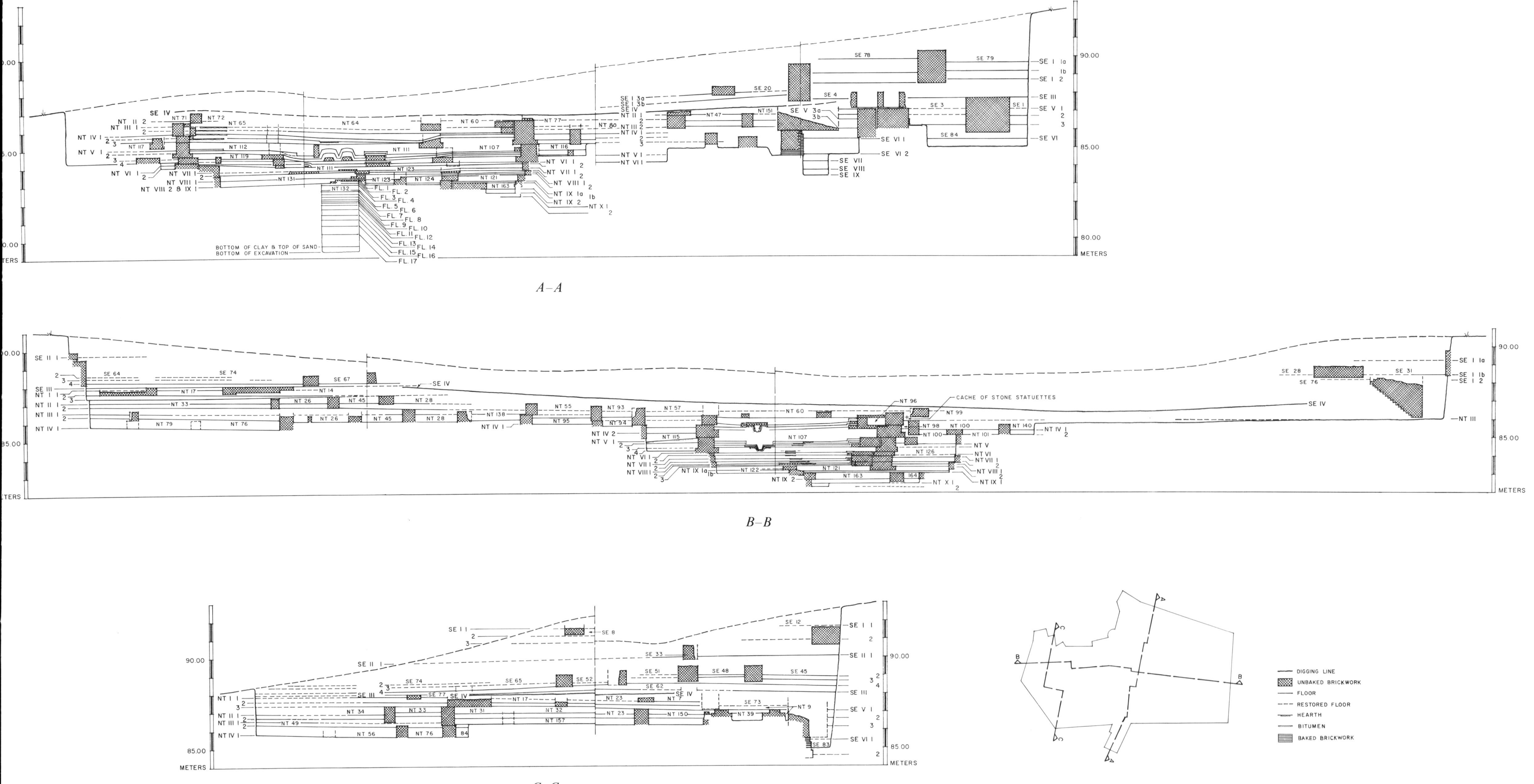

A–A

B–B

C–C

NT and SE Sections A–A, B–B, and C–C

PLATE 44

POTTERY FROM NT LEVELS. SCALES, 1:5, (2, 3, 6, 7, 11) AND 2:5

NO.	CAT. NO.	LOCUS	REMARKS
1, 3	3P 621	NT 165 IV	Top view and section-elevation; tan ware, buff slip under a light red wash strong on body and thin on shoulder and neck; incised decoration on shoulder. See *OIP* LXIII, C.526.471*f*
2	4P 262	NT 83 IV 1	Tan ware, buff slip; handle w. 2.1 cm., oval section. See *OIP* LXIII, B.516.271
4	3P 529	NT 96 IV	Tan ware, buff slip; one of nine similar vessels buried in altar; their measurements at rim d. 11.8–14.0, shoulder ridge d. 18.3–21.5 and h. 23.2–30.2, handle w. 3.4–4.8 and h. 3.0–4.4 cm.
5	3P 591	NT 60 V 1 (probably buried from IV)	Tan ware, buff slip
6	3P 537	NT 96 IV	One of three similar bowls used as lids for vessels (see Pl. 45:4); d. 15, h. 9.5–10.2 cm.

PLATE 45

POTTERY FROM NT LEVELS. SCALES, 1:5 (1, 3, 5) AND 2:5

NO.	CAT. NO.	LOCUS	REMARKS
1	3P 622	NT 98 IV 1	Tan ware, buff slip
2	3P 568	NT 69 III 1	Light yellow-brown ware, wet-smoothed; two more examples like this were found. See *UE* II, Pl. 264, No. 209*b* and *OIP* LXIII, C.527.362
3		NT 60 IV 1	Tan ware, wet-smoothed, bitumen-smeared; sherds of font vessel found on oval platform, see Pl. 42*F*. Earlier font vessel had high band rim, rope ridges
4	4P 264	NT 80 III 2	Tan ware, wet-smoothed
5	4P 257	NT 55 III 1	Tan ware, buff slip
6	4P 286	NT 48 II 2	Tan ware, buff slip
7	3P 564	NT 69 III 1	Tan ware, wet-smoothed
8	3P 616	NT 77 III 2	Tan ware, wet-smoothed. See *OIP* LXIII, B.533.230, 601.530, 652.500
9	4P 242	NT 3 III 1	Tan ware, light bright-red slip outside with vertical, close burnish. See *OIP* LXIII, B.556.540 and *Kish "A,"* Pl. LIV:57

PLATE 46

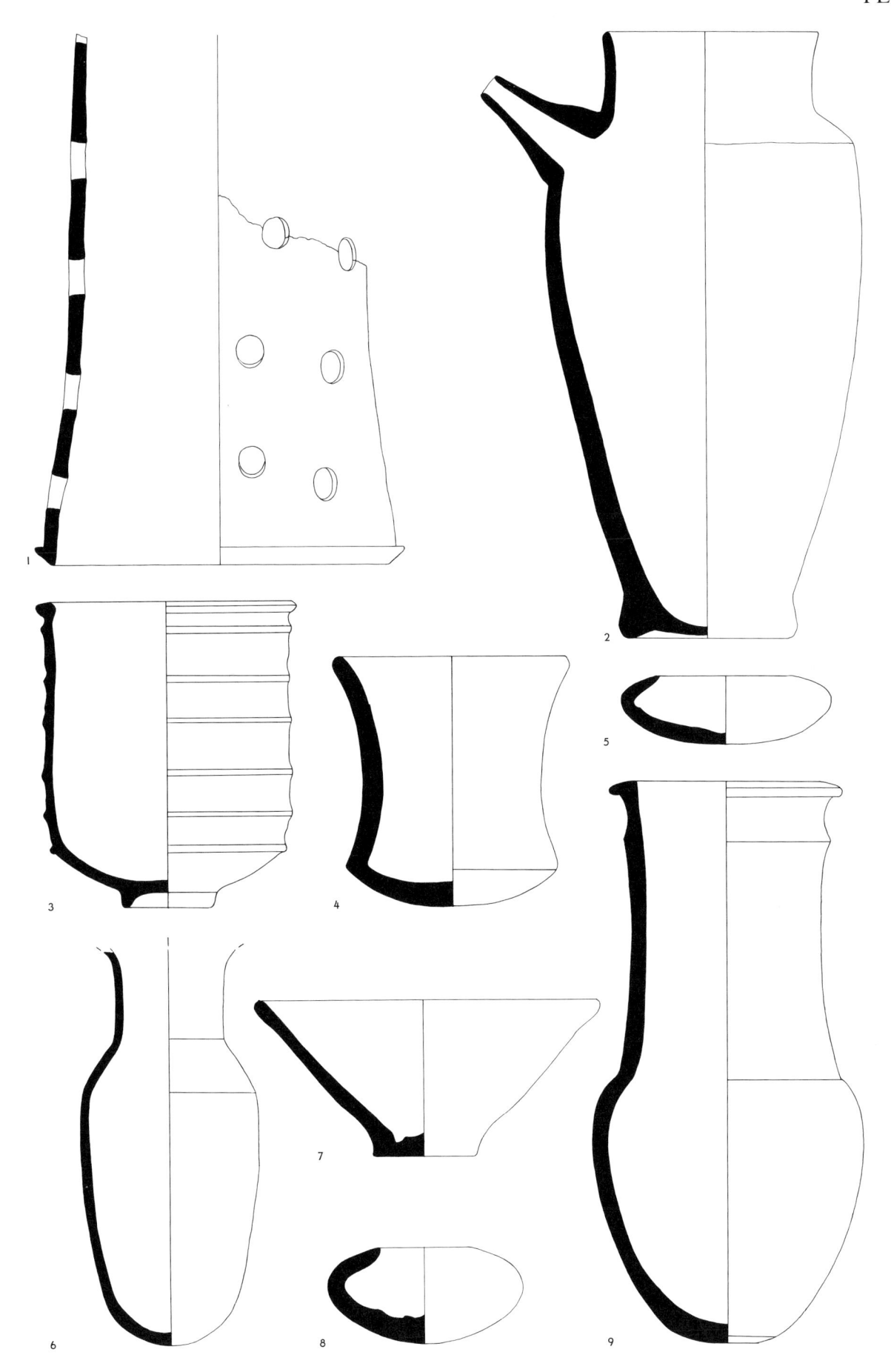

POTTERY FROM NT LEVELS. SCALES, 2:25 (3), 1:5 (6), AND 2:5

NO.	CAT. NO.	LOCUS	REMARKS
1	4P 290	NT 3 II 1	Greenish, overfired and warped
2	4P 291	NT 109 VI 2	Tan ware, buff slip; bottom full of bitumen
3	4P 221	NT 5 I 2	Steel gray ware, incisions chalk-filled
4	4P 275	NT I 1	Tan ware, buff slip
5	4P 240	NT 3 III 1	Tan ware, wet-smoothed
6	4P 295	NT 131 VIII	Buff stone; d. 13.0, h. 3.9 cm.
7	4P 219	NT I	Tan ware, buff slip outside. See *OIP* LXIII, C.053.312
8	3P 410	Debris above NT temple	Light whitish-gray stone
9	3N 512	NT 144 IV 1	Whitish-buff limestone
10	3P 401	Debris above NT temple	Pale brown stone
11	4NT 67	NT I	Sherd of white stone; inscribed; see p. 94

PLATE 47

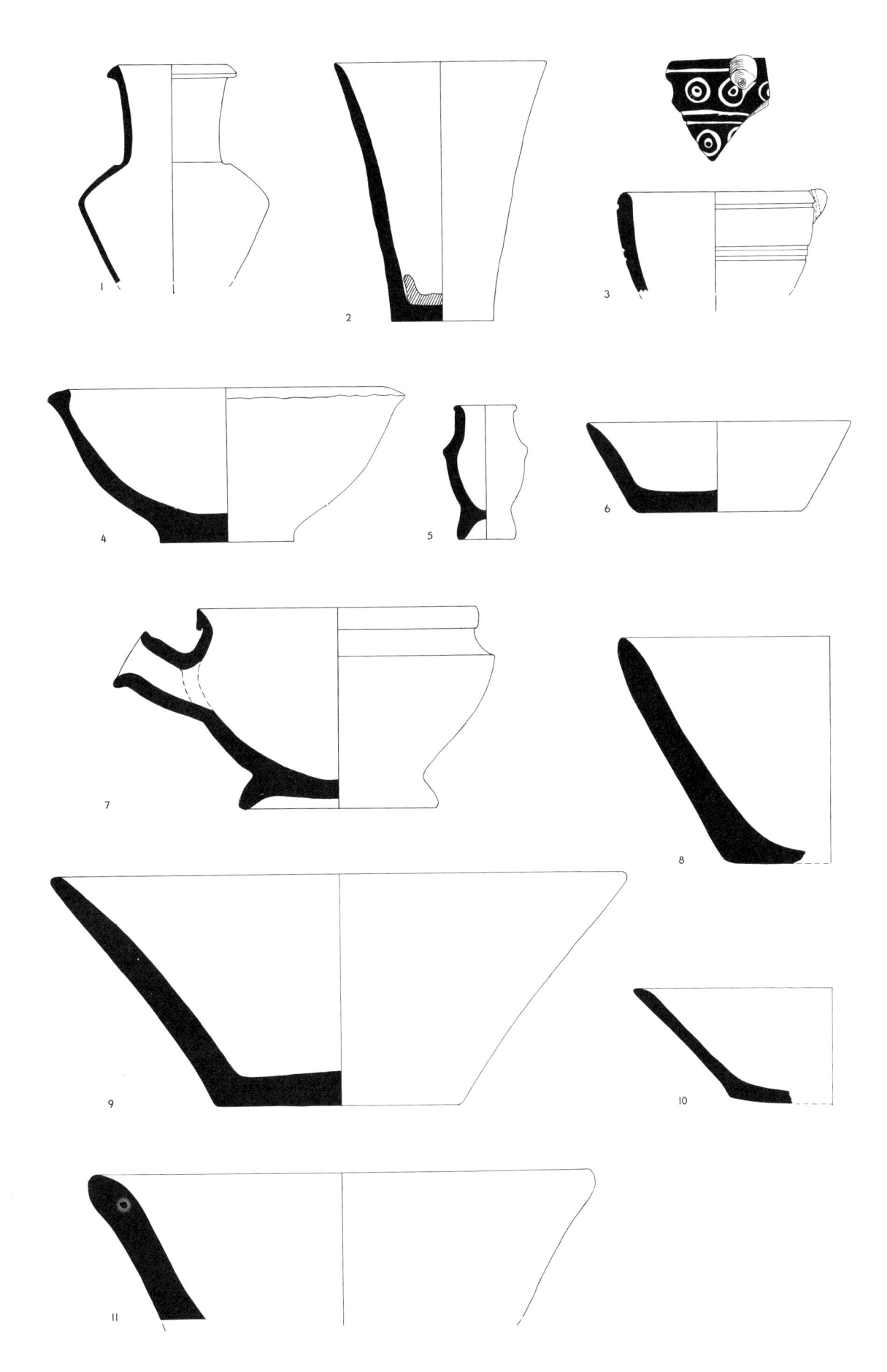

Pottery and Stone Vessels from NT Levels. Scales, 1:5 (1, 2) and 2:5

NO.	CAT. NO.	LOCUS	REMARKS
1	4NT 69	NT 33 II 2	Buff stone; inscribed; see pp. 76, 91
2	4P 261	NT 77 IV 1	Cream-colored limestone
3	4NT 1	SE I 2	Blackish-green steatite; inscribed; see pp. 49, 77, 92
4		NT 132 fl. 13	A series of vats or big bowls with diameters ranging from 30 cm. to more than 50 cm. is illustrated by Pl. 48:4–12.
5		NT 132 fl. 13	
6		NT 131 IX	
7		NT 121 IX	
8		NT 121 IX	
9		NT 132 fl. 11	
10		NT 41 II	
11		NT III 1	
12		NT 41 II	

PLATE 48

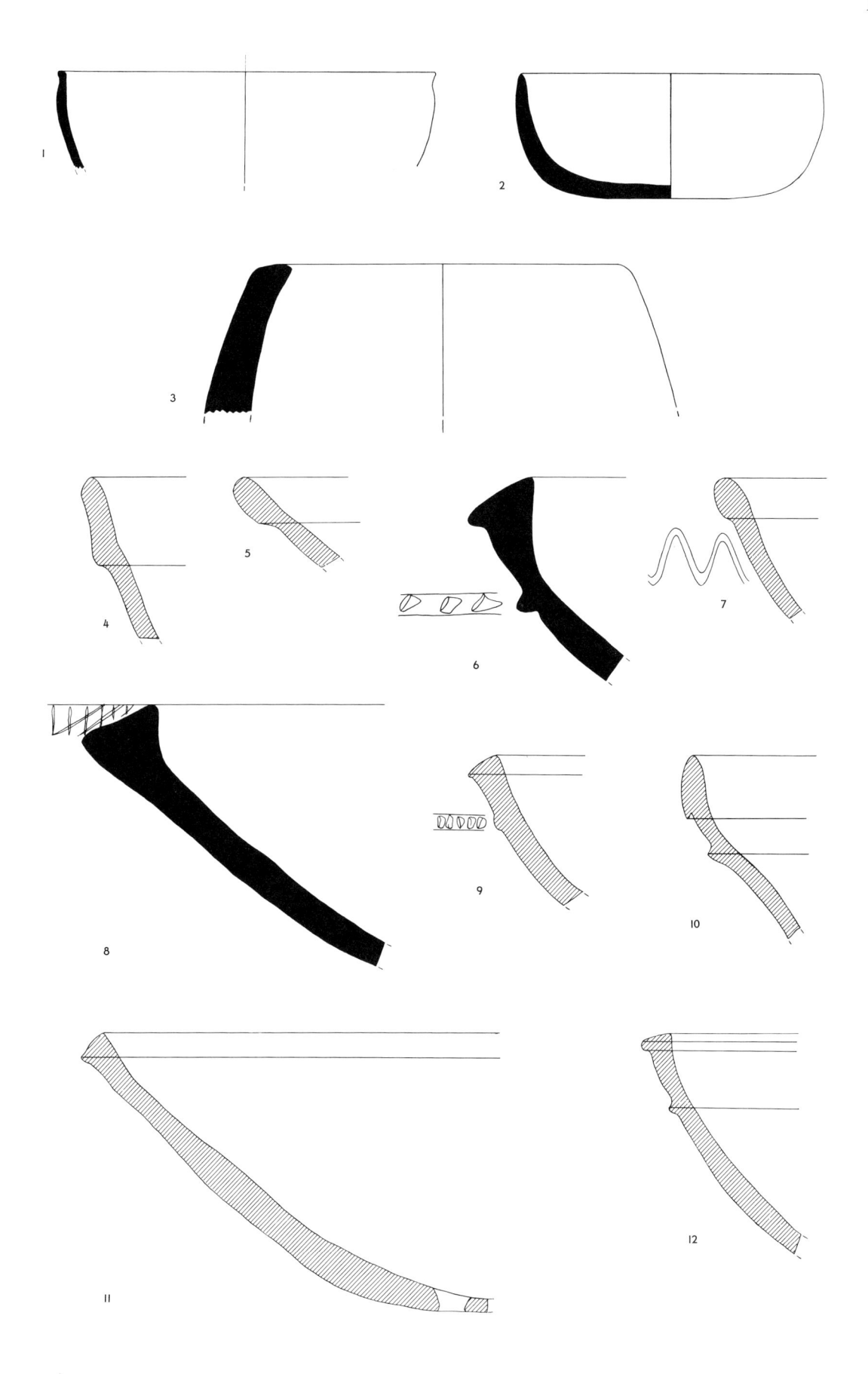

Pottery and Stone Vessels from NT Levels. Scale, 2:5

NO.	CAT. NO.	LOCUS	TYPE	RANGE AND FREQUENCY OF TYPE	REMARKS
1	4P 299	SE 85	73	3 in SE 85 (well)	Crudely made, solid or hollow base;
2	4P 300	SE 85	73		bottom of the plate formed by plugging the
3	4P 301	SE 85	73		narrow neck at top of the hollow base with a lump of clay. See Vol. I, Pl. 28:12
4	3P 285	SE 4 VI			Tan ware, buff slip
5	3P 281	SE 4 VI			Tan ware, buff slip
6		SE V 3			A variant of type 46. See Vol. I, Pl. 98:11–13
7		SE V 2			A variant of type 46. See Vol. I, Pl. 98:11–13
8		SE V 2			A variant of type 45B. See Vol. I, Pl. 98:4
9		SE V 2			A variant of type 46. See Vol. I, Pl. 98:11–13
10		SE V 2			A variant of type 43B. See Vol. I, Pl. 97:10
11		SE V 2			Pale brown with a very fine, smooth surface
12		SE V 2			Tan ware, white glaze; thick near rim with many small bubbles outside, thick glaze and bubbles more evenly distributed inside

PLATE 49

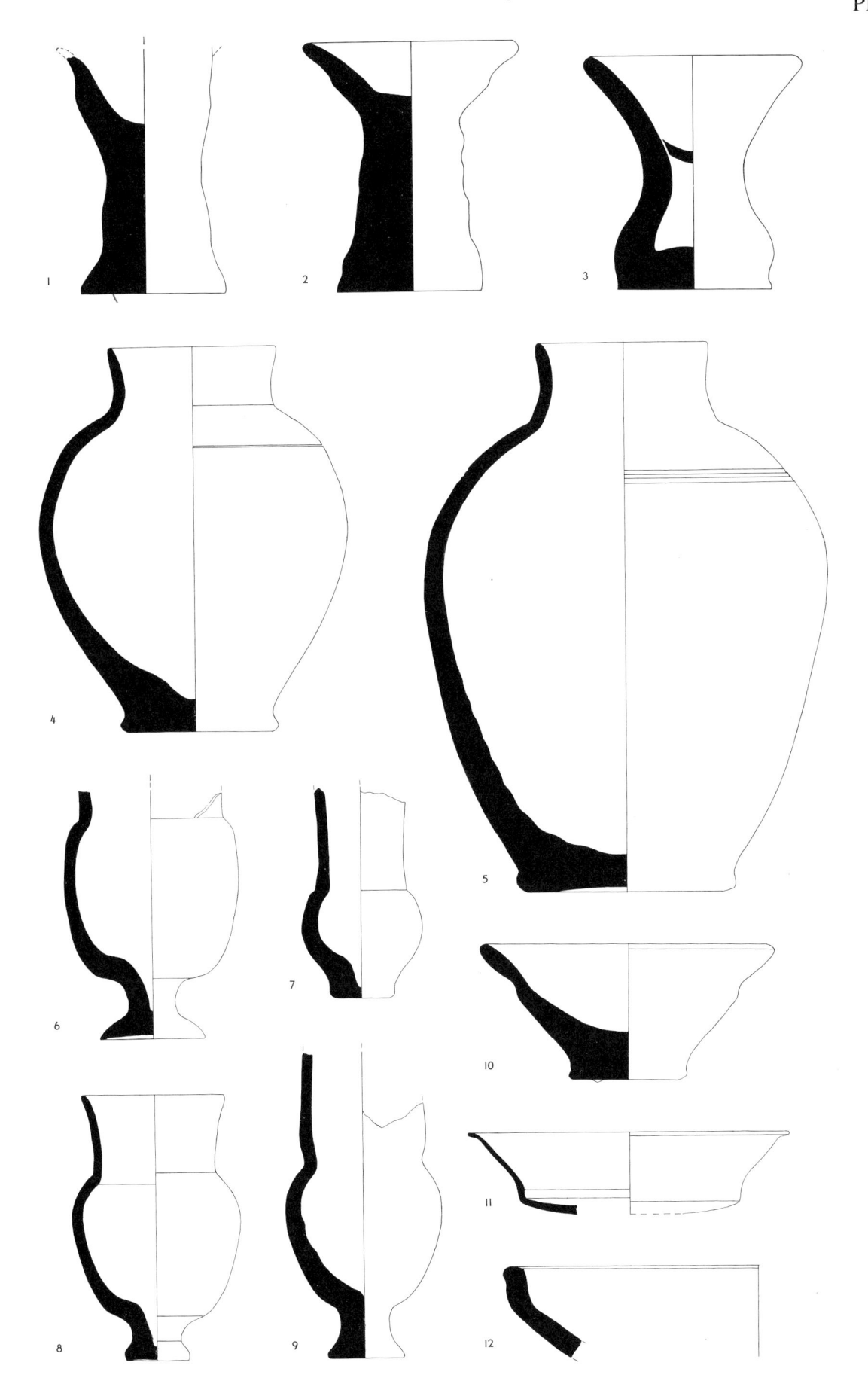

POTTERY FROM SE LEVELS. SCALE, 2:5

NO.	CAT. NO.	LOCUS	TYPE	RANGE AND FREQUENCY OF TYPE	REMARKS
1		SE V 2			Tan ware, buff slip
2		SE V 2			Buff ware, plain, irregular and poorly made; string-cut base
3	3P 277	SE V 2			Tan, very soft and flaky ware, buff slip outside and inside neck
4		SE V 2			A variant of type 47. See Vol. I, Pl. 98:14–16
5	3P 278	SE V 2			Tan ware, buff slip under traces of a light red wash or stain
6	3P 510	SE V 2			Tan ware, buff slip
7	3P 267	SE III 1			Tan ware, buff slip
8	3P 288	Unnumbered burial intrusive into SE 79 II	67		See Vol. I, Pl. 103:15–17
9	3P 341	SE V			Buff ware, plain, incised decoration
10	4P 102	SE II burial 4B 65A	67		See Vol. I, Pl. 103:15–17
11	3N 208	SE I burial 3B 48	67		See Vol. I, Pl. 103:15–17
12	4P 116	SE IV	74	3 in SE IV, 2 in SE III, 2 in SE II, 1 in SE I and 1 each in burials 4B 59 and 86	Usual ware, buff slip

PLATE 50

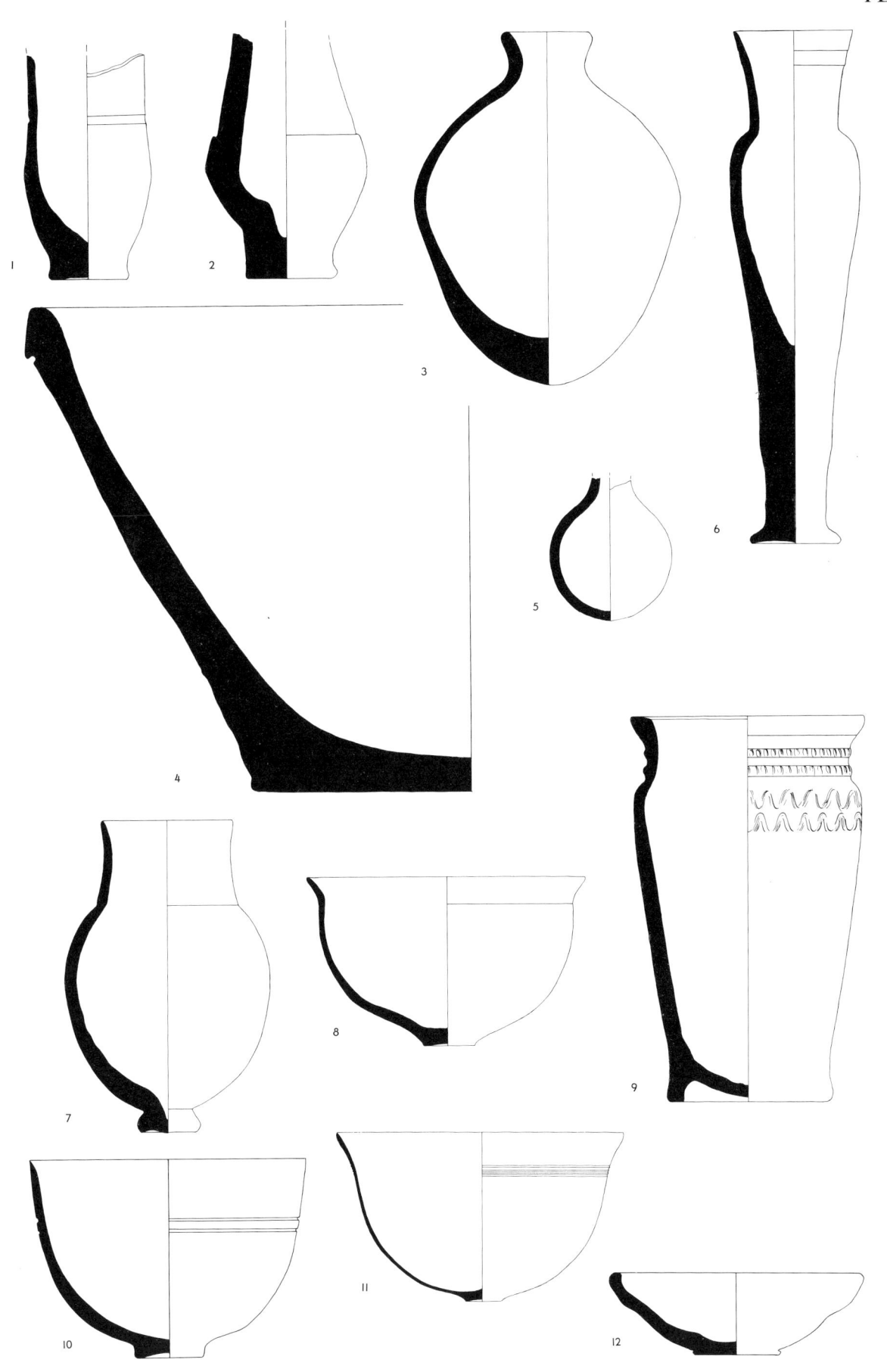

POTTERY FROM SE LEVELS. SCALE, 2:5

NO.	CAT. NO.	LOCUS	TYPE	RANGE AND FREQUENCY OF TYPE	REMARKS
1	4P 73	Unnumbered burial intrusive into SE 50 II 2	75	1 in SE II, 1 in SE II or I, 3 in unnumbered burials, 1 in burial 4B 67	Usually buff ware, plain or slipped. Two like 4P 47 (Pl. 51:2), rest with wide cylindrical neck, everted rim; h. 7.1–14, d. 7–12.5 cm.
2	4P 47	SE 44 II 2	75		
3	3N 211	SE I 1 burial 3B 40	75		
4	4P 75	Unnumbered burial intrusive into SE 50 II 2	75		
5	4P 87	SE 26 I 3	76	1 in SE I, 2 in SE II	Buff surface; h. 6.2–7.7, d. 4.9–6.4 cm.
6	4P 162	SE 71 II 4	76		
7	4P 74	Unnumbered burial intrusive into SE 50 II 2	70		See Vol. I, Pl. 104:11–18
8	4P 85	SE III	56		See Vol. I, Pl. 100:21–23
9	4P 51	SE 41 II 2	70		Buff and unglazed. See Vol. I, Pl. 104:11–18
10	3N 499	SE I burial 3B 93	70		Pale gray-blue glaze, three lug handles. See Vol. I, Pl. 104:11–18
11	4P 33	SE II 1	70		Buff and unglazed. See Vol. I, Pl. 104:11–18
12	4P 159	SE 71 II 4	59		Buff slip. See Vol. I, Pl. 101:15–20
13	4P 210	SE III or II burial 4B 104	59		Buff slip. See Vol. I, Pl. 101:15–20
14	4P 64	SE 42 II 4	72		Glazed. See Vol. I, Pl. 105:7
15	4P 204	SE II burial 4B 93	59		Buff slip. See Vol. I, Pl. 101:15–20
16	4P 209	SE III or II burial 4B 104	72		Glazed. See Vol. I, Pl. 105:7

PLATE 51

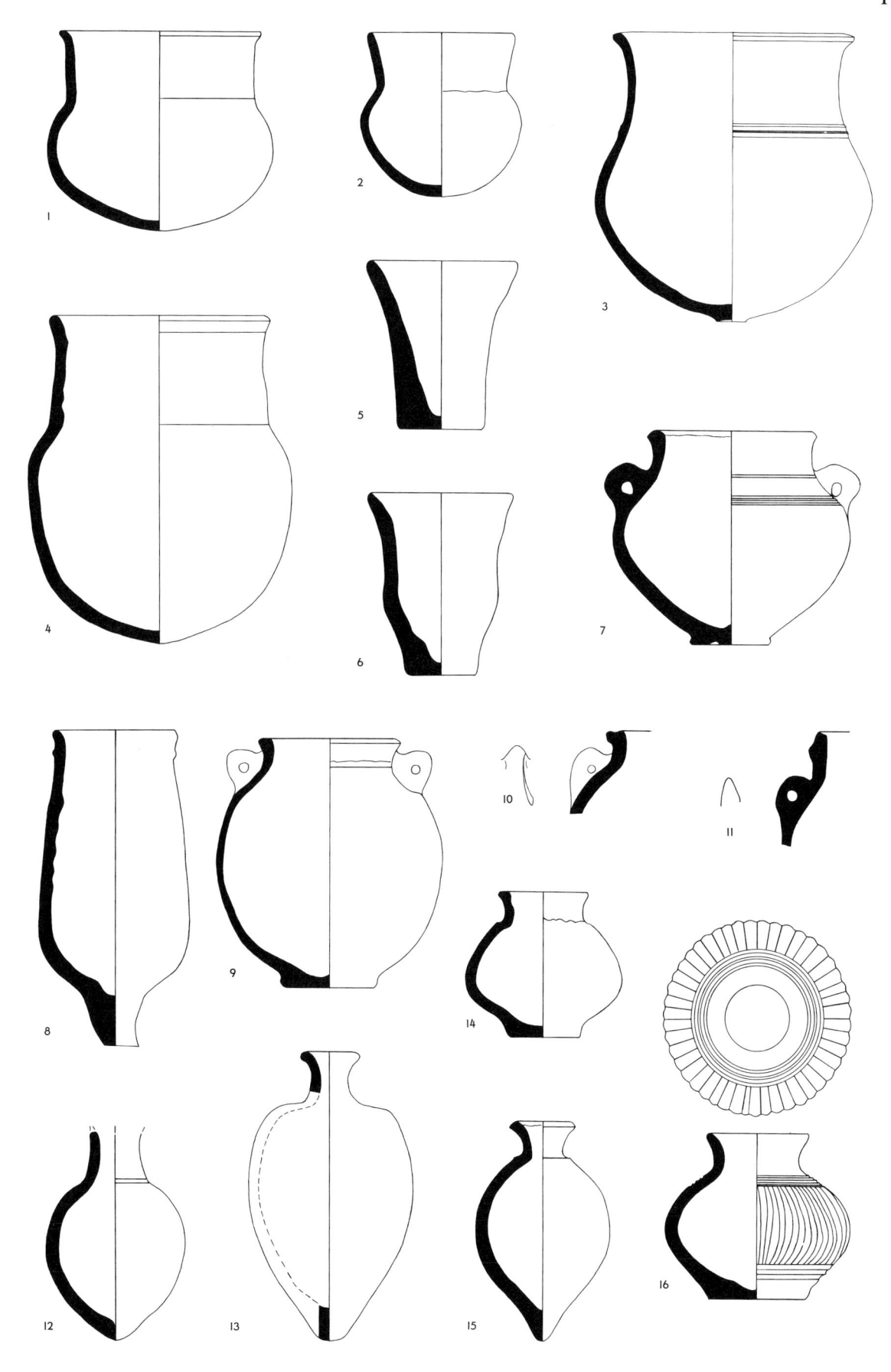

POTTERY FROM SE LEVELS. SCALE, 2:5

NO.	CAT. NO.	LOCUS	REMARKS
1	4P 18	SE 15 I 2	Type 60. See Vol. I, Pl. 102:1–9. Greek(?) inscription: probably ΔΙΦΙΛΟΥ
2	4P 101	SE II burial 4B 65*B*	Buff slip. Type 59. See Vol. I, Pl. 101:15–20
3	4P 12	SE I 2	Buff, light-blue glaze
4	4P 52	SE III 1	Buff surface. Type 63. See Vol. I, Pl. 102:18–19
5	4P 121	SE 56 III 2	White glaze, yellow on neck. Type 63. See Vol. I, Pl. 102:18–19
6	4P 15	SE I 1	Bluish-gray glaze
7	4P 84	SE 20 I 3	Tan ware, buff slip inside. One of two similar saucers; h. 4.7–5.3, d. 13.7–16.2 cm.
8	4P 7	SE II 1	Buff ware, plain
9	4P 16	SE surface	Buff, light-blue glaze
10	4P 45	SE II 1	Buff surface
11	4P 44	SE II 1	Tan ware, buff slip
12	4P 199	SE III	Buff surface
13	4P 256	SE III or II burial 4B 137	Tan ware, buff slip outside, incised line at shoulder
14	4P 2	SE 9 I 1	Buff, whitish-gray glaze
15	4P 25	SE I	Buff, pale gray slip
16	4P 20	SE III 2	Tan ware, buff slip

PLATE 52

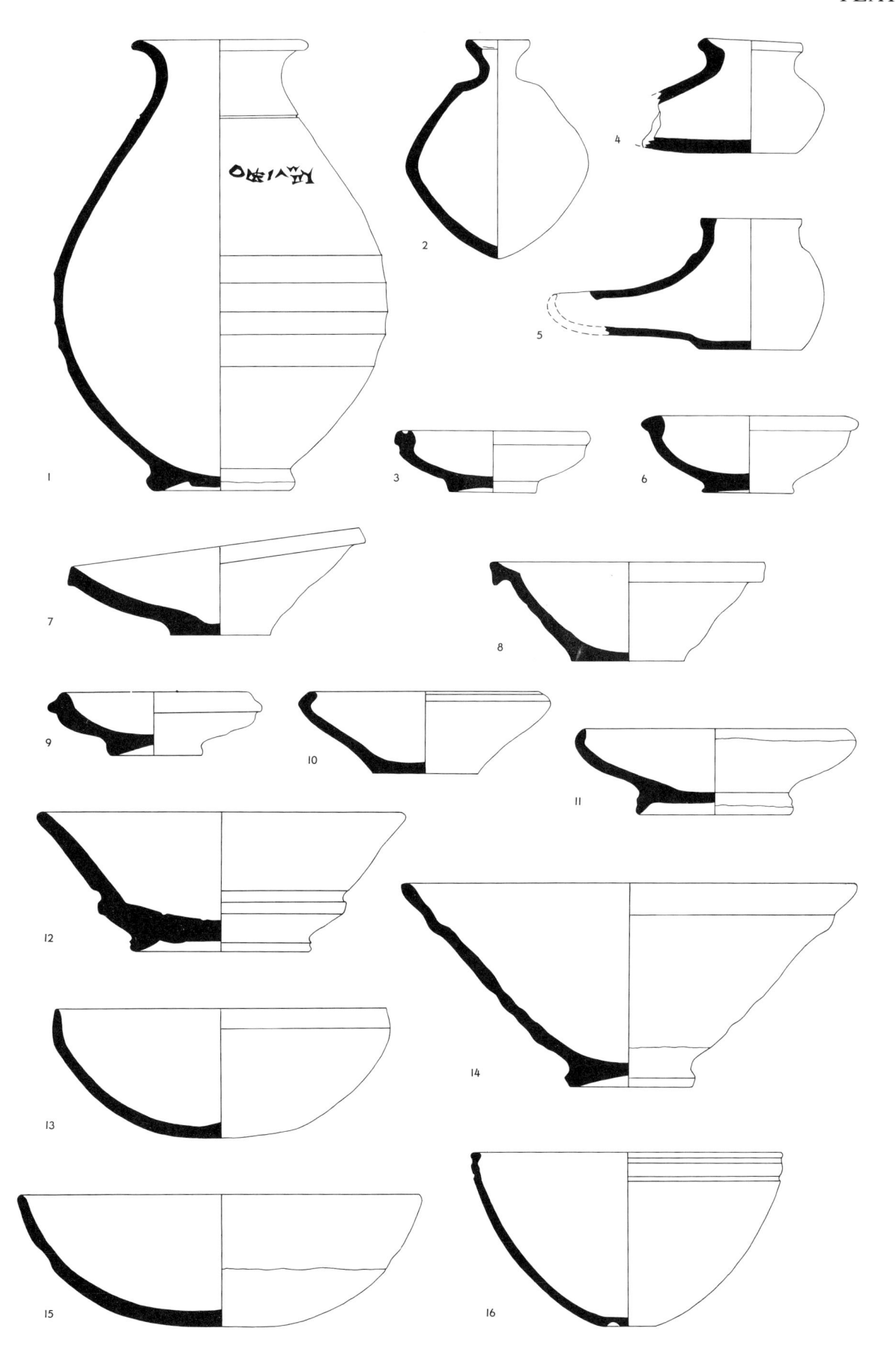

POTTERY FROM SE LEVELS. SCALE, 2:5

NO.	CAT. NO.	LOCUS	REMARKS
1	4P 230	SE III burial 4B 124	Tan ware, buff slip outside and inside rim
2	4P 49	SE 33 II 1	Tan ware, buff slip
3	4P 107	SE II burial 4B 65*B*	Gray ware, spaced horizontal burnish outside and inside
4	4P 30	SE II 2	Buff surface
5	4P 70	Unnumbered burial intrusive into SE 50 II 2	Buff surface
6	4P 71	Same as Pl. 53:5	Tan ware, buff slip
7	4P 72	Same as Pl. 53:5	Tan ware, plain
8	4P 172	SE 71 II	Buff ware, plain
9	3P 229	SE I 2	Tan ware, buff slip
10	4P 31	SE II 2	Tan ware, buff slip outside
11	4P 28	SE III	Buff surface
12	3P 228	SE I burial 3B 54	Greenish-buff, plain
13	4P 50	SE 41 II 2	Buff surface
14	4P 32	SE II 2	Buff, plain

PLATE 53

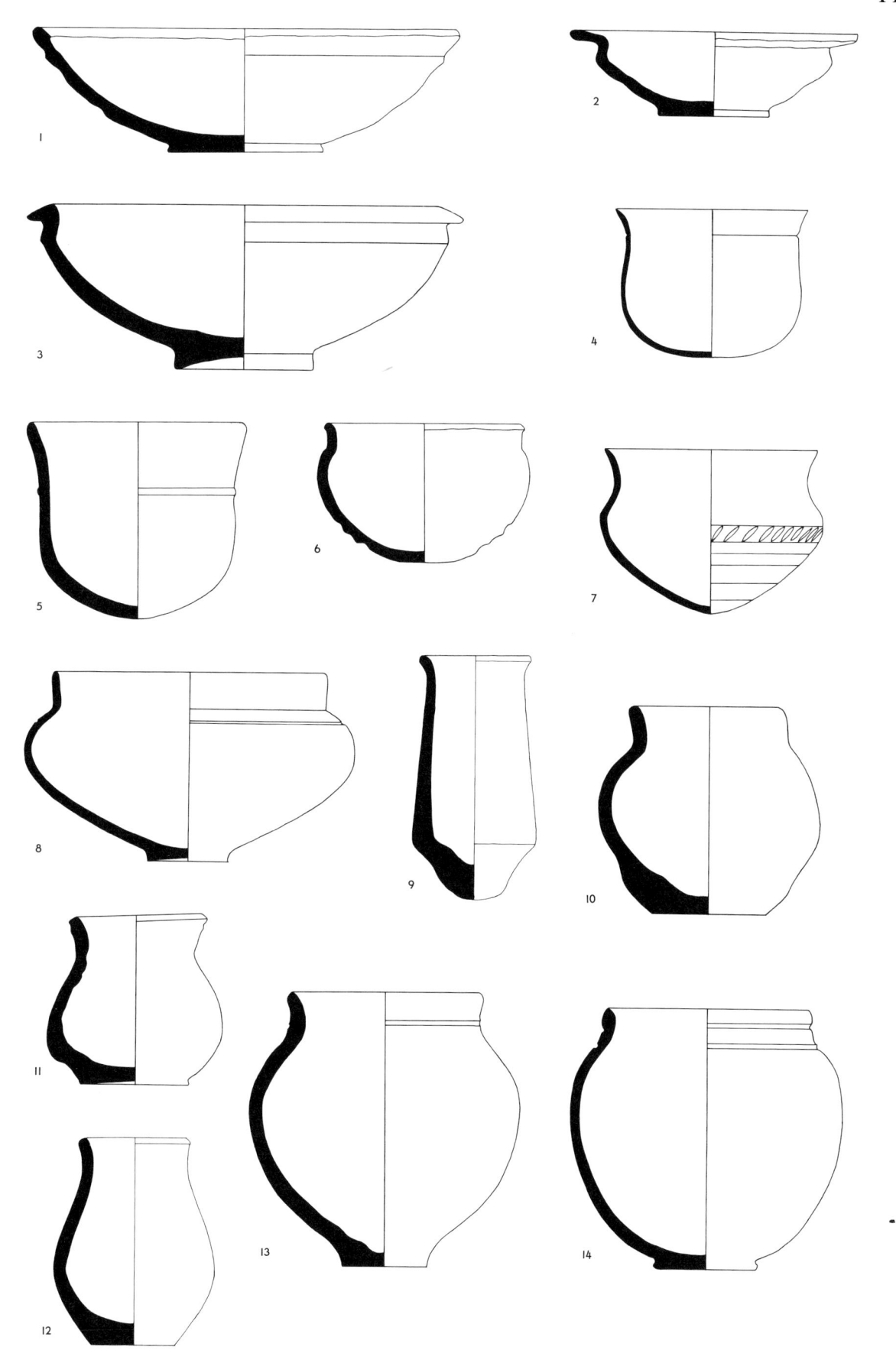

POTTERY FROM SE LEVELS. SCALE, 2:5

NO.	CAT. NO.	LOCUS	REMARKS
1	4P 54	SE 19 I 2	Drab buff, plain, incised line
2	4P 5	SE I 2	Buff, whitish-gray glaze
3	4P 222	SE III burial 4B 125	Buff surface
4	4P 65	SE 42 II 4	Buff, pale gray glaze
5	4P 8	SE surface	Buff, plain
6	4P 150	SE II burial 4B 83	Grayish glaze, dark green on neck
7	4P 197	SE II burial 4B 105	Buff surface
8	4P 186	SE III burial 4B 113	Blue-green glaze
9	4P 173	Intrusive into SE 71 II	Tan, plain
10	4P 163	SE II burial 4B 77	Buff surface. See Vol. I, Pl. 102:17

PLATE 54

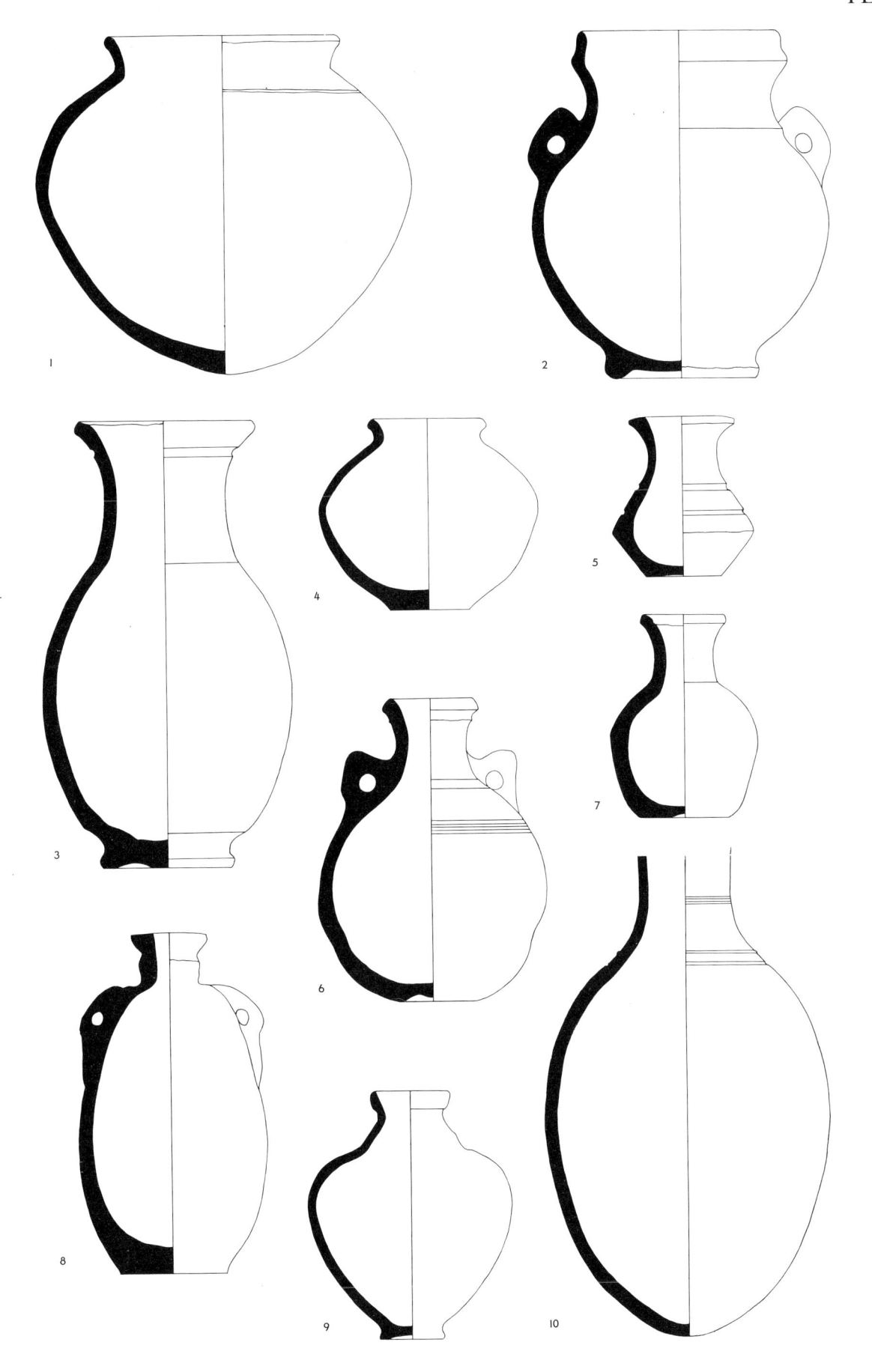

POTTERY FROM SE LEVELS. SCALES, 1:5 (9, 10) AND 2:5

NO.	CAT. NO.	LOCUS	REMARKS
1	3P 603	SE I burial 3B 93	Tan ware, buff slip
2	4P 106	SE II burial 4B 65*B*	Light gray surface
3	3P 613	SE II	Buff or tan ware, buff slip
4	3P 255	SE III	Beige, buff slip; two pairs of holes preserved
5	3N 489	SE I burial 3B 91	Alabaster
6	4P 143	SE II burial 4B 78	Buff surface, slight pouring lip; handle w. 2.1 cm.
7	4P 17	SE surface	Buff surface, handle w. 1.5 cm.
8	4P 220	SE dump	Tan ware, silver-white glaze; handle w. 0.8 cm.
9	4P 166	SE III	Buff or tan ware, buff slip
10	4P 59	SE III 1	Orange-tan ware, plain; handle w. 1.5 cm.

PLATE 55

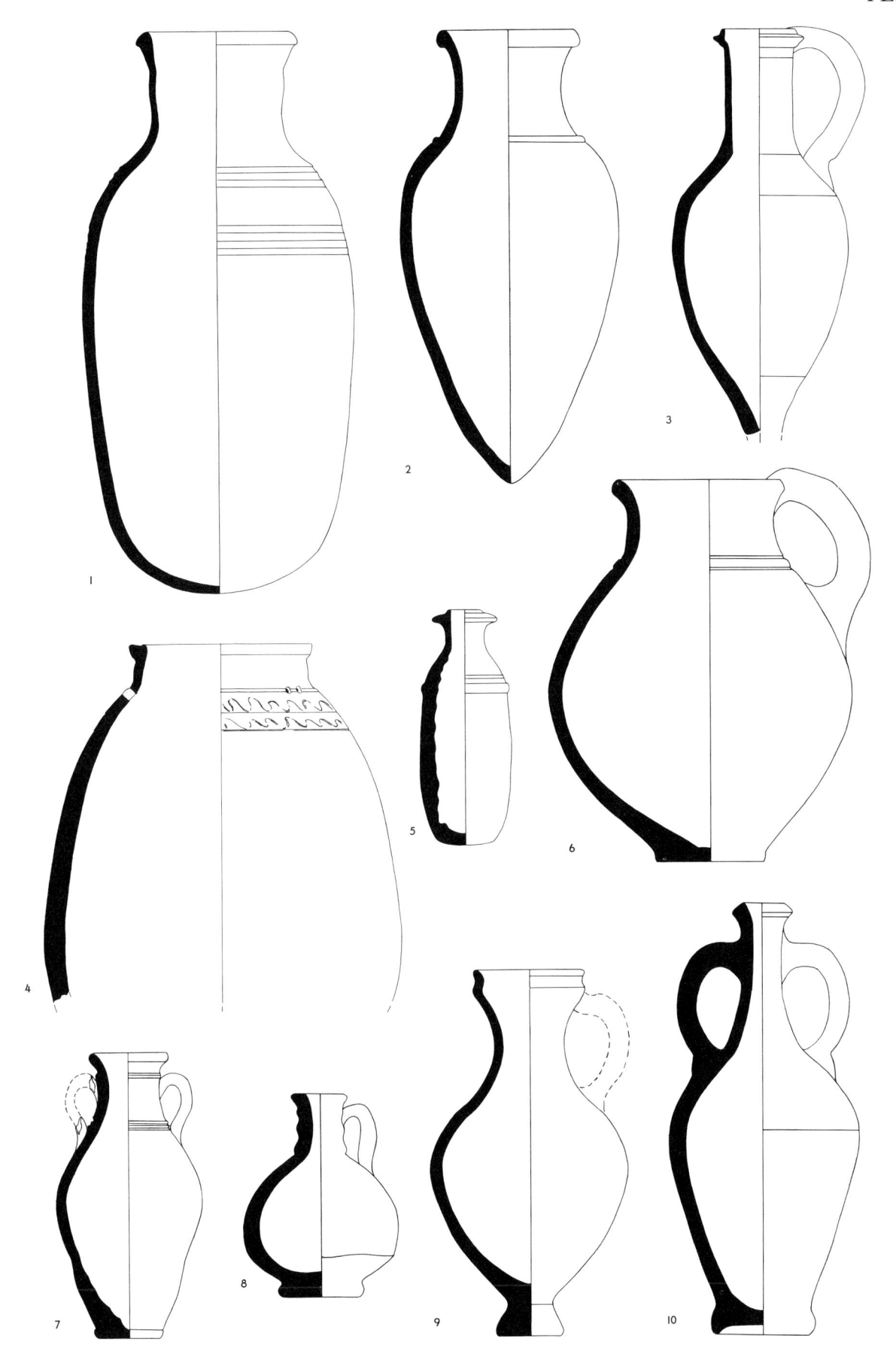

POTTERY FROM SE LEVELS. SCALES, 1:5 (4, 7) AND 2:5

NO.	CAT.NO.	LOCUS	REMARKS
1	4P 167	SE II 4	Buff surface, pouring lip
2	4P 10	Intrusive into SE I 2	Buff surface, slight pouring lip; handle w. 2.3 cm.
3	3N 492	SE I burial 3B 91	Alabaster
4	3N 365	SE (stratification uncertain)	Bronze, warped oval
5	4N 115	SE III burial 4B 119	Bronze. Drawing on right of section shows elevation of bottom with rosette and raised knob in center of rosette.
6		SE II burial 4B 74	Oval tub with handles
7		SE II burial 4B 90	Bowl, buff ware
8	4N 133	SE II burial 4B 77	Gray glass with white lines; pointed base
9	4P 139	SE III or II burial 4B 75	Handled lid of fine unbaked clay, with bowl similar to Pl. 56:7

PLATE 56

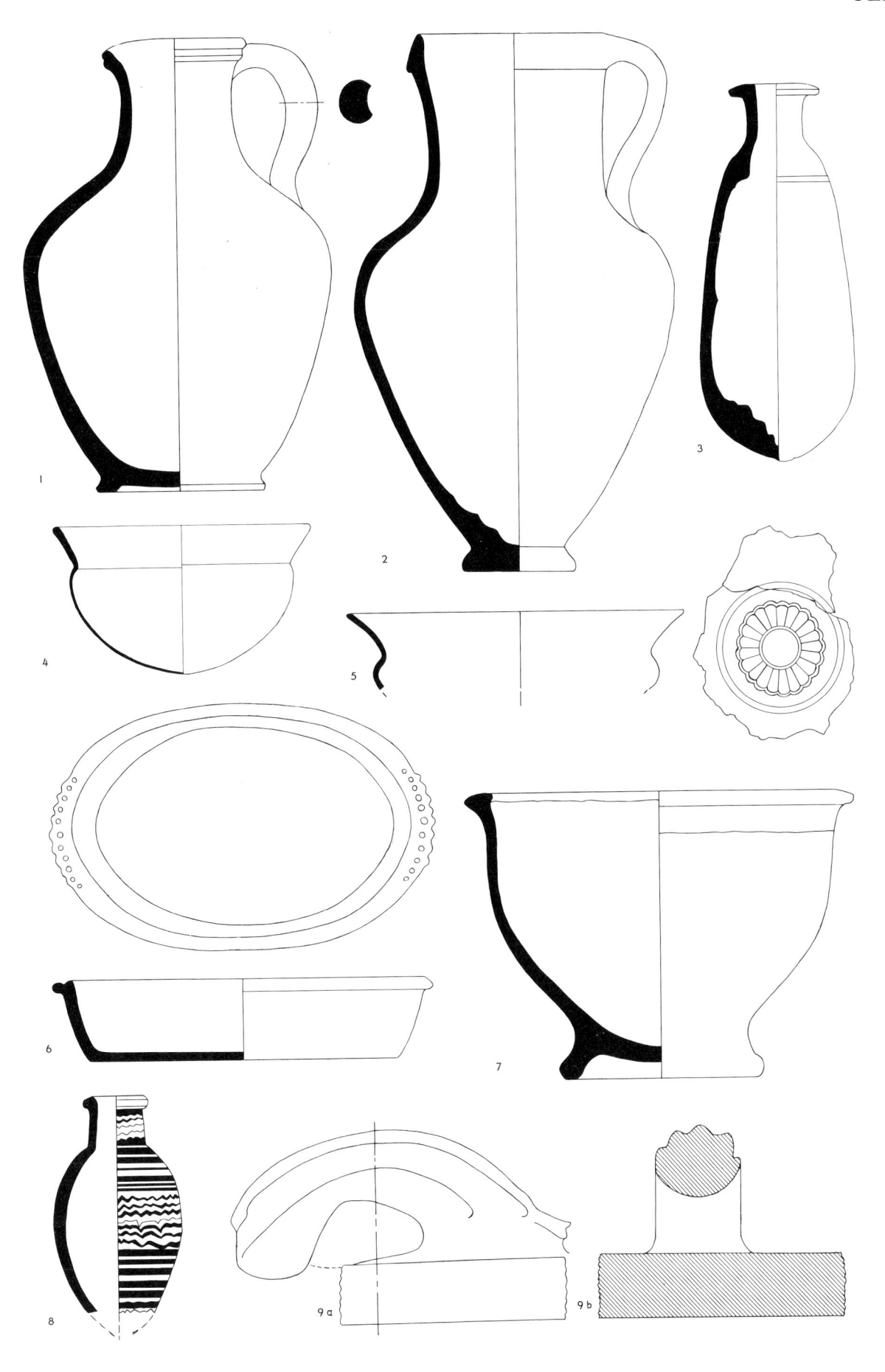

POTTERY, STONE, BRONZE, AND GLASS VESSELS FROM SE LEVELS.
SCALES, 1:10 (6), 1:5 (7), AND 2:5

NO.	CAT. NO.	LOCUS	REMARKS
1		Burial 4B 8	Pointed burial jar; tan ware, buff slip
2	4P 29	Burial 4B 1	Convex-base burial jar; plain buff, three strap handles
3	3N 479	SE surface	Light greenish-buff ware, blue-green glaze; strap handle with central groove, w. 2.9 cm.; incised design with vertical wavy line. Two more vessels of the same shape with blue glazes were found at the surface among the slipper coffins.
4		Burial 4B 10	Tan ware, buff surfaces; used as a cover for 4B 10; see Pl. 75:6
5		Burial 3B 65	Unglazed slipper coffin; soft and crumbly buff ware
6	4P 55	Unnumbered infant burial intrusive into SE 38 II	Convex-base burial jar

PLATE 57

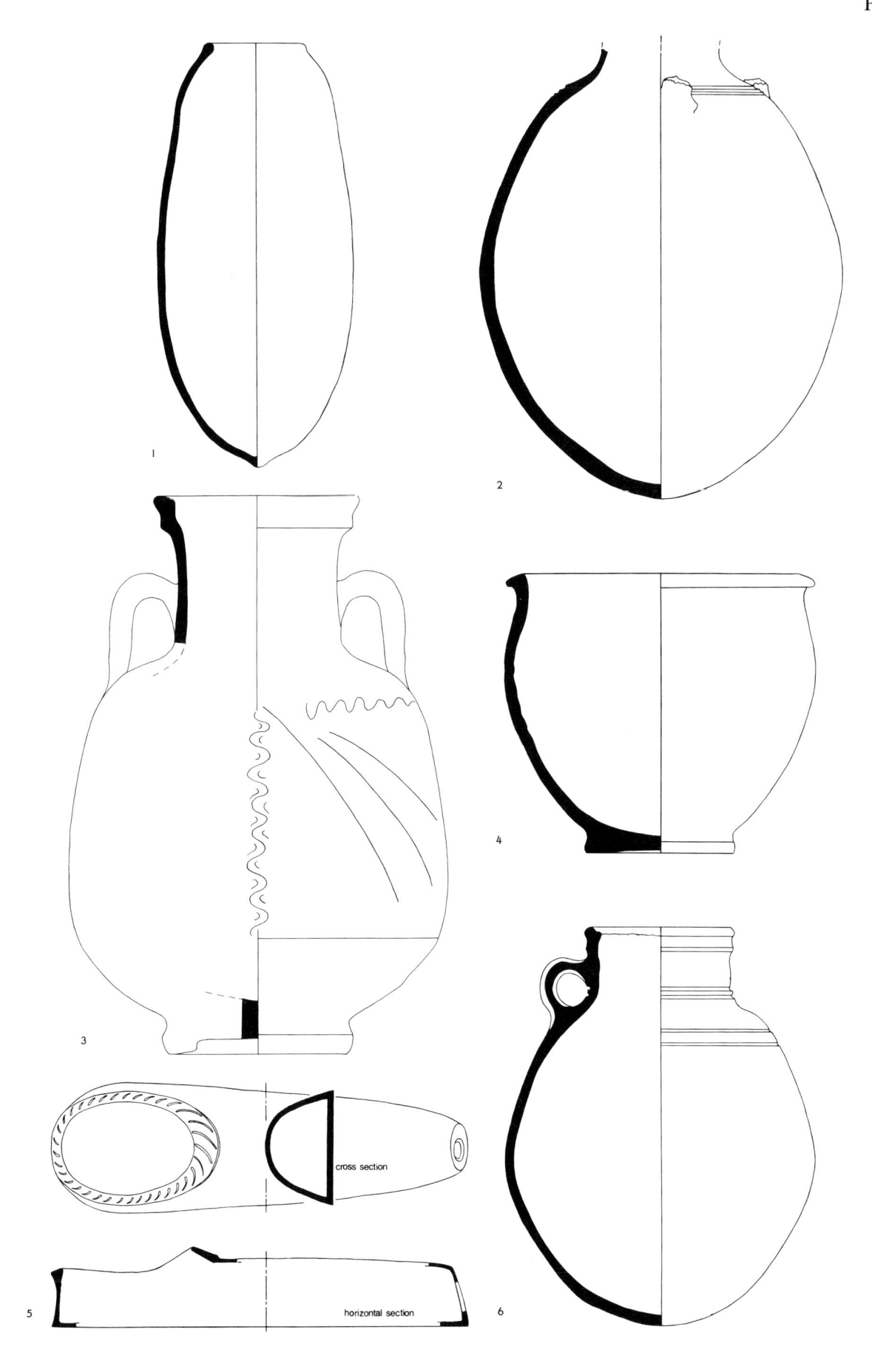

POTTERY FROM SE LEVELS. SCALES, 1:25 (5), 1:10 (1), 1:5 (2, 4, 6), AND 2:5 (3)

NO.	CAT. NO.	LOCUS	REMARKS
1	3P 549	SE surface	Tan ware, buff slip; comb incision and punctates
2	3P 583	Burial 3B 76	Tan ware, buff slip

PLATE 58

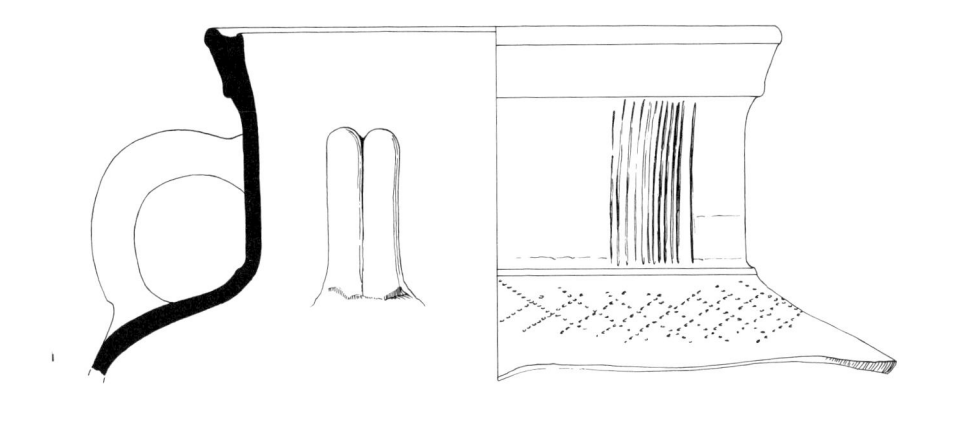

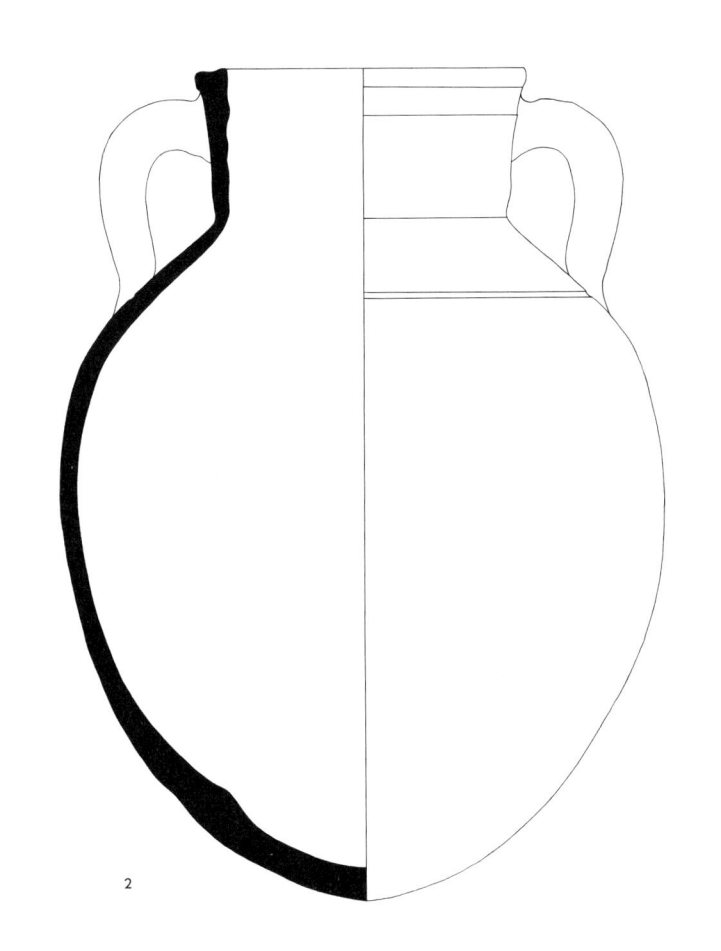

POTTERY FROM SE LEVELS. SCALE, 2:5

NO.	CAT. NO.	LOCUS	REMARKS
1	4N 186	NT 79 IV 1 south corner of room on floor	Bituminous limestone plaque with shell inlay border; center knob of two disks cemented with bitumen; one corner remade in bitumen, opposite corner broken; l. 33.4, w. 28.5, th. 4.0 cm. Same as in Pl. 67:2
2	3N 274	Debris above NT temple	White limestone or shell with greenish stone inset, perhaps discolored lapis
3	4N 210	NT 111 VI 2	Shell; six petaled flower; groove in center of each petal, dot in center; suspension broken
4	4N 213	NT 133 VIII 1	Greenish-gray steatite
5	4N 165	NT 27 II 2	Bronze, disk head
6	4N 118	NT 50 IV 1	Bronze
7	4D 374	NT 133 VII	Bronze; point tapers to edge
8	4N 184	NT 111 V	Shell; incised decoration
9	4N 107	NT 44 II 1	Crystal
10	4N 185	NT 118 V	Black stone, possibly steatite
11	3D 585	NT 100 IV 1	Gray stone, perforated diagonally
12	4N 128	NT 25 II 2	Black stone

PLATE 59

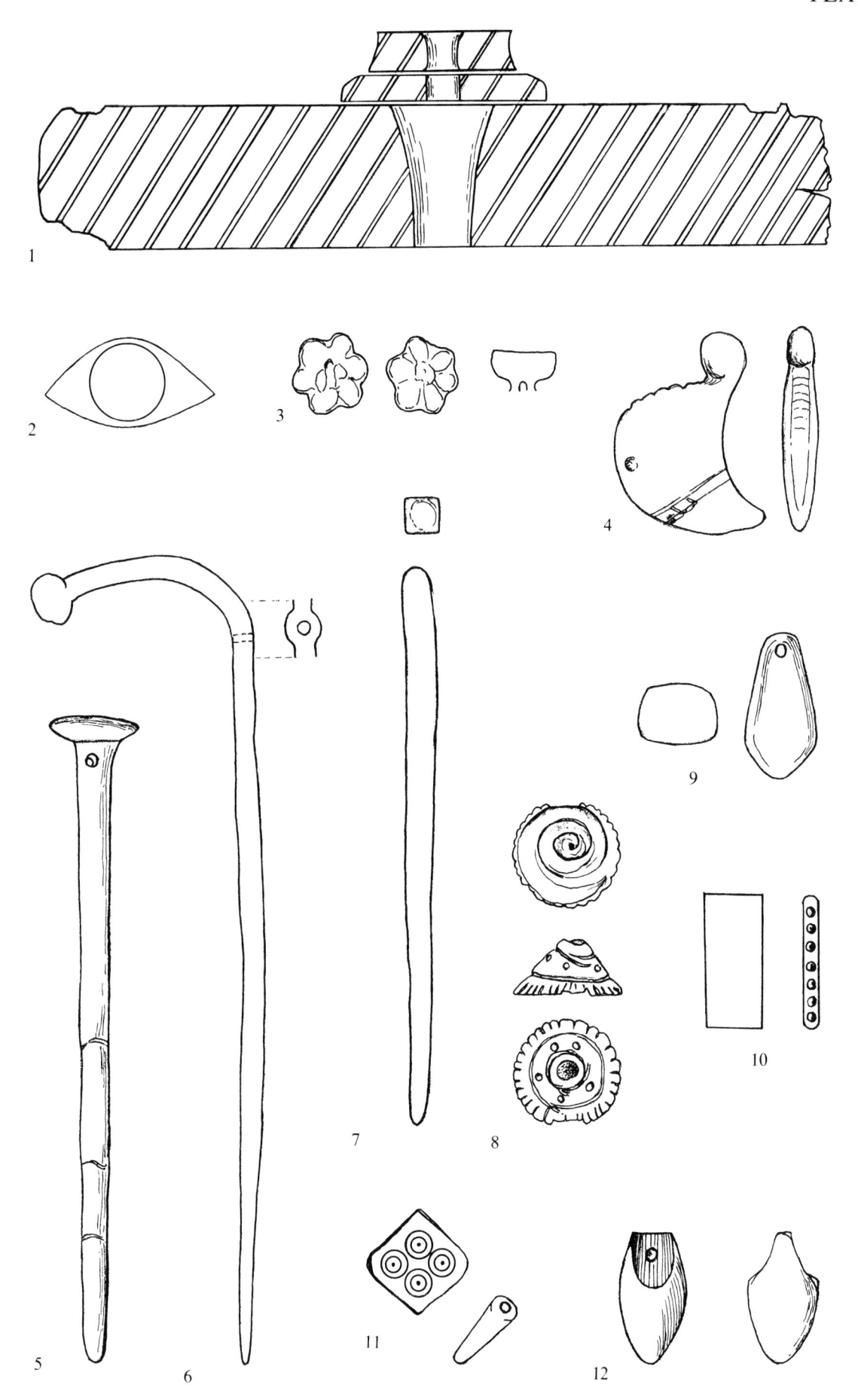

OBJECTS FROM NT LEVELS. SCALES, 1:2 (1) AND 1:1

NO.	CAT. NO.	LOCUS	REMARKS
1	4N 146	NT 81 IV 1	Bone, high polish
2	4N 163	NT 27 II 2	Bronze; flat sheet, edges thinned at tip
3	3D 563	SE I 2	White stone
4	4N 145	SE III 1	Bronze
5	4N 95	NT 46 II 1	Bronze chisel
6	3N 392	NT 100 IV	Tan ware
7	4N 164	NT 27 II 2	Bronze
8	4N 150	SE III or II burial 4B 120	Four iron arrowheads with lentoid section; l. 9.4–10.9, w. 2.1–2.4, th. 0.5–0.7 cm.
9	4D 230	SE III or II burial 4B 109	Iron; wood handle, traces of curved scabbard
10	4N 149	SE III or II burial 4B 120	Iron
11–14	4D 202	SE 71 II	Fragments of metal implements: bronze rod in bronze sleeve (Pl. 60:11), bronze tube with end filled with lead plug (Pl. 60:12–13, bronze chain and eye (Pl. 60:14)
15	4N 18	SE 41 II 2	Bronze rod
16	4N 51	Kiln in SE 40 II 2	Gray ware, plain
17	4N 68	SE 58 III 2	Buff ware, plain

PLATE 60

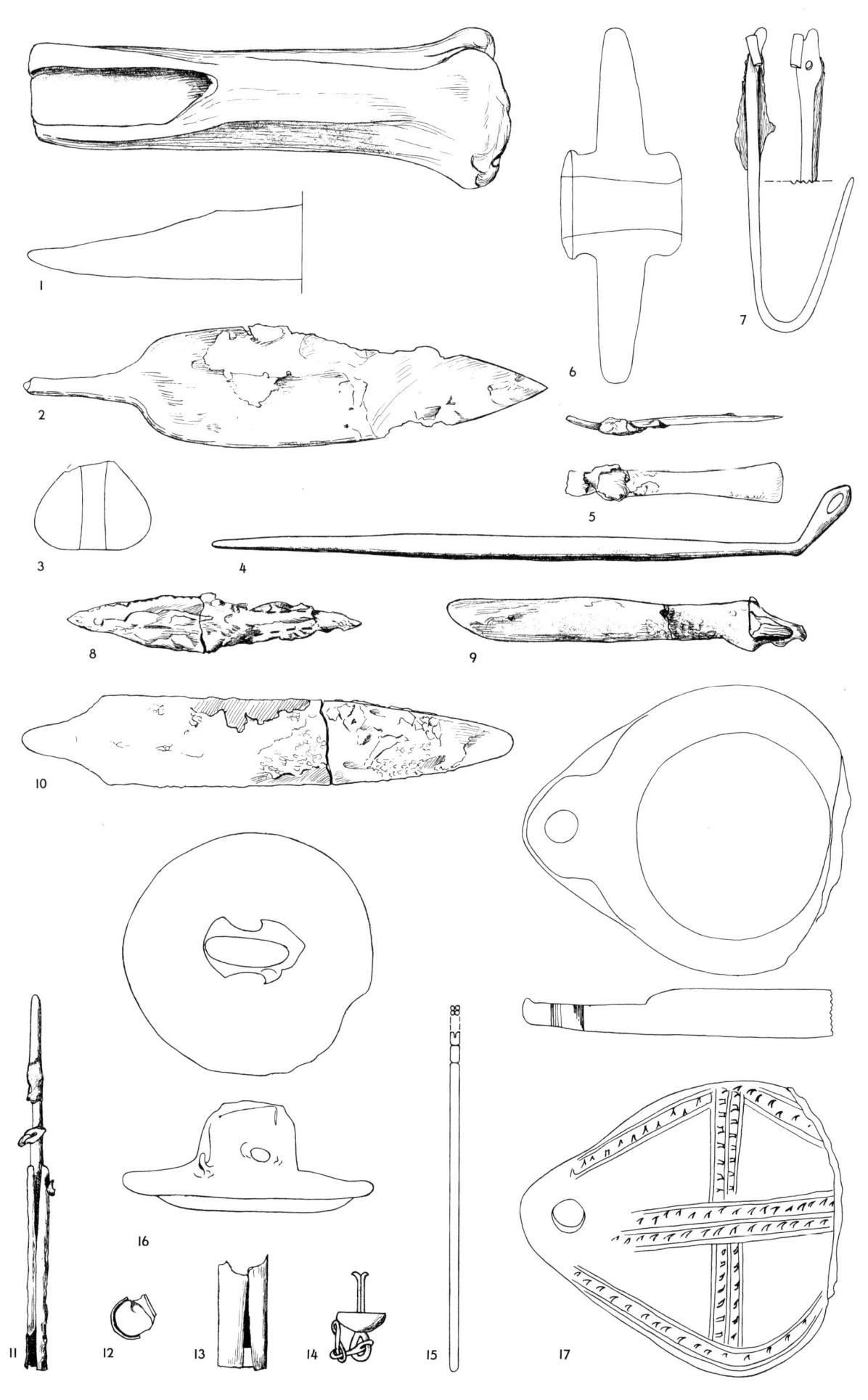

OBJECTS FROM NT AND SE LEVELS. SCALES, 1:4 (6) AND 1:2

NO.	CAT. NO.	LOCUS	REMARKS
1	4N 44	SE 52 II 3	Gold-mounted bead with amethyst cylinder
2	4N 7	SE I 3	White frit disk; flat face with depressed circle filled with yellowish frit
3	4N 52	SE II burial 4B 65*A*	Two silver earrings; hollow ball with openwork circles in middle band, four balls on square platform at bottom
4	4N 117	SE III burial 4B 103	Bronze bracelet
5	4N 49	SE I burial 4B 64	Thin bronze crescent; th. 0.15 cm.
6	4D 336*a*	SE III or II burial 4B 128	Bronze shaft ring on pithy wood
7	4D 336*b*	SE III or II burial 4B 128	Bronze stave top
8	3N 196	SE 78 II 2	Pot firing separator; buff, plain
9	4N 28	SE 24 I 3*b*	Bone arm and hand
10	4N 61	SE 67 II 4	Bone knob

PLATE 61

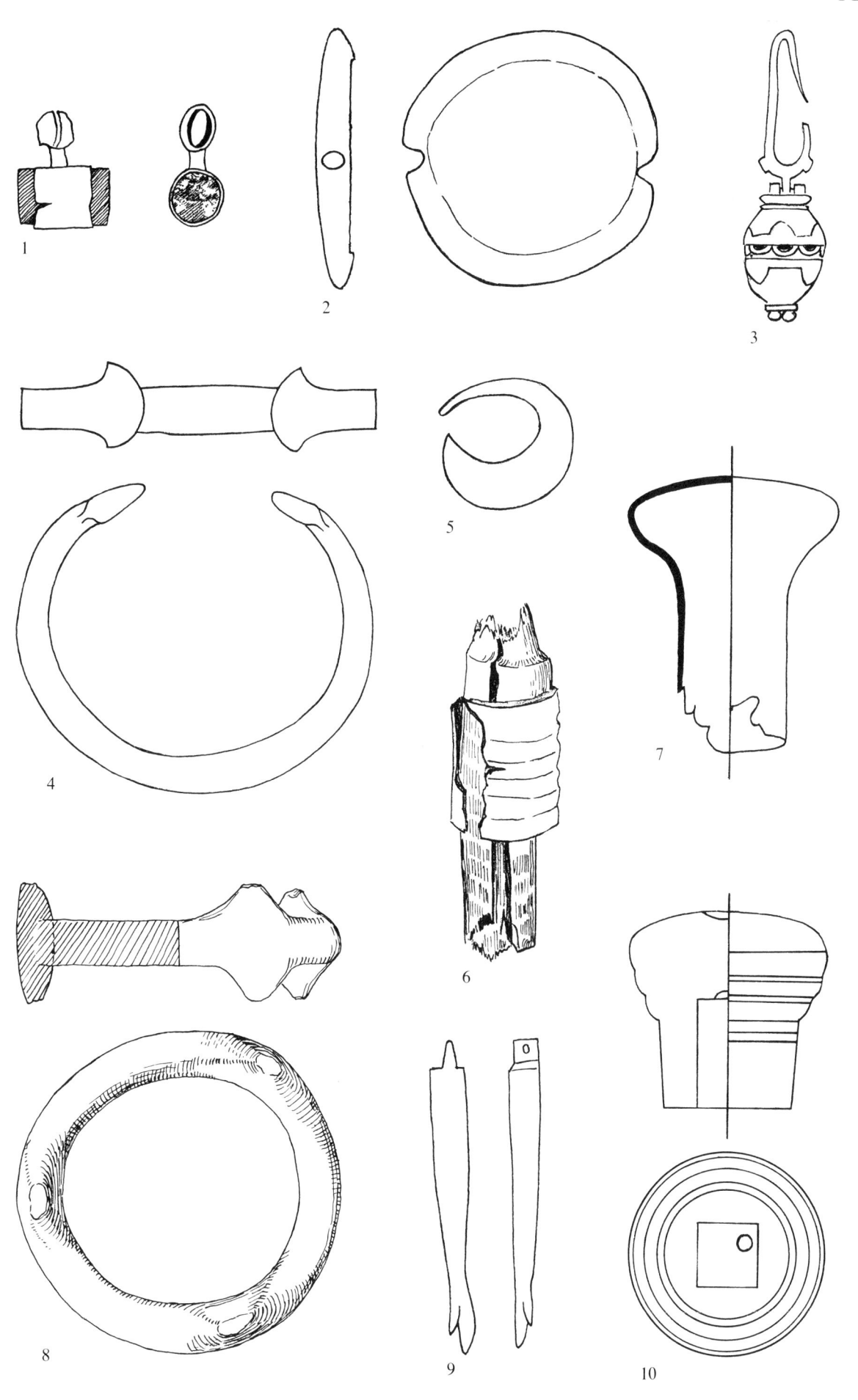

Objects from SE Levels. Scale, 1:1

NO.	CAT. NO.	LOCUS	REMARKS
1	4N 25	SE 44 II 2	Iron chisel
2	3N 426	SE surface	White frit
3	4N 73	Burial 4B 6 intrusive into SE 23 I 3	Black stone pendant
4	3N 437	Burial 3B 87 intrusive into SE 76 *ca.* I 2	Bronze pendant with a flat back and loop
5	4N 13*a*	SE surface	Frit; streaked yellow, red, and black
6	4N 13*c*	SE surface	Incised shell
7	4N 13*b*	SE surface	Frit; 5 beads streaked black and white, yellow and white, black, green, and red
8	3N 483	SE surface	Bone spoon handle
9	3N 397	Burial 3B 66 intrusive into SE 81 *ca.* I 3	Tool in thin bronze sheet, th. 0.1 cm.
10	4N 109*b*	Burial 4B 135 intrusive into SE 81 *ca.* I 3	Silver with carnelian bezel
11	4N 10	Burial 4B 6 intrusive into SE 23 I 3	Two gold earrings
12	4N 15	Burial 4B 38 intrusive into SE 76 *ca.* I 3	Two very thin gold leaves near skull
13	4N 9	Burial 4B 6 intrusive into SE 23 I 3	Bronze bracelet on left wrist, similar bracelet on right wrist

PLATE 62

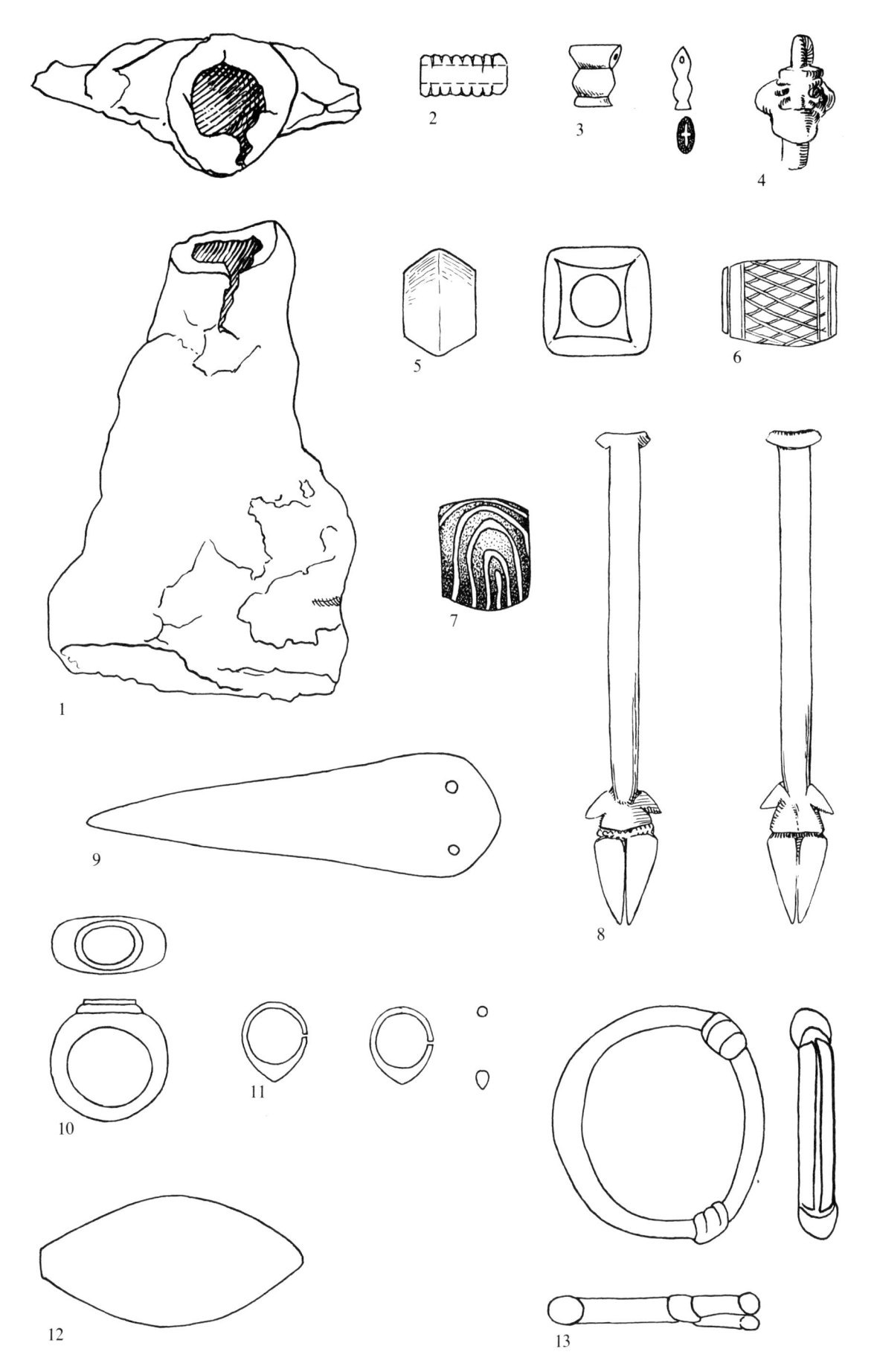

OBJECTS FROM SE LEVELS. SCALE, 1:1

NO.	CAT. NO.	LOCUS	REMARKS
1		NT II	Jar sherd with rugose slip. See Vol. I, Pls. 86:13 and 148:5
2	4N 138	NT 53 III 1	White stone cylinder seal; Early Dynastic III; h. 1.4, d. 0.7 cm.
3	4D 298	NT 43 II 2	Seal impression; lower part of crossed animals
4	4D 378	NT 132 fl. 17	Seal impression; handled vases with birds between. See Frankfort, *Cylinder Seals,* Pl. IVg; early Protoliterate
5	4D 315	NT 57 IV 1	Seal impression; cf. Pl. 63:10
6	4N 174	NT 106 V 2	Cylinder seal; Early Dynastic II; h. 2.6, d. 2.1 cm.
7	4D 199	NT 21 II 1	Seal impression; rear of erect bulls
8	4N 153	NT 80 III 2	Cylinder seal; white, soft, chalky stone in bad condition; probably bulls rampant either side of gate; to right worshiper facing right to seated figure; Akkadian; h. 2.5, d. 1.7 cm.
9	4D 245	NT 43 II 1	Seal impression; procession of erect animals
10	4N 101	NT 33 II 2	Barrel-shaped shell bead; diamond design; l. 3.0, d. 0.85 cm.
11	4D 129	Debris above NT I	Seal impression
12	4N 105	NT dump	Burned steatite cylinder seal; worn, with one end broken; winged gate; Akkadian; preserved h. 2.5, d. 1.2 cm.
13	4D 257	NT 42 II 1	Seal impression
14	4D 254	NT 42 II 1	Seal impression
15	4D 260	NT 43 II 1	Seal impression; procession of erect animals

PLATE 63

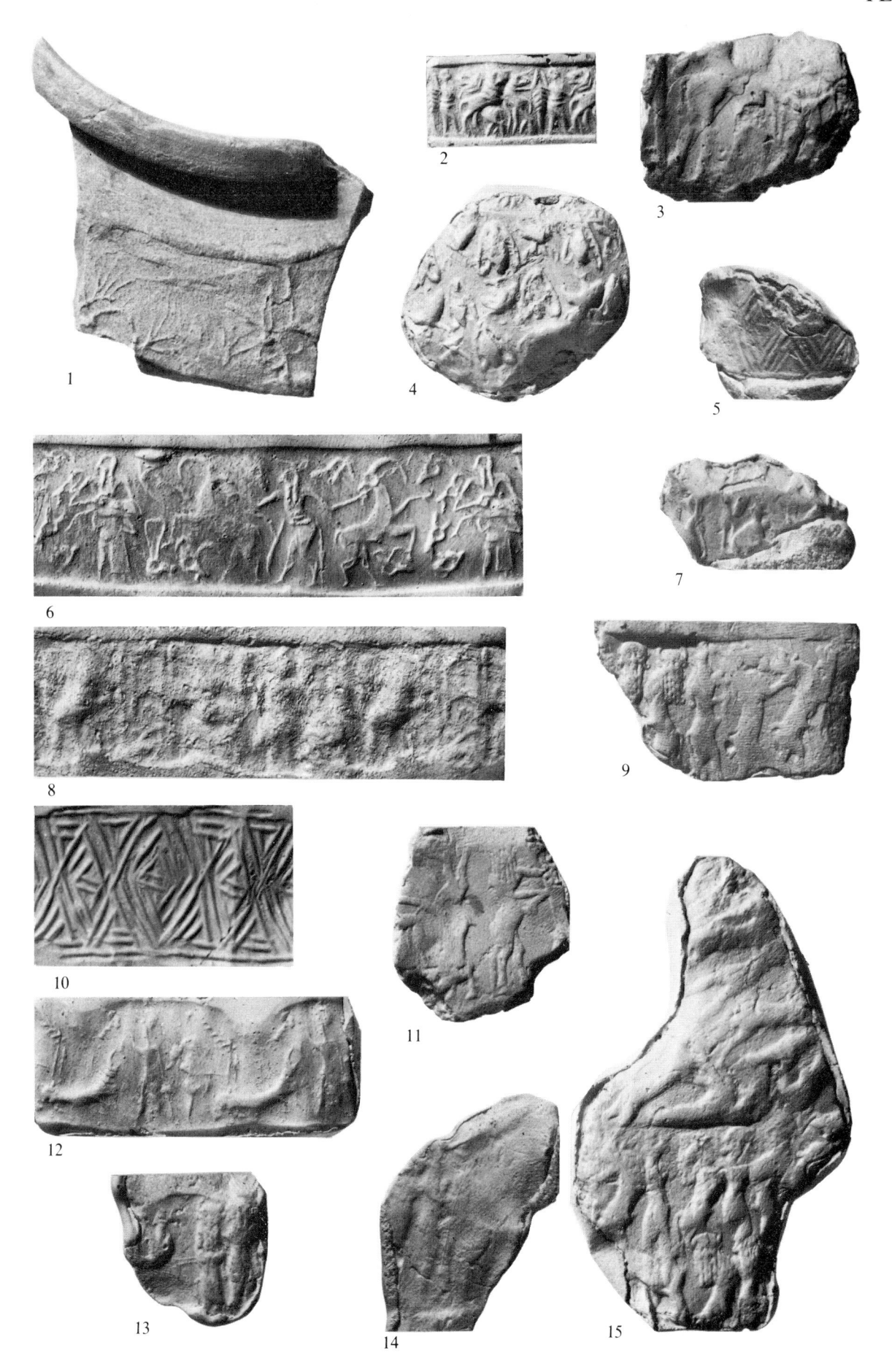

POTSHERD, CYLINDER SEALS, SEAL IMPRESSIONS AND BEAD FROM NT LEVELS.
SCALE, ca. 2:3 (1) AND ca. 1:1

NO.	CAT. NO.	LOCUS	REMARKS
1	4NT 270	NT 43 II 1	Seal impression, from same seal as the impression in Pl. 64:4; see p. 95
2	4D 309	NT 5 II 2	Seal impression; lower part of erect animals
3	4NT 269	NT 43 II 1	Seal impression; inscription between antithetical groups, something on dragon below inscription: *Íl bur-šu-[ma] lugal*; see p. 94
4	4NT 268	NT 1 I 2	Seal impression; antithetical groups; inscription: *Íl nu-èš*; see p. 94
5	4D 157	NT 43 II 1	Seal impression
6	4D 274	NT 43 II 1	Seal impression
7	4D 278	NT 43 II 1	Seal impression
8	4D 303	NT 43 II 1	Seal impression; animals and central human
9	4D 300	NT 43 II 2	Seal impression; contest scene
10	4D 275	NT 43 II 1	Seal impression
11	4D 286	NT 43 II 1	Seal impression; contest scene
12	4D 218	NT 43 II 1	Seal impression
13	4D 204	NT 43 II 1	Seal impression

PLATE 64

SEAL IMPRESSIONS FROM NT LEVELS. SCALE, *ca.* 1:1

NO.	CAT. NO.	LOCUS	REMARKS
1	4D 205	NT 43 II 1	Seal impression
2	4D 250	NT 42 II 1	Seal impression
3	4D 255	NT 42 II 1	Seal impression
4	4D 151	NT 1 I 2	Seal impression
5	4D 146	NT 1 I 2	Seal impression
6	4D 119	Debris above NT I	Seal impression
7	4D 195	NT 41 II 2	Seal impression; central figure with "arms" down, a rectangle above shoulders, faced by men on both sides, tree to right
8	4D 148	NT 1 I 2	Seal impression; procession of figures in uncertain action
9	4D 131	Debris above NT I	Seal impression
10	4D 154	NT 6 I 2	Seal impression; mythological scene
11	4D 136	Debris above NT I	Seal impression
12	4D 273	NT 43 II 1	Seal impression; probably winged gate
13	4D 181	NT 9 I 3	Seal impression; figures seated back to back
14	4D 304	NT 43 II 1	Seal impression; ploughman below ziggurat building; Early Dynastic III
15	4D 251	NT 42 II 1	Seal impression; procession of bull-men

PLATE 65

SEAL IMPRESSIONS FROM NT LEVELS. SCALE, *ca.* 1:1

NO.	CAT. NO.	LOCUS	REMARKS
1	4D 258	NT 42 II 1	Seal impression; bull-harp in uncertain scene
2	4D 240	NT 41 II 2	Seal impression; contest scene; Early Dynastic III
3	4D 267	NT 43 II 1	Seal impression; from the same seal as the impression in Pl. 65:15; procession of bull-men
4	4D 264	NT 43 II 1	Seal impression; procession of bull-men with standards
5	4D 266	NT 43 II 1	Seal impression; procession of erect animals
6	4D 147	NT 1 I 2	Seal impression; procession of men
7	4D 208	NT 43 II 1	Seal impression; repeated, paired bull-men in contest
8	4D 323	NT 48 II 2	Seal impression; lion or dog and ibex separated by branch
9	4D 239	NT 20 II 1	Seal impression; hatched animal
10	4D 287	NT 43 II 1	Seal impression. See Frankfort, *Cylinder Seals*, Pl. XXV*b*
11	4D 101	Debris above NT I	Seal impression
12	4D 252	NT 42 II 1	Seal impression; worshiper facing god to right, geometrical figure to left
13	4D 214	NT 43 II 1	Seal impression; from the same seal as the impression in Pl. 66:12
14	4D 297	NT 43 II 2	Seal impression; left to right: a ribbed vertical, erect bull, man with bow(?), erect hatched lion
15	4N 111	NT 60 III 1	Gypsum; base and back with feet of a statuette; left side of base broken, left foot abraded; l. 12.6, w. 7.8, preserved h. 5.3 cm.
16	4N 155	NT 87 IV 1	Plaque in bituminous limestone cut out for inlay figures; upper register with skirted figure to right, lower register with head to right; preserved h. 11.7, preserved w. 7.0, th. 2.2 cm.

PLATE 66

SEAL IMPRESSIONS AND STONE SCULPTURES FROM NT LEVELS.
SCALES, *ca.* 1:2 (16), *ca.* 2:3 (15), AND *ca.* 1:1

NO.	CAT. NO.	LOCUS	REMARKS
1	4N 110	NT 74 III 1	Calcite; part of two registers of a very weathered plaque. Top register with skirted figure at left facing right, right arm before face; offering stand between him and deity whose forefoot and skirt are preserved; probably drinking scene as in *OIP* LX, Pl. 65; preserved l. 11.9, preserved h. 12.8, th. 1.9 cm.
2	4N 186	NT 79 IV 1	Bituminous limestone plaque with shell inlay border; same as in Pl. 59:1
3	3N 402	NT 99 III 1	White gypsum; worn inscription on back (see p. 78); bitumen in eyes, two pieces of light green steatite inlay in left eyebrow; possibly vertical grooves on side locks; see *Archaeology* V, cover; h. 75.8, at elbows w. 23.7, at skirt bottom w. 22.0, th. 23.5 cm.; for discussion, see p. 72
4	3N 328	Debris above NT temple	Gypsum; rectangular base curved at back; back a solid sheet and not separate from rear of legs; toes indicated; preserved h. 6.1, w. 5.8, th. 4.0 cm.
5	3N 405	NT 99 III 1	Gypsum; oxidized, more ocher color in thin crust on surface; slight vertical fluting on beard; waist projects below hands; preserved h. 8.9, preserved w. 10.7, preserved th. 4.6 cm.

PLATE 67

1

2

3

4   5

STONE SCULPTURES FROM NT LEVELS. SCALES, *ca.* 1:5 (3), *ca.* 1:4 (2), AND *ca.* 2:3

NO.	CAT. NO.	LOCUS	REMARKS
1, 2	3N 402	NT 99 III 1	Gypsum statuette; see Pl. 67:3
3	3N 401	NT 99 III 1	Pinkish buff stone; broken at neck, on left side above elbow, on right side at wrist, and at bottom above knees; vertical leg line on back; preserved h. 11.0, preserved w. 7.6, th. 2.6 cm.
4	3N 406b	NT 99 III 1	Gypsum; vertical perforation from bottom to between ankles; see Pl. 70:1; base l. 10.7, w. 10.6 cm.

PLATE 68

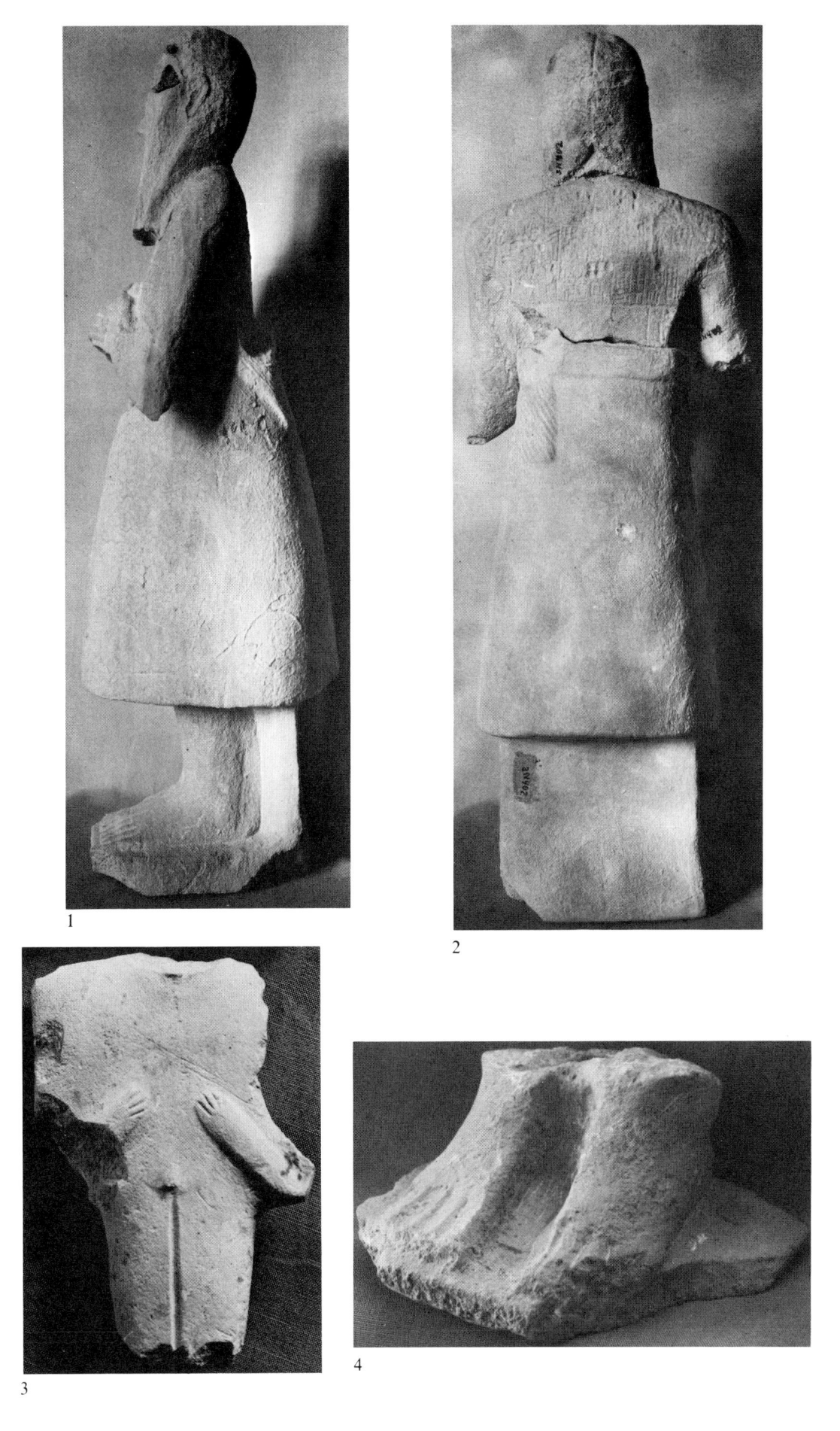

STONE SCULPTURES FROM NT LEVELS. SCALES, *ca.* 1:5 (1, 2) AND *ca.* 2:3 (3, 4)

NO.	CAT. NO.	LOCUS	REMARKS
1, 2	3N 404	NT 99 III 1	White gypsum; breasts rounded and moderately pronounced; sides curved and planes not sharp; right hand over left, probably with right thumb projecting up; hands may have held something; two perforations in bottom probably to attach legs; patch or possibly inset on back, for surface at left projects beyond plane of skirt; short illegible inscription on right shoulder; preserved h. 24.0, w. (restored) 11.0 cm.
3–5	3N 511	Debris above NT temple	Light brown limestone, granular surface; base and left foreleg of reclining bull broken; h. 10.9, l. 7.6, th. 4.0 cm.; cups: h. 4.2, rim d. 4.7 cm.

PLATE 69

Stone Sculptures from NT Levels. Scales, *ca.* 1:2 (1, 2) and 2:3 (3–5)

NO.	CAT. NO.	LOCUS	REMARKS
1	3N 406a	NT 99 III 1	Gypsum; vertical grooves on belt with lined tassel at left rear; imbricated triangles (as in *OIP* LX, Pl. 35) on skirt; long tassels on skirt border; perforation in bottom; see Pl. 68:4; preserved h. 17.0, base w. 12.6, th. 14.0 cm.
2, 3	3N 403	NT 99 III 1	Gypsum; fragmentary head; cylindrical perforation in neck; apparently hair bun at back of head; preserved h. 6.2, preserved w. 3.5, preserved th. 6.1 cm.
4	3N 476	Debris above NT temple	White gypsum or alabaster; inner line of upper arms indicated front and back; perforated at top and bottom; preserved h. 4.5, w. 2.6, th. 1.5 cm.
5	4N 86	Debris above NT temple	White gypsum; back and left side lost, most of left forearm missing, surface lost below chest; preserved h. 10.1, th. 5.1 cm.
6	3N 510	NT IV 1	Black and white marble bead or stamp seal(?); flat triangular cross section; l. 5.5, h. 4.7, th. 0.9 cm.
7	3N 481	Debris above NT temple	Bronze; tip of horn broken; missing below neck; h. 4.0, w. 3.2, th. 1.7 cm.
8	3N 275	Debris above NT temple	Calcite; feet of statuette; preserved h. 3.2, w. 6.2, th. 2.6 cm.
9	4D 249	NT 42 II 1	Figurine head; unbaked light-brown clay; incised eyes, nostrils, and mouth line

PLATE 70

STONE SCULPTURES AND OTHER OBJECTS FROM NT LEVELS.
SCALES, *ca.* 2:3 AND *ca.* 1:1 (6, 7, 9)

NO.	CAT. NO.	LOCUS	REMARKS
1	4N 26	SE II 1	White stone cylinder seal; lion to left of indistinct vertical element; l. 1.7, d. 0.8 cm.
2	4N 54a	SE II burial 4B 62	Glazed frit cylinder seal; traces of pale blue surface; l. 2.0, d. 1.2 cm.
3	4N 74	SE II burial 4B 76	Pale yellow frit scaraboid; l. 1.3, w. 1.0, h. 0.7 cm.
4	4N 60	SE 58 III 1	Baked-clay cylinder seal; tan ware
5	4N 122	NT 32 II 2 below burial 4B 117	Clay sealing with string perforation; worshiper before triangular-topped vertical rising from horizontal line; d. 2.3, th. 0.7 cm.
6	4N 123	NT 32 II 2 below burial 4B 117	Stone disk stamp seal; bull going left; d. 2.1, th. 1.4 cm.
7	4N 139a	SE III or II burial 4B 117	Yellow faience scaraboid; l. 1.3, w. 0.9, h. 0.5 cm.
8	4N 139b	Same as 4N 139a	Yellow faience scaraboid; l. 1.3, w. 0.9, h. 0.9 cm.
9	4N 139c	Same as 4N 139a	Yellowish stone scaraboid; l. 1.3, w. 1.2, h. 0.5 cm.
10	4N 139d	Same as 4N 139a	Carnelian scaraboid; l. 1.3, w. 1.2, h. 0.9 cm.
11	4N 131	NT 48 II 2	Glass stamp seal; truncated cone with rounded top, perforated near top; probably two figures fighting; h. 1.8, d. 0.8 and 1.4 cm.
12	4N 130	SE II burial 4B 91	Worn black stone cylinder seal; left to right: figure with lines from shoulders, two worshipers, seated figure facing left; probably Ur III or Isin-Larsa; l. 1.5, d. 0.8 cm.
13	4N 157a	NT 161 I 3	Chalcedony scaraboid stamp seal; l. 1.4, w. 1.4, h. 0.9 cm.
14	3N 215	SE V 2	Reddish stone cylinder seal; symposia in upper, probably birds in lower register; Early Dynastic; l. 3.2, d. 1.5 cm.
15	3N 238	SE V 3	Mold-made male figurine. See Vol. I, Pl. 130:11
16	3N 237	SE V 3	Mold-made figurine
17		Locus unknown	Vat
18		SE 29 I 1	Oval tub in foreground, drainage jar in background
19	3N 493	Burial 3B 98 intrusive into SE 75 ca. I 3	Pale green glass bottle; 3P 610, 611 similar; may be Parthian; h. 13.1–14.2, d. 3.1–3.5 cm.
20	4D 17	SE dump	Female figurine; tan ware, plain; traces of salt or plaster; nose and outline of face alone indicated
21	3P 609	SE surface	Glass bottle; gray surface
22	3P 608	SE surface found with 3P 609	Glass bottle; white
23	3N 480	SE I	Double-mold figurine; high headdress; back of the block is also worked

PLATE 71

BAKED-CLAY FIGURINES AND OTHER OBJECTS FROM NT AND SE LEVELS.
SCALES, UNKNOWN (17, 18), *ca.* 2:5 (19, 21, 22), *ca.* 2:3 (15, 16, 20, 23), AND *ca.* 1:1 (1–14)

NO.	CAT. NO.	LOCUS	REMARKS
1	4N 81	SE 62 III	Convex back
2	3D 698	SE II	Tambourine player
3	4D 50	SE 25 I 3	Flute player, probably female; hollow; front and back separate pieces
4	3N 473	SE I	Flute player
5	4D 60	SE 24 I 3	Female figurine
6	4N 63	SE IV or III	Convex back
7	3D 690	SE surface	
8	4N 62	SE IV or III	Slightly convex back
9	4D 19	SE II 1	
10	3N 190	SE dump	Head; 3 examples; tan, plain, or buff slip; perforated vertically from top of head through neck; h. 6.2–7.0, w. 3.0, th. 3.0–4.0 cm.
11	4D 192	SE IV or III	Horns on cap, beard line across cheeks; preserved h. 6.3 cm.
12	4D 18	SE II 1	Horse and rider; handmade, with a somewhat exaggerated profile of the mold-made type
13	4D 128	SE 66 II 3	Plaque; probably jar at lower left side
14	3D 697	SE II	Figure on horse

PLATE 72

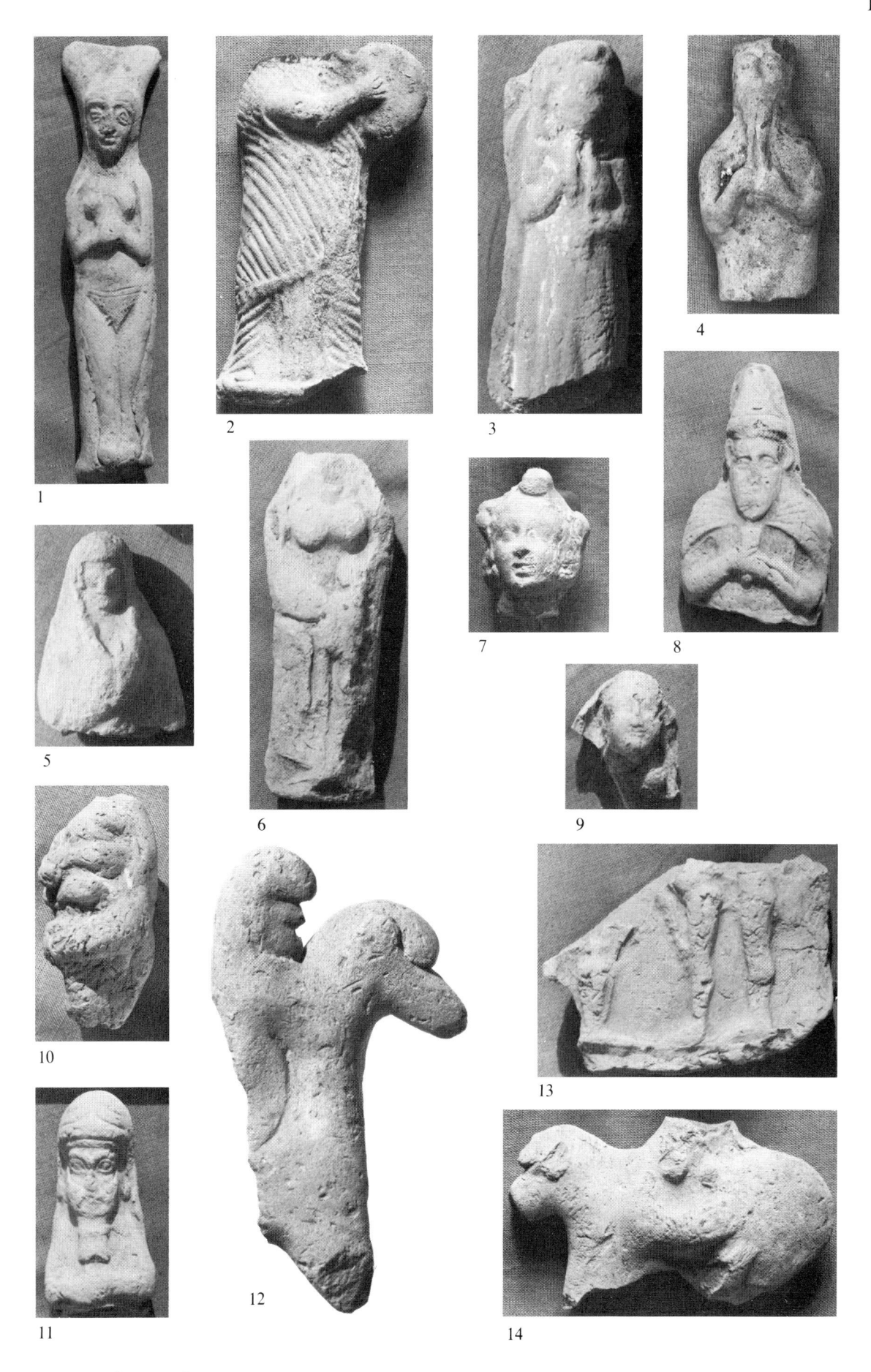

BAKED-CLAY FIGURINES AND PLAQUE FROM NT AND SE LEVELS. SCALE, *ca.* 2:3

NO.	CAT. NO.	LOCUS	REMARKS
1, 2, 4	3N 177	SE II	Buff ware; traces of blue paint on beard; base hollowed; preserved h. 4.2, w. 2.9, th. 4.0 cm.
3	4N 43	SE 55 III	Monkey figurine; buff surfaces; convex back; h. 6.6 cm.
5	3N 185	SE II	Tan ware, plain; base of rhyton
6	4N 69	SE 61 III 2	Mold (with impression at left); buff ware, plain; flat surfaces; l. 10.5 cm.
7	4N 64	SE dump	Greenish buff, plain; h. 8.3 cm.
8	4N 67	Intrusive into NT I	Plaque; grayish brown ware, plain; slightly convex back; l. 8.8 cm.
9	4N 65*a*	SE III	Mold (with impression at right); tan ware, buff surfaces; plano-convex with flat back; preserved h. 7.0 cm.

PLATE 73

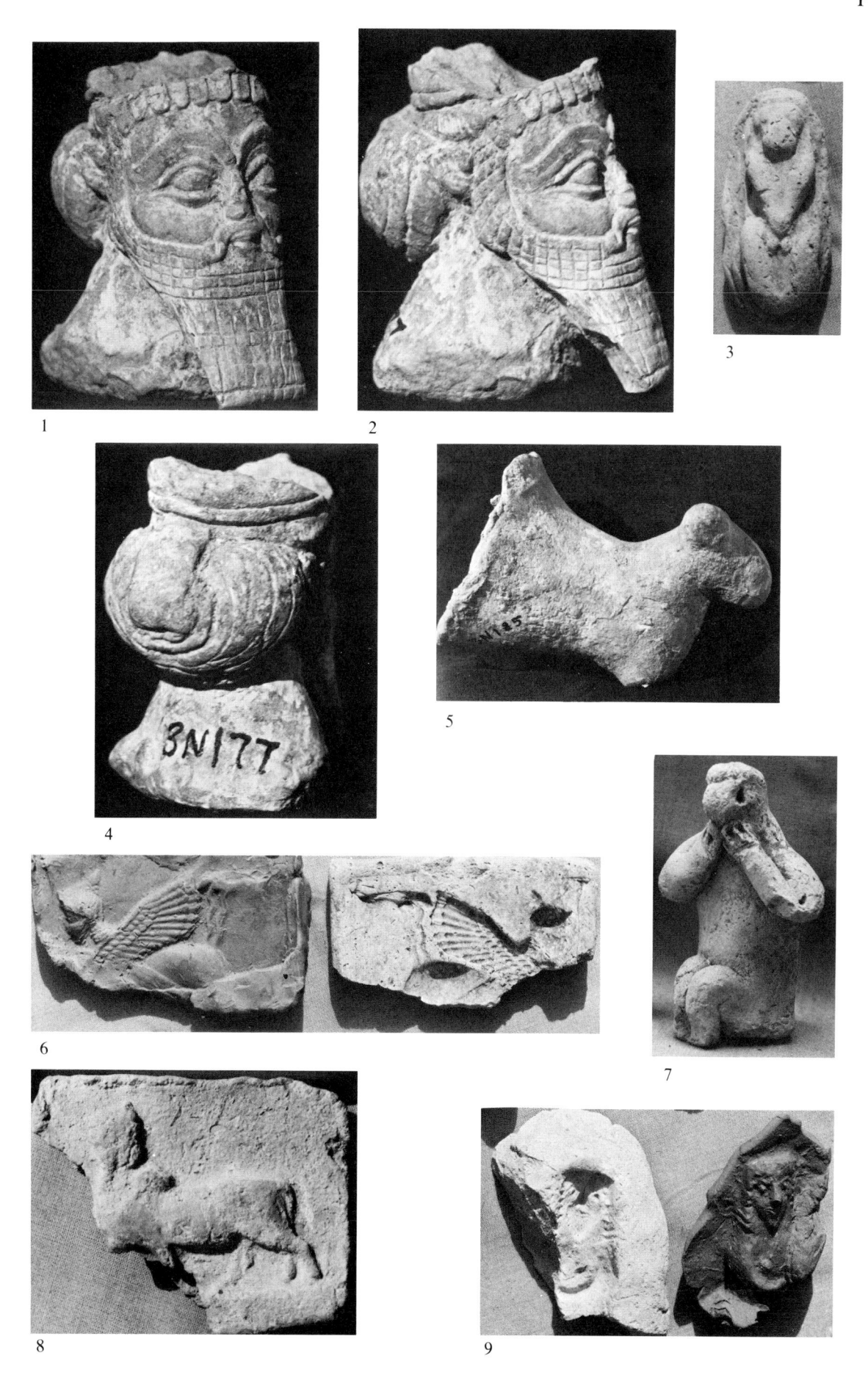

BAKED-CLAY FIGURINES, PLAQUE, AND MOLDS FROM SE LEVELS.
SCALES, *ca.* 1:2 (6, 9), *ca.* 2:3, AND *ca.* 3:2 (1, 2, 4)

NO.	CAT. NO.	LOCUS	REMARKS
1	4D 3	SE I 2	Preserved h. 8.2 cm.
2	4D 143	SE III 1	Hollow body (from jar?); incised mouth; nostrils; preserved h. 5.6 cm.
3	4N 30	SE 49 II 4	Buff ware, pale green glaze; l. 7.3 cm.
4	4D 201	SE 68 II 4	Tan ware, buff slip
5	4N 94	Intrusive into NT 9 I 2	Bronze; division between front paws; h. 1.9 cm.
6	4N 31	SE 40 II 4	Buff ware, plain; moderately convex back; l. 11.6 cm.
7	4N 22	SE I 3	Pale yellow frit; head broken at longitudinal perforation, arms at sides, marks on chest, navel hole, vertical lines on skirt, feet below; rectangular sectioned rib up back; preserved h. 2.4 cm.
8	4N 42	SE II burial 4B 56	Necklace composed of elements found in burial. Beads: type 1a numerous in silver, d. 0.45–0.6 cm.; six carnelian, type 3a with hexagonal plan, l. 0.45, d. 0.55 cm.; seven amethyst, type 3a, l. 0.5, d. 0.6 cm. Pendants: carnelian ball in gold net; two frit cylinders with three gold circlets with granulated design from which hang plano-convex gold drops with granulated edging, another similar but with one central drop; one fragmentary with plain gold circlet; two gold circlets
9	4N 39, 40	SE II burial 4B 56	Pair of silver bracelets; l. 7.5, h. 5.9, th. 0.6 cm.
10	4N 37	SE II burial 4B 56	Two silver earrings; the larger, d. 5.8, th. 0.3 cm., has balls suspended from wire, then a row of triangles with openwork between them, and then two inner wires; the smaller, d. 3.2, th. 0.2 cm. has one grape cluster
11	3N 505	SE surface	Bronze spatula, perhaps for applying kohl
12	4D 1	SE I 1	Brick stamp, on brick in facing wall; stamp measures 5.7 × 6.3 cm.
13	4D 51	SE 25 I 2	Carved plaster
14	4D 42	SE surface	Carved plaster
15	4D 43	SE dump	Carved plaster

PLATE 74

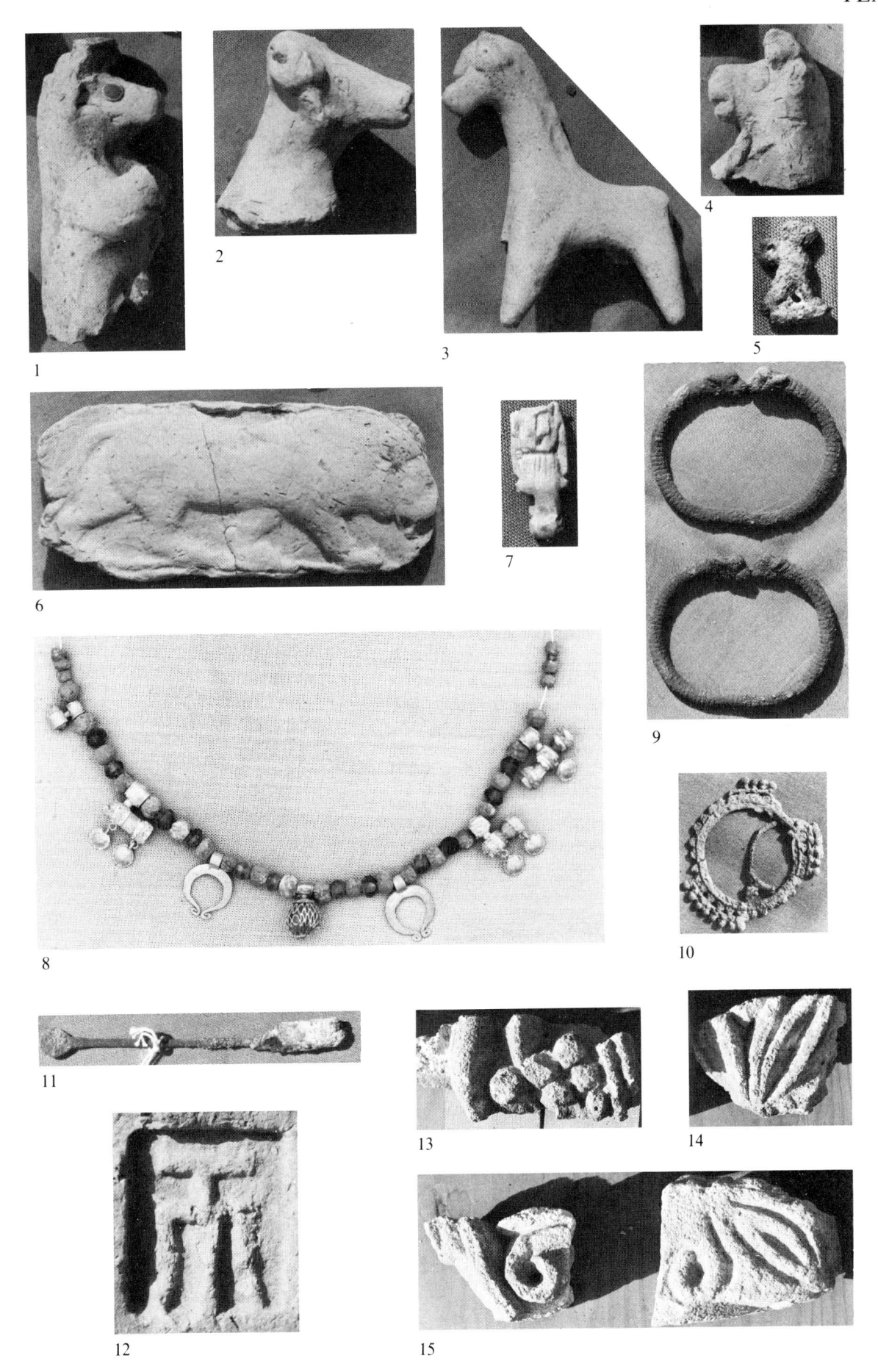

BAKED-CLAY FIGURINES AND OTHER OBJECTS FROM SE LEVELS.
SCALES, *ca.* 1:3 (13–15), *ca.* 1:2 (5, 7, 9–12), AND *ca.* 2:3

NO.	BURIAL NO.	LOCUS	REMARKS
1	4B 61	SE II intrusive into SE 47 II 4	Burial in ring-base jar, capped with circle of fine clay 11 cm. thick
2	4B 60	SE II intrusive into SE 49 II 4	Burial in funnel-bottom jar. See Vol. I, Pl. 157:8
3	3B 91	SE I intrusive into SE 64 II 2	Burial in long tub with rounded ends and lid; coffin of soft buff ware
4	4B 28	Intrusive into SE 16 I 2	Same type as in Pl. 75:3; covered with unbaked-brick gable
5, 7	3B 81	Intrusive into SE 81 *ca.* I 3	Burial in slipper coffin; soft and coarse buff ware, blue-green glaze; l. 215, h. 32 cm.
6	4B 10	Intrusive into SE 29 I 1	Burial in convex-base jar; soft and crumbly buff ware, two handles, obliquely incised dots on shoulder; h. *ca.* 40, d. 35 cm.; covered by bowl; see Pl. 57:4
8	3B 94	Intrusive into SE 75 *ca.* I 3	Burial in glazed slipper coffin; l. 200 cm.; two adult skeletons, one over the other
9, 10	3B 66	Intrusive into SE 81 *ca.* I 3	Burial in slipper coffin

PLATE 75

BURIAL JARS AND SLIPPER COFFINS FROM SE BURIALS

NO.	BURIAL NO. OR CAT. NO.	LOCUS	REMARKS
1	4B 36 and 4B 38	Intrusive into SE 76 *ca.* I 3	Burials in glazed slipper coffins; on left, 4B 36 has two pointed jars over opening; l. 215, h. 40 cm.; on right 4B 38 has two-part lid
2, 3	4B 36	Intrusive into SE 76 *ca.* I 3	Burial in glazed slipper coffin
4, 5	4N 72	SE surface	Aramaic incantation bowl; d. 16, h. 7 cm.

PLATE 76

SLIPPER COFFINS AND INCANTATION BOWL FROM SE LEVELS

NO.	CAT. NO.	LOCUS	REMARKS
1–3	4N 17	SE surface	Aramaic incantation bowl; d. 15, h. 7 cm.
4	4D 58	SE III 1	Brazier or incense burner; h. 10.8 cm. See Vol. I, Pl. 99:5–6
5	3D 692	SE surface	Figurine head
6	4D 11	SE I 2	Male figurine head

PLATE 77

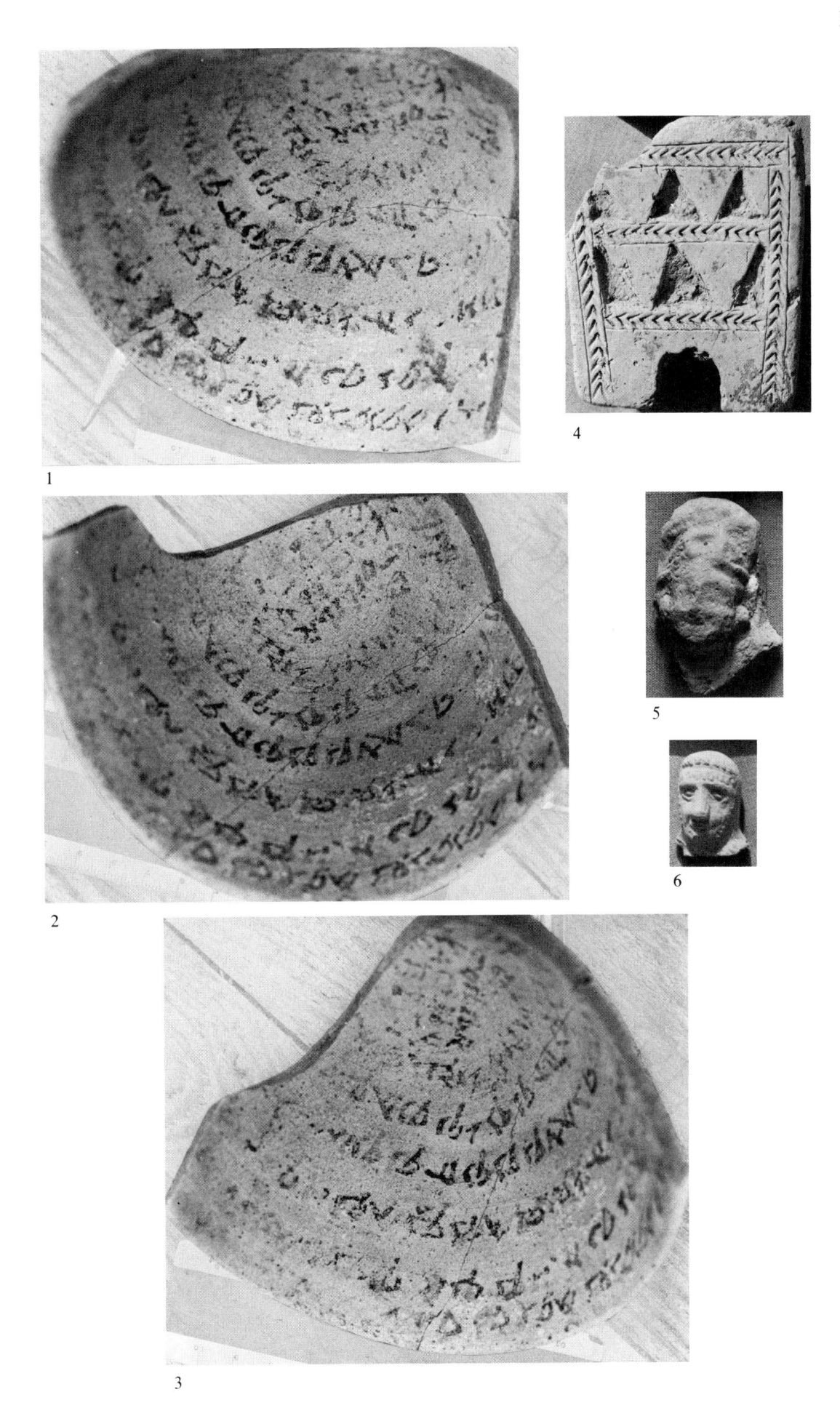

INCANTATION BOWL AND OTHER OBJECTS. SCALES, *ca.* 1:2 (4) AND 2:3 (5, 6)